International seafarers and transnationalism in the twenty-first century

MANCHESTER
1824

ress

New
Ethnographies

Series editor
Alexander Thomas T. Smith

Already published

The British in rural France: Lifestyle migration and the ongoing quest for a better way of life
Michaela Benson

Ageing selves and everyday life in the North of England: Years in the making
Catherine Degnen

Chagos islanders in Mauritius and the UK: Forced displacement and onward migration
Laura Jeffery

Integration, locality and everyday life: After asylum
Mark Maguire and Fiona Murphy

An ethnography of English football fans: Cans, cops and carnivals
Geoff Pearson

Literature and agency in English fiction reading: A study of the Henry Williamson Society…
Adam Reed

Devolution and the Scottish Conservatives: Banal activism, electioneering and the politics of irrelevance
Alexander Smith

International seafarers and transnationalism in the twenty-first century

Helen Sampson

Manchester University Press
Manchester and New York

distributed in the United States exclusively
by Palgrave Macmillan

Published by Manchester University Press
Oxford Road, Manchester M13 9NR, UK
and Room 400, 175 Fifth Avenue, New York, NY 10010, USA
www.manchesteruniversitypress.co.uk

Distributed in the United States exclusively by
Palgrave Macmillan, 175 Fifth Avenue,
New York, NY 10010, USA

Distributed in Canada exclusively by
UBC Press, University of British Columbia, 2029 West Mall,
Vancouver, BC, Canada V6T 1Z2

British Library Cataloguing-in-Publication Data is available

Library of Congress Cataloging-in-Publication Data is available

ISBN 978 0 7190 9553 5 paperback

First published by Manchester University Press in hardback 2013

This paperback edition first published 2014

Printed by Lightning Source

In memory of Richard K. Brown, the extraordinarily kind man who first introduced me to sociology

Contents

List of tables and figures

Tables

Figures

Acknowledgements

I would like to thank all of the people who helped me with this research and who made me welcome aboard the ships I sailed on, as well as during my time in India, and in Hamburg.

I am grateful to Tony Lane for introducing me to the occupation of seafaring, to Nelson Turgo for hunting down last minute references for me, and to Louise Deeley for considerable help with the presentation of the final manuscript.

I would also like to thank colleagues, friends and family who read, and commented on, parts of this text or who offered encouragement from the 'sidelines', most particularly: Jose Ricardo Ramalho, Ray Hudson, Michael Bloor, Lionel Cliffe, Chris Jones, Tony Novak, Michael Burawoy, Anne Kennedy, Diana Sampson and David Walters. I owe the greatest debt of gratitude, however, to Huw Beynon for his brave and unfailing critique, his encouragement, and for looking after 'the family' during so many absences.

The research which underpins this book was undertaken as part of an ESRC-funded study of transnationalism at sea (ref. L214252036). In connection with the study, work was undertaken in multiple settings by a team of researchers (Michael Bloor, Geoff Bourne, Erol Kahveci, Tony Lane, Helen Sampson, Torsten Schroeder, Michelle Thomas). However, this book is based solely upon my individual experience amongst communities in India and on board five different multinationally crewed ships. In relation to the work I undertook in Hamburg and Northern Germany I thank both Torsten Schroeder and Nelson Turgo for their assistance and contribution.

Permission to reproduce 'Sea Fever' by John Masefield (Chapter 3) was kindly granted by The Society of Authors as the literary representative of the Estate of John Masefield.

'I wanna go home', words and music by Van Morrison and Lonnie Donegan © 2010, reproduced (in Chapter 5) by permission of EMI Music Publishing Ltd, London W8 5SW and Conexion Music Ltd, 10 Heathfield Terrace, London W4 4JE.

Series editor's foreword

At its best, ethnography has provided a valuable tool for apprehending a world in flux. A couple of years after the Second World War, Max Gluckman founded the Department of Social Anthropology at the University of Manchester. In the years that followed, he and his colleagues built a programme of ethnographic research that drew eclectically on the work of leading anthropologists, economists and sociologists to explore issues of conflict, reconciliation and social justice 'at home' and abroad. Often placing emphasis on detailed analysis of case studies drawn from small-scale societies and organisations, the famous 'Manchester School' in social anthropology built an enviable reputation for methodological innovation in its attempts to explore the pressing political questions of the second half of the twentieth century. Looking back, that era is often thought to constitute a 'gold standard' for how ethnographers might grapple with new challenges and issues in the contemporary world.

The *New Ethnographies* series aims to build on that ethnographic legacy at Manchester. It will publish the best new ethnographic monographs that promote interdisciplinary debate and methodological innovation in the qualitative social sciences. This includes the growing number of books that seek to apprehend the 'new' ethnographic objects of a seemingly brave new world, some recent examples of which have included auditing, democracy and elections, documents, financial markets, human rights, assisted reproductive technologies and political activism. Analysing such objects has often demanded new skills and techniques from the ethnographer. As a result, this series will give voice to those using ethnographic methods across disciplines to innovate, such as through the application of multi-sited fieldwork and the extended comparative case study method. Such innovations have often challenged more traditional ethnographic approaches. *New Ethnographies* therefore seeks to provide a platform for emerging scholars and their more established counterparts engaging with ethnographic methods in new and imaginative ways.

Alexander Thomas T. Smith

Figure 1: A well-maintained gangway

1

All at sea

It was April 1999 when I first stood on the edge of a quayside surveying the organised mayhem that constituted the unloading of a refrigerated fruit ship. In front of me forklift trucks scuttled about like strangely formed stag beetles, their pattern of movement a mystery to my untrained eye. Lorries littered the quay patiently waiting to be filled, their cavernous insides craving a cargo. Beyond the chaos, locked to the concrete apron of the wharf, towered a rusty hulk. It was the ship that I was supposed to board – but how?

I carefully studied the vessel through gaps in the traffic, painfully conscious that to get to it I would have to dodge the vehicles and would quite likely fail and get shouted at, my arrival on board made all the more humiliating, all the more public. I flinched inwardly at the thought. There was certainly no doorway conveniently carved into the ship's side that one could step into from the quay. No, it looked very much as though I was going to have to climb the perilous-looking metal steps that descended at a steep angle from the decks. This contraption (the gangway) looked rather feebly attached to the ship and ran parallel to its side seemingly suspended at the top, unlike a ladder which might reassuringly lean at an appropriate angle against whatever one was about to climb up to. I don't like heights, or ladders, at the best of times and I eyed the gangway with disfavour and a large dollop of suspicion. Was the netting slung beneath it meant to reassure me? Certainly it looked unlikely to be able to perform the useful function of catching anyone who fell – its mesh gaping and sagging and in need of much repair. The knot of anxiety in my stomach tightened but I mentally braced myself and began to walk towards the looming metal shape which looked to be both unseaworthy (to my unpractised eye), and unwelcoming.

At the time, I lived in Manchester nowhere near to the sea and my research was focused upon issues of education and underachievement, unemployment, and issues relating to disability. The idea of research on board a cargo ship was so different, and so exciting in prospect, that I had forgotten to feel nervous about it until those moments standing on the quayside considering the little rusty reefer (refrigerated cargo ship) that was to provide me with my first taste of the life of a modern-day seafarer.

The ship did not disappoint. Contrary to my fears, the crew of Swedish and Filipino seafarers welcomed me into their lives and for forty-two days I lived and worked alongside them, painting the ship with them, venturing ashore to the sea-men's bars with them, laughing with them, even dancing and singing with them. For seafarers, of necessity, learn to make their own entertainment to pass the time. Confined aboard, they know how to rub along with one another and lighten the oppressive atmosphere of their institutionalised, routinised and regimented work-ing lives.

A major motivation in going to sea, and the only one for many people, is the high income that can be earned over a relatively short period of time. This is par-ticularly true for seafarers in the developing world who, as a consequence of the globalisation of the shipping industry, can earn tremendous salaries relative to their shore-based counterparts. Thought of as 'easy money' by many non-seafar-ers, such incomes are in fact hard-earned and often come at a high 'price'. Seafaring is a dangerous field of employment where accidents are prevalent and mortality rates higher than in comparable shore-based occupations (Hansen 1996, ICONS 2000). In many parts of the world, including India, it is also one carrying high risks of unemployment and of debt accumulation. Additionally the personal costs in terms of loneliness, isolation and the development of emotional gulfs between regularly employed seafarers and their families, need to be taken into account (Thomas, Sampson and Zhao 2003, Thomas 2003).

Those who work aboard ships are largely invisible to those ashore and this is particularly the case in Europe now that crewing practices have changed. Today many companies are based in European and other OECD countries but the crews recruited to serve on their ships are hired from developing nations in the Far East, China, India and so forth. Seafarers work for long periods aboard vessels, often on contracts of nine months and sometimes longer. They move from ships back to shore, attempting to combine both work and life in their communities despite the disconnected nature of these two realms. This is not uncommon amongst migrant workers, and seafarers serve as an illustration (sometimes an extreme example) of people attempting to traverse borders and maintain a meaningful presence in more than one social 'world'.

The questions addressed here have salience in relation to migration and the ways in which migrants manage their lives, perceive themselves, and relate to oth-ers. These represent major issues for the twenty-first century which extend way beyond the illustrative example of seafaring. The social composition of contempo-rary communities is constantly changing as people move to find work – a major driver of migration. The places which emigrants leave may be affected as much as those to which people move. Increasingly, it may be possible for people to neither fully depart from one place nor to fully arrive in another but to retain a co-pres-ence in two societies at once. The lives of transborder travellers and the ways in which they may be embedded in, or marginalised from, societies and groups are increasingly important to social scientists as migration on a global scale continues to remain a central feature of modern life. Thus the consideration of 'transnation-als' and 'transnationalism' has developed into a major area of enquiry within social science enveloping a variety of groups of people and new ideas.

As this literature has developed, there has been criticism from some authors that accounts of transnationalism have become 'diluted' by a remoteness from the lived experiences of workers and those affected in their everyday lives by the process of globalisation and transnationalism:

> The earlier promise of ethnographies investigating the cultural and social effects of transnational identities in third world societies … has lately been diluted by an American cultural studies approach that treats transnationalism as a set of abstracted dematerialized cultural flows, giving scant attention either to the concrete, everyday changes in people's lives or the structural reconfigurations that accompany global capitalism …[W]hat has often dropped out of this approach is an interest in describing the ways in which people's everyday lives are transformed by the effects of global capitalism, how their own agencies are implicated in the making of these effects, and the social relationships in which these agencies are embedded. (Ong and Nonini 1997: 13)

In the spirit of this critique and the writings of authors contributing to texts such as *Global Ethnography* (Burawoy, Blum, George *et al.* 2000) this book seeks to contribute to the rectification of such deficiencies by adding to the works identifying and describing the 'real' lives of workers, affected by globalisation, as they themselves understand them. As such it considers the lives of groups of workers from Ghana and Cape Verde searching for shipboard jobs from bases within North Germany. It describes the worlds of seafarers aboard international cargo vessels and it goes beyond this to consider the shore-based communities from within which seafarers regularly depart using the illustrative case of two regions in India (Goa and Mumbai).

I undertook shipboard research on different kinds of vessel in connection with the project which largely informs this book. Since then, I have continued to undertake fieldwork aboard multinationally crewed cargo ships in connection with various studies at the Seafarers International Research Centre. My latest voyage, for example, was with Swedish officers and Filipino ratings, in late 2011, aboard a container roll-on/roll-off (ro-ro) vessel crossing the North Atlantic. Given that it is impossible to separate myself, or my ongoing learning, from the writing of this account, the continuing fieldwork aboard ships is undoubtedly influential. However, this account specifically draws upon the field notes[1] and interview transcripts from just five ships. Two of these were refrigerated cargo ships (reefers), two were product tankers (carrying refined product) and one was a bulk carrier (a bulker). The ships varied in age and flag, and they were operated by different companies. The main criterion for selection was that the vessels included in the research should be carrying crews of mixed nationality. Throughout the text pseudonyms are used, not only for individual people but also in place of vessel and company names.

The longest voyage I undertook aboard a single vessel was forty-two days. The shortest was just two weeks. All the crews that I sailed with were male[2] and although some of the vessels could have been carrying the wives of senior officers, in as much as this was permitted by some companies, none were. This had implications for the safe conduct of the research, which I have written about with Thomas elsewhere (Sampson and Thomas 2003). It may also have had implications for the substantive research findings, but this is very difficult to assess. In general, seafarers welcomed the opportunity to talk about themselves and seemed particularly comfortable to do this with me, a female researcher. In different ways they commented, on all of the vessels, that having a woman on board raised the standards of general behaviour, particularly with regard to personal hygiene. Beyond this, however, it appeared that seafarers soon forgot to think of me as an 'outsider' and did not pay particular mind to my gender. Living aboard a ship rather than merely visiting on a daily basis, and then returning home, accorded me something of the status of a 'seafarer' notwithstanding the different nature of the work that I was engaged in. In sharing the voyage with seafarers, I was subjected to the same living conditions, the same exposure to motion and noise, the same exposure to boredom, the same remoteness from family and friends, the same risks associated with sinking or drowning. In many senses, and of course quite literally, we were all 'in the same boat'. Institutionalised living and the sense of separation from the rest of the world combined to speed up the process by which I was assimilated into the daily consciousness of most seafarers as just 'part of the furniture'. Daily language quickly came to contain many swearwords. Interaction and joking was periodically obscene. Visits to seamen's bars continued as usual, as often as not with me 'in tow'; I took part in both dangerous and dirty activities (open lifeboat launches and inspections of ballast tanks for example) and generally I was accorded the temporary status of 'seafarer' as opposed to 'landlubber'. In discussions with my male colleagues, and having read their research field notes, I have been unable to detect any significant difference in the content of the data we gathered about transnationalism which I can attribute to our differences in sex. It is undoubtedly the case, however, that the research process itself was affected by issues of gender and that the research environment was a challenging one for a lone female researcher (Sampson and Thomas 2003).

Inevitably ethnicity and language also impact upon the research process in multi-ethnic settings and I was horrified to be told on my first research voyage, by a Filipino seafarer, that on seeing me climb the gangway, he had assumed that I was 'a racist'. His explanation for this was something to do with my long hair and dark sunglasses. Given that, at the time of negotiating physical access to the ship, I was extremely apprehensive, it may also have had something to do with the seriousness of my expression. The assumption had been made from a distant vantage point, however, and in the absence of any interaction between myself and any seafarer (I was literally just arriving). Shocking as this was to learn, in mixed nationality settings these kinds of misconceptions and first impressions are relatively easy to overcome, given time and opportunity, and seafarers were active in testing them out for themselves. In contrast, language barriers can pose a greater challenge.

English was the working language of all the ships I sailed on (Sampson and Zhao 2003). However, the language required to function in the job (particularly for those lower in the hierarchy i.e. 'ratings' as opposed to 'officers') is not the equivalent of the language required to discuss complex feelings and issues. I spent a great deal of time working alongside ratings and socialising with them in their free time. In doing so I became familiar with their modes of expression and I had a great deal of opportunity to tease out the meaning that lay behind many of the things they described. In the formal interviews that I also draw upon in writing this book, however, I found that much less meaning could be captured in the bare words constituting a transcript. While this problem could also arise with officers, their proficiency in the English language garnered more detailed, and richer, formal interview transcripts.

Additionally, I conducted fieldwork and interviews with seafarers' families in India in two locations (Goa and Mumbai). Using connections established through training centres and via seafarers who had participated in on-board fieldwork, I made contact with seafarers' partners in India and then followed a multiple web of connections using a snowballing technique in relation to the conduct of formal interviews. In addition I immersed myself as fully as possible in the life of the local community of seafarers in Goa and was included in a variety of social activities including weddings, Christmas festivities (including a family Christmas Day dinner with a chief engineer), and a very large silver wedding anniversary party.

Finally, I conducted fieldwork and interviews in Hamburg and Bremen building upon the work of my co-worker Torsten Schroeder.[3] In conducting this part of the research much use was made of seafarer hostels and the cheap bed and breakfast establishments frequented by seafarers. The local missions to seafarers were a great help as were local seafarers with local knowledge of Bremen and Hamburg.[4] Snowball sampling was, again, an important element in the conduct of formal interviews.

The ethnographic approach here is 'new' in as much as the research design was adapted to facilitate the study of a dispersed group of migrant workers who may come together in transient groups aboard ships for just a single voyage and who are sometimes employed from contract to contract by different ship operators. In these circumstances, attempting to track the same workers from a vessel back to their communities would be both impractical and overly intrusive. In essence it would involve following each individual seafarer back to their home (their family house) as the seafarers aboard a vessel never hailed from the same communities, even where they came from the same countries. Similarly, the process would be impractical if operated in reverse. Shipboard access is extremely difficult (and lengthy) to negotiate with operators and furthermore it is often only at the last minute that individual seafarers know what vessel they will next board, and when. The logistics alone rendered such approaches impossible.

The barriers experienced in accessing workers in both their workplaces, and in relation to their families and communities, are not unique to studies of seafaring nor to those of transnationalism. In his study of a Japanese advertising agency, for example, Brian Moeran notes that 'I rarely put in the long hours of overtime that was customary for my informants. Nor did I ever meet them in their home environment' (Moeran 2006: 119). In this research there was a similar separation and I was not able to meet any of the seafarers I sailed with in their homes, although I did meet one or two in other contexts (for example at industry conferences) following completion of the shipboard study. While it was impossible to track individuals from the workplace to their home communities, it was possible to research the life and work of seafarers aboard ships, the lives of seafarers and their families in shore-based communities, and the lives of seafarers hunting for work in hub ports such as Hamburg, by visiting each setting independently. This approach does not accord with the traditional approaches of anthropology in the construction of ethnographies and it may well be criticised on these grounds, and also as a consequence of the relatively short periods of fieldwork undertaken in each of the multiple sites that were involved. However, it nevertheless allows for the construction of a compelling, and arguably well-informed, sociological account of seafarers' lives on board ships and ashore. From a methodological point of view there are undoubtedly some 'costs' attributable to the multi-sited approach, but in the context of an occupation such as international seafaring, it is the only conceivable way in which a broad understanding of life and work can be attained.

The attempt to construct a multi-sited ethnography was undertaken in the spirit of the work of researchers who have tracked professionals working in globally diffuse occupations, such as Ulf Hannerz in his study of foreign media correspondents (Hannerz 2003, 2004), and also those who have utilised multi-sited ethnography when considering different dimensions of transnationalism (for example Roth 2009, Tapias and Escandell 2011).[5] It follows 'flows' of seafarers across borders in the spirit of multi-sited ethnography as proposed in a seminal article on the topic by George Marcus (Marcus 1995) but it does not follow individual trajectories, careers, or families. In short, it is based wholly on an interest in the life and work of a particular occupational group but in attempting to capture the different dimensions of such lives as fully as possible, it is not confined to a single occupational, or community, setting.

Since the mid-twentieth century, workplace ethnographies have become relatively accessible, although some authors have suggested that they are less common today than in the 1970s and 1980s (Strangleman and Warren 2008). A variety of writers have sought to describe the daily lives of workers in broad terms, as well as in relation to more specific issues such as professional assimilation (Becker, Geer, Hughes *et al.* 1961), industrial relations (Beynon 1973), gender (Pollert 1981, Westwood 1984, Chung 1988) and social relations in multinational firms (Sedgwick 2007). However, ethnographies of seafarers working aboard commercial cargo vessels[6] remain uncommon and in this respect this work might also claim to be 'new', though not entirely unique.

This study constitutes an account of the daily lives of real people (although throughout I make use of pseudonyms) and within it I have developed the idea of 'structured space' in making sense of their experiences and perceptions. As such, the text engages with aspects of life which appear to be neglected in relation to discussions of transnationalism and migration more generally. In collecting data from transmigrant seafarers searching for work in Germany (but originating from Ghana and Cape Verde), from seafarers aboard vessels which spend much time beyond national borders, and with the families of seafarers in India, I have been struck by the ways in which the possibilities for embeddedness are constrained and shaped by factors quite beyond the control of individuals. This is in contrast with the findings of studies emphasising the individual characteristics of migrants in connection with their successes or failures in integrating with, or remaining embedded in, both 'host' and 'home' societies. In relation to seafarers and their families close attention reveals the ways in which national laws, workplace hierarchies, cultural norms and cultural porosity all work together to structure the social spaces available to migrant workers, be they short-term overseas contract workers or longer-term residents.

I have therefore introduced the term 'structured space' to allow for a concentration upon the externalities shaping the lives of migrants in contemporary society rather than on the individual attributes which tend to be the focus for much enquiry in this area – education, class, networks, that is to say, social, financial, human and cultural capital. Without a doubt, such attributes impact upon the experiences of migrants, and there are a wealth of data in the public domain to support this, but the opportunity to consider these issues in three different contexts has clearly highlighted the overwhelming importance of the structure of the spaces seafarers inhabit when considering their degree of integration/exclusion. The structure of social space is, then, a hugely significant element in influencing the possibilities open to migrant workers, to asylum seekers, and to overseas contract workers. It is this, arguably more than anything else, which determines the lives which migrants and transmigrants end up living, in the societies and places they move to, or move into. It impacts significantly on embeddedness and marginalisation. What emerged clearly from the analysis of these data was the extent to which the structure of space is the key factor which facilitates or blocks the 'expenditure' of human, financial, social and cultural capital. It thereby dominates the more individual characteristics of migrants, their networks and the various kinds of access to capital that they 'possess', as an explanatory factor concerning social integration and exclusion.

The lives of contemporary seafarers have been strongly influenced by the rise of a globalised labour market and, while some aspects of seafaring remain immutable, the impact of the globalisation of the industry has been significant and can be seen to drive other globalised processes such as regulation, and the stretching of social frontiers. Thus the discussion of the potential for seafarer transnationality, which is presented, is rooted in an understanding of the shipping sector as globalised. Transnationality is considered against this background but is not seen to be an inevitable outcome of globalisation. The industry is subject to globalising processes and is arguably at the forefront of globalisation but this does not necessarily produce transnational social relations. Transnationality varies with context and is particularly influenced by the kind of social spaces that workers, in this case seafarers, inhabit. A central argument of this text is that the 'structure' of the spaces occupied by migrants and transmigrants impacts significantly on the types of social relations they develop and the extent to which these can be described as transnational.

In undertaking this, the book is divided into chapters which present empirical material and chapters which relate such material to prevailing theoretical contexts and seek to build from these in the development of ideas about transnationalism and social space. Thus following on from this introduction, Chapter 2 begins with a consideration of transnationality. Transnationalism has become almost as broadly used a term as globalisation and the chapter begins by considering its scope and establishing a working definition which delimits its meaning. It continues by briefly outlining the possible ways in which different groups of seafarers, those aboard ships and transmigrants, might be thought of in relation to debates about diaspora and transnationalism and it highlights the importance of the spaces they occupy and how these are conceptualised. The chapter then considers issues of differential access to the possibilities of transnationalism and goes on to discuss the ways in which the spaces inhabited by seafarers, and other potential transnationals, are constrained and thereby 'structured' by legal, political, and social, means, focusing upon and explaining the concept of 'structured space' in more detail.

Chapter 3 outlines the process of globalisation as it is manifested in the shipping industry. It considers the functions of flag states and the relationship between vessel ownership and registration. It presents data which shed light upon the factors which fleet personnel managers consider, and the pressures they are subject to, when selecting crews, and it goes on to outline the particular role of ship management companies and crew agencies, and their origins and development. In doing so, it highlights the extent to which the decline in the numbers of small ship owners, and their replacement with multinational owner-operators and ship management companies acting for shareholders or finance houses, has impacted upon the relationship between employers and employees in the shipping sector. This relationship and the contractual basis of seafarers' employment in the sector, which is increasingly organised on a temporary 'per voyage' basis, is key to understanding the development of both working and social relationships on board vessels which are characterised by a highly skewed distribution of power linked closely to occupational hierarchy.

Chapter 4 introduces data on the experiences of groups of transmigrant seafarers who travelled from developing regions of the world to parts of Europe, in this case Northern Germany, to seek work aboard European-flagged ships prior to the globalisation of the seafarers' labour market in the 1960s, 1970s and 1980s. The chapter discusses the ways in which globalisation has impacted upon these groups and develops the idea of the significance of constrained, or structured, social space. The experiences of the seafarers described also serve to highlight the ways in which globalisation has impacted not just upon European labour markets and the terms and conditions available to seafarers from OECD nations but more widely to include seafarers, for example, from Ghana, Cape Verde, and the Philippines.

In Chapters 5, 6 and 7, seafarers' lives aboard vessels are explored. Here the impact of globalisation, as it is experienced as a consequence of the crewing practices of ship operators, is considered. Such crewing practices mean that contemporary seafarers find themselves working in multinational crews where their colleagues from other nations are in competition with them for jobs and where differential rates of pay and conditions are in place such that crew members of the same rank may work for different wages and according to different terms in relation to leave and leave-pay. The environment in which seafarers live and work is notionally governed by the 'flag' of their vessel and as a result of long contracts (often nine months for ratings and sometimes longer) they often spend more of their working lives aboard such mixed nationality, hierarchically structured, vessels than in their 'home' communities. In the spirit of calls to further consider the experiences of workers employed in transnational corporations (TNCs) (see for example Kim 2004) the chapters describe living and working arrangements considering issues of nationality, hierarchy and transnationality.

The book moves towards a conclusion with an account (in Chapter 8) of the lives of seafarers' partners and the impact upon them of the globalisation of the industry from which their household incomes are derived. The empirical work underpinning these accounts was undertaken in India (in Mumbai and Goa) where many seafarers reside and careful attention is paid, throughout, to issues of transnationalism by 'contact'. The question of whether transnational households are associated with transnational employees is carefully considered in response to the literature, touched upon in Chapter 2, relating to the idea of transnational social fields. Furthermore the impact of the life and work of seafarers upon their families is discussed in broader terms in order to offer a sense of some of the lived consequences of the globalisation of the shipping industry and the concomitant development of a global labour market for seafarers.

The book concludes with a detailed consideration of the ways in which the lives of the three groups considered – working seafarers, transmigrant would-be seafarers, and seafarers' families – shed light upon the impact of globalisation on a workforce and 'its' connections. The potential for globalisation to produce a set of positive outcomes as a consequence of the rise of a transnationalism that facilitates 'two-way inclusion', as opposed to exclusion and marginalisation, is considered. The book concludes that such beneficial effects are scarce but that the legal, social and political dimensions of social spaces are key to the establishment of contexts for marginality or alternatively 'substrates' for inclusion and transnationalism. The argument suggests that nation states retain an important role in relation to the mediation of the experiences of life and employment in globalised sectors by structuring the spaces which migrants, transmigrants, and transnationals, inhabit.

Notes

1   I make fairly extensive use of field notes throughout the chapters, particularly describing life on board ship. They are generally used in two ways. They either describe physical settings or they describe interaction. Such use is intended to allow the reader to get a clearer picture of 'the scene' and to allow them to judge for themselves whether the interpretation placed on such findings seems reasonable. In this, the use of field notes echoes that made by Becker, Geer, Hughes *et al.* (1961). Further, field notes have an immediacy that is lost in later writing-up when an author's *post hoc* interpretation and analysis adds to the layers through which any observational data is filtered.

2   Women seafarers are rarely employed aboard cargo ships and tend to be concentrated in a number of large and more progressive companies (see Belcher, Lane, Sampson *et al.* 2003 for more information on women at sea).

3   With his prior agreement, I have combined Torsten's interview material with my own in writing about the experiences of seafarers searching for work in Hamburg.

4   And here I owe a particular debt of gratitude to my friend Hajo whose full name is omitted out of respect for his modest preference to always stay 'on the sidelines' and out of the 'limelight'.

5   NB unlike this research, in their work Tapias and Escandell were able to interview members of the same families and communities in two different countries.

6   Seafaring is an occupation and life which differs markedly to that experienced by those making a living from fishing, which is the subject of many ethnographies.

2

Transnationality and structured space

Migration is a major feature of modern society (Arnold 2012). In 2005, the number of international migrants was reported by the Migration Policy Institute to stand at a record level of 195 million which is suggested to be more than double the level recorded in 1960 (Fix, Papademetriou, Batalova *et al.* 2009).

Migration is often conceived of in the public imagination as an 'opportunity' (sometimes a 'lifeline') for people travelling to new countries and a challenge or even a threat to the residents of the countries to which they travel. There is plenty of evidence of the benefits which migrants bring to 'host' cultures and economies, as 'replacement migrants' in many European countries with declining populations for example (Arnold 2012). Similarly, there are very many examples of migrant deprivation, experiences of racism (Mclaughlin 1999), and exclusion. Nevertheless, this rather simplistic conceptualisation of migration (as opportunity and/or threat) somehow persists and is promulgated, in many parts of Europe, by the popular press.

In the days when travel was by foot, by cart, and/or by sail, migration tended to be an enduring affair whereby families travelled to new lands, severed many of their ties with their old communities, and settled permanently in order to start new lives. In the twenty-first century, however, the face of migration has changed to become a somewhat more fluid, and sometimes transient, affair as people not only relocate on a permanent basis but may also move from place to place, or shift between locations, where they nevertheless maintain connections. As always, however, both politics and economics drive and facilitate migration, and labour markets play a key role in where people move to and for how long.

In recent decades, the globalisation of the seafarer labour market has allowed many seafarers from across the world to join the ranks of temporary migrant workers in both skilled and relatively unskilled roles (as officers and as ratings). Such workers directly access the global labour market for seafarers via crewing agents established in their homelands. These agencies operate as third party crew suppliers to ship operators who have outsourced and offshored their labour requirements. Even before the rise of the global labour market, employment aboard ships provided the impetus for many would-be seafarers to travel to (primarily European) hub ports to seek work. Some of these seafarers stayed in the countries concerned (in Holland for example), achieved resident status, and secured land-based work. Others lived as transmigrants in countries such as Germany where they sought work on board ships while being granted only limited access to employment markets ashore.

In many ways, the globalisation of the seafarer labour market has been a process which has impacted negatively on seafarers as a group (for example, wages have fallen, leave periods have been reduced, temporary contracts have largely replaced permanent ones). Nevertheless, it also carries with it the possibility of positive change. Research on other groups of migrants suggests, for example, that seafarers from new labour supply countries could have been transformed into groups of 'transnationals' as a consequence of their relatively regular employment in multinational crews and/or their experiences of searching for work in 'foreign' hub ports. Transnationality has generally been described in positive terms, as an improvement on the possibilities of migrant marginalisation, ghettoisation and isolation. However, whether this is invariably the experience of transnationals remains open to question. Transnationality may not necessarily bring opportunities but could rather pose challenges to individuals striving to retain a presence in more than one community.

The idea of transnationality

Traditionally, the terms 'home' and 'host' have been used by anthropologists and social scientists seeking to conceptualise migration in bi-polar terms. Within this paradigm, migrants were studied in relation to receiving, or host, societies and in relation to sending, or home, societies without a great deal of specific attention being given to the linkages between the two. In the 1990s, however, the idea of transnationalism was refined and developed and became an extremely active area of social enquiry. The linkages between home and host societies and the identities of migrant workers became a central concern for those studying transnationality and today the active stretching and shaping of the definition of transnationality remains an ongoing, and contested, process.

The idea of the transnational individual emerged at a time when discussion of transnational corporations became a focus for social science in conjunction with discussions of globalisation. In some of the earlier accounts of transnationalism which emerged, transnationals were conceptualised as closely interlinked with transnational corporations. In this context, transnationals were primarily seen as occupational groups (employees of transnational corporations) operating within an international arena, slipping effortlessly across boundaries, and interacting with colleagues and associates who operate in similarly transnational environments. Hannerz, for example, describes such transnationals as:

> Transnational cultures today tend to be more or less clear-cut occupational cultures (and are often tied to transnational job markets) ... These cultures become transnational both as the individuals involved make quick forays from a home base to many other places – for a few hours or days in a week, for a few weeks

here and there in a year – and as they go, they find others who will interact with them in the terms of specialized but collectively held understandings. (Hannerz 1990: 243–4)

Such 'transnationals' were not necessarily seen to be cosmopolitan in nature in either an elitist, enlightenment, or a postethnic sense (Hollinger 1995). Indeed Hannerz has suggested that migrant workers, in general, are typically *not* cosmopolitan in nature:

> Most ordinary labour migrants do not become cosmopolitans either. For them going away may be, ideally, home plus higher income; often the involvement with another culture is not a fringe benefit but a necessary cost, to be kept as low as possible. A surrogate home is again created with the help of compatriots, in whose circle one becomes encapsulated. (Hannerz 1990: 243)

Thus for Hannerz and writers of a similar perspective, transmigrants may never move beyond interaction with their direct associates and colleagues when they are abroad and may never make any 'real' contact with the majority of people occupying the territorial spaces which they flit in and out of. However, they frequently have the opportunity to do so and *may* periodically choose to step out of their transnational 'bubbles' to become genuinely 'cosmopolitan' (Hannerz 1990).

This conceptualisation deviates from that contained within the main body of work relating to discussions of transnationalism as it stands today. In 2012, a significant quantity of literature emphasises the importance of the real existence and presence of transnationals in more than one society. In this, writers have moved away from notions of people parachuting in and out of societies or maintaining an encapsulated presence in enclaves or 'social bubbles' – to all intents and purposes cut off from the culture and day-to-day life of the majority of the population. In contrast, therefore, the current concept of transnationality is generally taken to describe labour migrants who maintain 'multi-stranded' relationships with their 'home' societies that incorporate 'familial, economic, social, organizational, religious, and political' (Basch, Glick Schiller and Szanton Blanc 1995: 7) links and ties. In the course of this process cultural and social distinctions are said to become blurred (Kearney 1999a) as communities (Faist 2000) come to span state boundaries utilising new technology and telecommunications, as well as benefiting from the development of free trade laws and a better international transport infrastructure (Portes 1996).

The idea of spanning territorial boundaries is critical here alongside a notion of living life in more than one social space. In contrast to migrants described as having assimilated into host societies (the corollary being that they have largely disconnected from 'homelands'), transnationals may be seen as having a foot in two cultures, two societies, two countries, at the same time. They live physically, mentally and emotionally, in more than one place engaging in a series of ongoing cross-border movements (Mitchell 2000) which may or may not involve physically traversing space.

New technology is seen by many to be at the heart of transnationality (Vertovec 1999) which may represent a kind of 'speeded up' version of diasporic relations which are already defined by many as incorporating a degree of transnational exchange. In discussing Filipino Americans, for example, Okamura suggests '... diasporas should be understood as consisting of transnational linkages between an immigrant/ethnic minority and its homeland (or cultural center) and its counterpart communities in other host societies' (Okamura 1998: 14).

The overlap in terminology can be problematic here, however, as diasporas and transnational communities, while closely related, are clearly conceptually different. Diasporas are primarily located in a physical world that is located beyond the borders of members' increasingly (over time) 'imagined' homelands. Many diasporas emerge as a result of the exclusion of people from their homelands. Such exiles have no option but to cut all links and ties with their homelands which they one day may hope to return to. Many scholars suggest that diasporas are specifically characterised by suffering: that members of diasporas have all endured a traumatic event associated with being effectively exiled (Faist 2000). However it is not clear how reference to a common collective experience of general 'trauma' is helpful conceptually except in marking the extent to which members of diasporas are excluded from their 'homelands' which increasingly become 'imagined' places. In this context, their links with others outside their homeland may be far stronger than those within their homelands. Conceptually it seems unreasonable to exclude other groups sharing these characteristics (exclusion, lack of contact with homelands and stronger contacts with other 'exiles' than members of homeland communities) on the basis that they have not been subject to mass upheaval – war, torture, trauma. While controversial, a broader use of the term diaspora is useful, therefore, when considering this concept alongside the idea of transnationality.

Thus, members of a diaspora, whatever its origins, may maintain some cross-border links with their homeland but these are generally irregular and infrequent. This contrasts with the notion of the transnational who, by definition, maintains considerable cross-border linkages, networks and emotional and financial relationships. Some Filipinos, for example, might helpfully be characterised as part of a Filipino diaspora: they may cling to a Filipino identity yet may never return to the Philippines, severing all direct connections with their homelands or alternatively relying on telecommunication and the sending of 'balikbayan' boxes packed with gifts for relatives in the Philippines (Okamura 1998). They do not in this sense reside in more than one geocultural space, and they may have stronger links with other expatriate nationals than with those who remain 'at home'. Indeed, Rafael has described how Filipino 'Balik Bayans' are in some senses 'outsiders' (he refers to their 'spectral presences') in the Philippines, no longer at 'home' in their imagined homelands (Rafael 2000). By contrast others who seek work abroad from the Philippines may develop a web of intricate cross-national relationships and connections which mean that the reality of their lives and their identities is characterised by duality as they reside physically and emotionally in more than one national space and culture. These workers might be said to be transnationals.

However as the concept of transnationalism has been developed and stretched, it has been argued, by some, that it is not necessarily the case that people need to physically traverse borders in order to engage in transnational activity or to occupy transnational space (Faist 2000, Bunnell 2007). However, within this text, and the conceptualisation of transnationalism that runs through it, the physical crossing of borders is considered an important aspect of the definition of transnationality in relation to individuals for whom, it is argued, there should be the maintenance of a meaningful presence in more than one society. Transnationals who *rarely* physically travel back to their 'homelands' are *unlikely* to be able to maintain such a presence over a *long period of time*. Thus, this account suggests that physical travel and a material presence in two societies is required, in most cases, for the development of medium to long-term transnationality: that in considering transnationals it is important to recognise that they are by definition embedded within more than one social world; that they are neither fully assimilated into the culture of the society they have moved to, nor are they divorced from it. An important aspect of this conceptualisation of transnationality is considered to be the two-way flow of information, cultural values, knowledge, and even capital (Portes 1995), between 'migrants' and their 'original' communities. This takes place in the context of communities that have a genuine presence in host societies facilitating a meaningful two-way exchange and the possibility of the emergence of cultural hybridities and multiple identities (Vertovec 1999).

One element of this exchange is well known and relates to remittances being sent from migrants to their 'homes', i.e. their countries of origin, from their countries of domicile. The importance of remittances to the economies of 'sending' nations has been documented extensively in relation to Pakistan (Ballard 1987), Haiti, Dominican Republic, Brazil, Ecuador and Mexico (Levitt and de la Dehesa 2003), El Salvador and China (Landolt and Da 2005) and the Philippines (Sampson 2003) amongst others. Such has become their importance that governments of sending nations have frequently sought to encourage the return of remittances not only to families but to national 'causes' or projects. Levitt and de la Dehesa describe in some detail the mechanisms by which different example nations have sought to 'capture' and make use of dollar remittances, suggesting that the most developed of these approaches are successful in channelling dollar remittances from foreign-based migrants into 'public works' programmes. They explain:

> To attract money from nationals abroad, governments have adopted policies ranging from investment funds that pay higher rates to matching funds for investments in public works. The most elaborate and successful of such programmes is that instituted by the Mexican government. Since its creation in 1990, the DGMCA [General Directorate from Mexican Communities Abroad] has fostered the development of hometown and home-state organizations which raise funds for public projects in Mexico. (Levitt and de la Dehesa 2003: 592)

Similarly both China and El Salvador are examples of states which, having initially resisted emigration, have now come to embrace it. In the People's Republic of China (PRC) successful economic migration has come to be understood as a patriotic act while in El Salvador migrants, once characterised as traitors, are now described as 'distant brother[s]' (Landolt and Da 2005: 637).

However, while remittances are a very important factor in encouraging states to make efforts to retain links with migrant labour (Faist 2000), capital can also move in the other direction, i.e. from, so-called, 'sending countries' to 'receiving countries'. For example, in the 1980s, capital flowed into the UK as British-Chinese entrepreneurs obtained financial backing for new ventures from friends and relatives in Hong Kong who were fearful of a recession and the then colony's more general future prospects (Benton and Gomez 2000). Less welcome flows may also occur in relation to political influences and ideas. In relation to their 'home' societies transmigrants may come to occupy a position of considerable significance. They, like refugees, may have a significant political (as well as an economic) impact. In discussing the importance of Timorese refugees in highlighting the plight of East Timor and putting it onto the international political agenda Goodman has suggested that:

> As globalization accelerates, transnational pressures play an increasingly important role in political culture. Cultural linkages created by migration can be sustained and reproduced, allowing migrant groupings to maintain a role as movers for social change. Such linkages open up possibilities for mutual engagement or dialogue across the external-internal boundaries of nation statehood (Goodman 1997: 457).

In these processes the technologies of communication are once again of supreme importance. This two-way flow of finance, of people, of knowledge, and so forth, is central to the idea of transnationality and has perhaps driven the development of the notion of transnational 'social fields' (Levitt and Glick Schiller 2003). This terminology encapsulates the imagery of a large-scale arena in which activities freely take place obliterating the meaning of borders or national frontiers. The terminology may take us too far from the realities of transnationalism and the barriers which are necessarily presented to, and to varying extents overcome by, the majority transnationals, however. It is important to note that these barriers never completely 'dissolve' for most transnationals although they may, or may not, be successfully overcome by them.

It is not only with respect to transnational social fields that the concept of the transnational has been arguably over-stretched. Crang, Dwyer and Jackson (2003) imaginatively argue for the application of the term transnational to space. In doing so they argue that the ontological definitions of transnationality that have been adopted require revision in order to broaden the approach to whom, or what, can be seen as transnational. The attractive implication of their work is that engaging (very loosely) in transnational space or being involved with organisations that can be described as having transnational 'biographies' renders an individual, or a group of individuals, 'transnational'. Crang et al argue that the efforts to delimit the concept of transnationalism risk the difficulty, as they frame it, that:

> transnationals and transnational communities all too easily become synonymous with national 'ethnic minorities' … while overlooking the transnational connections of so-called national 'majorities'. (Crang *et al.* 2003: 444)

There are several aspects of this argument that are problematic. Perhaps most importantly, the suggestion that transnational communities may become synonymous with ethnic minorities is unsustainable. A strict definition of transnationality works against such a situation not in favour of it. Employing the definition of Portes, for example, many ethnic minority groups, well assimilated into new homelands and with only imagined connections to a 'motherland' of origin, speaking only one language and not participating in a meaningful way in the everyday life of two nations, are excluded from being defined as 'transnationals'.

Portes and others have sought to retain a clear meaning for the term transnational suggesting, for example, that it should only be applied to people who move easily between two countries, have homes, economic, political and cultural interests in two nations, and effectively retain 'a simultaneous presence in both' (Portes 1997: 16). This account supports such efforts to maintain a specific definition for transnationality.

Seafarers and transnationality

Research on transnationality may be founded on a notion that transnationalism has emerged as a consequence of transformations in the broader global economy – the globalisation of industry and the rise of the transnational corporation, for example. Alternatively, it may be that researchers see the development of transnationalism as driven by innovation in the realms of information and communications technology (ICT). Here while the relevance of development in ICT is acknowledged, an emphasis is placed upon the importance of transformations in the global economy and specifically the emergence of global labour markets in driving transnationality.

Some industries have 'globalised' faster or more extensively than others but in shipping we have a prime example of one that is highly globalised. Seafarers are recruited all over the world via both formal and informal mechanisms. The use of crewing agents with a mandate to supply competent and qualified seafarers is widespread among ship owners. However, it is still possible to access the seafarer labour market informally and especially in large port cities such as Rotterdam and Hamburg. The nature of the informal seafarer labour market has therefore led to the formation of port-based communities of migrant, and immigrant, seafarers seeking new or better jobs at sea (working conditions and salaries vary dramatically from ship to ship). Such communities may be transnational or they may come to form part of various diasporas. In some cases they may incorporate both transnational and diasporic characteristics. In this context, their position, their national or transnational orientations, and the characteristics of the 'spaces' they occupy are of great interest. Similar questions are presented by seafarers at sea. They may be seen as 'cosmopolitan' transnationals in Hannerz's sense or they can be, more compellingly, conceptualised as occupying different kinds of locations. Arguably while the term 'hyperspace' is both helpful and appropriate in conceptualising such arenas of work and life (Sampson 2003) so too might be the disputed concept of a transnational social field.

Cosmopolitanism can be used to refer to people or communities that are open to strangers/difference (Werbner 1999) while the term 'hyperspace' (Kearney 1999b) may be applied to deterritorialised locations such as airports, the offices of multinational corporations, or franchise enterprises. When considered in isolation from their local environments, hyperspaces are characterised by monotonous and universal features. They are in many senses culturally indeterminate reflecting neither one culture nor another. For example, the office of a multinational shipping company in Manila may closely resemble similar premises in Singapore or Glasgow. Such offices may be staffed with multi-ethnic personnel and the culture of the surrounding environs may only slightly permeate the office 'shell' to reach the generally homogenous transnational corporate space. Furthermore, we would not expect a hyperspace to reflect the culture of corporate owners, which in any case may be very difficult to establish.

Within these terms ships may well qualify as hyperspaces. They share common uniform features regardless of their ownership, management, trading region, or crew complement. On a merchant cargo ship one neither feels in Europe, nor in Asia, nor in the USA, nor in any other identifiable world region: a feeling accentuated by a ship's separation from land. These are not precisely cultural vacuums but they may reflect an occupational rather than a recognisable geo-spatial culture. In the context of a global shipping industry it is therefore useful to explore the extent to which multinational cargo ships can be described as deterritorialised 'hyperspaces'. In doing so it is helpful to compare seafarer 'communities' ashore with those at sea. In terms of their 'residents' it is worth considering the kinds of spaces seafarers occupy. Whether, for example, these are cosmopolitan spaces or spaces on the 'edge'; spaces of oppression or of resistance (hooks 1990). For while the notion of transnationality is a seductive one we need to be alert to the possibility that transnationals, far from being present in more than one culture or society, are in fact rendered absent from all societies and cultures becoming 'spectral presences' (Rafael 2000) in their 'homelands' and in the places which they have 'newly populated'.

Inequalities and transnationality

In examining the ways in which barriers to social participation, and integration, are overcome (or not) attention has begun to be given to ideas of power and access to power. For example, Massey's useful idea of power geometry (Massey 1994) has been applied to issues of transnationalism amongst seafarers (Sampson and Schroeder 2006). Similarly writers have begun to pay attention to the policies of 'sending' and 'receiving' countries and the impact these may have on the experiences of transnationals (Levitt 2001, Landolt and Da 2005). The work of such writers reminds us, should we require a reminder, that transnationality is not an option that is uniformly available to all migrants parted either temporarily or permanently from their extended families and 'homelands'. In addition to what might be termed structural issues, returned to later, there are also issues of social capital and of micro-familial relationships, cultural capital and mere happenstance that effect the extent to which individuals are able to develop transnational lives. Landolt and Da offer us, for example, contrasting case studies of families from the PRC who are successful in traversing transnational social/physical space and those who are not. For some it seems 'time-space compression' does shrink the social world and allows for the emergence of transnationality; for others, however, physical distances cannot be overcome and may split families apart. Landolt and Da describe how their research illustrates that:

> While some families are able to shrink and bridge distances, others experience dramatic ruptures in their family network. There is not only one type of transnational families, but rather a continuum of familial arrangements, families may shrink and successfully bridge long distances or their multi-local transnational practices may be ruptured, fragmented and even interrupted for substantial periods of time. (Landolt and Da 2005: 647)

The difficulties faced by migrants in attempting to enter into host societies were identified long ago by authors such as Irvin Child (1943) who identified the risks faced by migrants in attempting to be assimilated: risks of rejection by the mainstream 'host' society and simultaneous rejection by the minority 'home' society for perceived treachery and betrayal. In developing this work in a more contemporary context Richard Alba (2005) has highlighted a critical element in this process in bringing attention to the question of what we might think of as the porosity of host societies. Discussing second-generation immigrants in the USA, France and Germany, Alba describes what he terms 'bright' and 'blurred' boundaries across which migrants find it more or less difficult to pass. Bright boundaries are those where individuals find themselves clearly placed upon one side or another, whereas he describes blurred boundaries in opposition to these as:

> The counterpoint to a bright boundary is one that is or can become blurred in the sense that, for some set of individuals (generally members of the ethnic minority), location with respect to the boundary is indeterminate or ambiguous. This could mean that individuals are seen as simultaneously members of the groups on both sides of the boundary or that sometimes they appear to be members of one and at other times members of the other. (Alba 2005: 25)

While Alba discusses the assimilation of second-generation migrants his focus upon the structures of society which he identifies as producing bright or blurred boundaries, facilitating or resisting assimilation (religion, language, citizenship and law), alerts us to the possibilities that transnationality is equally likely to be more or less possible in different social settings. Similarly the work of Portes and his colleagues in presenting evidence from the Children of Immigrants Longitudinal Study should remind us that it may be 'easier' for transnationals to be located in some (marginal) parts of their host society than others. The risk being, for example, that they can only integrate into marginalised populations in specific geographic areas such as the inner cities (Portes, Fernandez-Kelly and Haller 2005, Portes and Zhou 1993). This transnationalism at the 'edges' of society shares some equivalence with 'downward assimilation' (Portes et al 2005) in as much as neither condition challenges the concept of transnationalism or assimilation per se but both highlight the qualitative differences found within the experiences of assimilation and transnationalism and raise questions about when assimilation at the margins can be considered assimilation in society, and when transnationalism at the edges can be regarded as genuine transnationality. In this sense, we may regard transnationality as depending upon the 'structure' of the spaces in which transnationals are bi-located, on the permeability of new 'host' societies and on the adhesiveness of 'home' societies. In contrast to the argument of Faist who suggests that exclusionary forces in immigrant host societies encourage migrants to maintain links to 'home' thereby facilitating the development of transnational communities, here it is suggested that where 'host' societies remain impermeable, or only partially permeable, and 'home' societies prove to be 'non-sticky', individuals traversing national boundaries might as easily find themselves amongst the dispossessed as find themselves part of a transnational community. A study by Leichtman of Lebanese migrants to Senegal highlights such a situation. He presents evidence to suggest that the Senegalese residents are hostile to Lebanese migrants, that the Lebanese in Senegal face discrimination and that they do not 'feel' Senegalese (Leichtman 2005: 668–9). Yet concurrently the Lebanese second and third-generation migrants do not feel Lebanese either, taking a rather negative view of the residents of their 'motherland' in relation to values and 'mentality'. Leichtman explains:

> 'We are not like the Lebanese of Lebanon', they say. 'We have a different mentality.' When asked to define what this means, they respond unanimously that the Lebanese of Lebanon are materialistic and shallow, care only about a person's outside and not their inner values, and are less tolerant than they are. (Leichtman 2005: 671)

Similarly, in a study of Kurdish migrants settling in Denmark, Christiansen uncovered surprisingly negative views of the values and attitudes of villagers who had remained 'at home'. He reports that:

> their focus is constantly on practices in Turkey and among their compatriots that they view critically. For instance, the way that strangers ask you questions in a very direct manner (rather than being more reserved and discreet); or the highly de-regularised nature of the traffic in Konya; or the way that the permanently resident villagers are just waiting, rather than working, relying on migrants to provide an income for them; the way that staff in offices and shops unrestrainedly talk to their friends on the phone rather than serving clients and customers etc. (Christiansen 2008: 99)

In Denmark such critical views were often associated with individuals motivated to achieve high levels of integration with Danish society which perhaps required a distancing from the values of their 'home' communities. In the case of the

Lebanese discussed by Leichtman, such negative views appeared to arise from a combination of visits back home and experiences of 'betrayal' by family members remaining in Lebanon – the squandering of remittances intended for the purchase of land and property for example. A loss of status in Lebanon as a result of relative impoverishment in Senegal, rocketing prices and increasing affluence in Lebanon, were also regarded by Leichtman as important. Whatever the reasons, however, the account is one in which the migrants described no longer feeling a part of their 'homeland' and those that returned to Lebanon often did not remain there for long or curiously settled in 'enclaves' of similarly returned Lebanese migrants to Senegal. Leichtman acknowledges that second and third-generation Lebanese migrants to Senegal are *not* embedded in the everyday social activities of both 'homeland' and 'hostland' but nevertheless conceives them as transnationals on the basis that they:

> Maintain transnational characteristics through their self-identification and definition by others, their 'imagining' of their motherland, and their upholding of political and religious identities. (Leichtman 2005: 681)

However, this arguably stretches the concept of transnationalism too far. For the concept to carry a distinct meaning it is necessary to preserve some of its specificity and essence. Perhaps the mistake here has been for authors to study transnationality with too strong a focus on linkages, of *any* kind, 'back home', or alternatively to pay exclusive attention to embeddedness in 'host' societies (Leichtman 2005: 680). The strength of the concept of transnationalism lies in its notion of embeddedness in the daily activities of *both* home and host societies. Therefore, studies of transnationalism need to focus on linkages with both countries (or places) of residence and countries of origin. Such linkages need to be considered from both a qualitative and a quantitative perspective to consider not just how often people, or money, or knowledge, etc. flow back and forth across a boundary but also what significance or meaning is attached to such movements and what the potential consequences may be. Where ties and involvement are, to all intents and purposes, prevented, severed, meaningless, or latent, transnationality in relation to people, communities and identities cannot be argued for.

Structured space

In accounting for transnationality, and the possibilities for transnationalism, much thought needs to be given to what can be conceived of as the 'structured social spaces' in which migrants find themselves, i.e. the legislative constraints under which they are placed, the cultural and material confines which may result from discrimination, prejudice, unemployment (possibly enforced), and the threat of violence which all impact hugely on their ability to become transnationals. The importance of such factors is demonstrated clearly in the findings from North Germany (presented in a later chapter), where seafarers' transnational possibilities differed greatly according to differences in the structured spaces they occupied.

Similarly, seafarers aboard vessels occupied very different social spaces to those occupied by transmigrant seafarers located ashore in Germany (as described in Chapter 4). The term 'structured space' is therefore introduced to encourage consideration of the kinds of spaces available to would be transnationals and the kinds of factors shaping such spatial opportunities. This definition diverges from previous usage of the idea of 'structured space' which has usually referred in social science to space structured by architecture or 'cultural landscapes' (see for example Schmidt and Voss 2000). In relation to issues of migration and transnationality, structured space might be considered as a continuum. At one end of such a continuum, impermeable and impervious social structures, which exclude migrants, can be seen to produce homogenous cultural spaces where migrants are effectively absent, even if physically present, and more permeable porous social structures resulting in the creation of heterogeneous multicultural, multinational and multiethnic spaces at the other end. The archetypal heterogeneous space being: 'hyperspace' (Kearney 1995).

As described in some detail in Chapter 4, in Germany, Cape Verdean transmigrant seafarers live lives of extreme exclusion. The rules governing social security payments and employment ashore in Germany produced an environment, at the turn of the century, in which transmigrant Cape Verdean seafarers were marginalised at the very edges of society. This contrasted with the experiences of other transmigrant seafarers within Germany who occupied differently structured spaces by virtue of their passports and associated rights (this was, for example, the case for Cape Verdean, Portuguese passport holders).

Transmigrant seafarers are not alone, however, in experiencing extreme marginalisation and there are strong parallels with the Cape Verdean seafarers' experiences to be found in accounts of asylum seekers in Ireland (Luibheid 2004), and elsewhere, suggesting that the notion of structured space might usefully be applied more broadly. Luibheid for example writes that:

> The combined effect of Direct Provision and Dispersal is to ensure that, although asylum seekers may physically remain in Ireland while their cases are considered, they are largely excluded from meaningful participation in Irish life. (Luibheid 2004: 337)

Others too have noted such marginalisation (hooks 1990, Fabricant 1998, Yegenoglu 2005) and Massey's concept of power geometry (Massey 1994) highlights the perceived need to conceptualise the inequalities in power that result in people being more or less able to thrive in a period of globalisation. Yegenoglu reminds us not to make assumptions about the progressive and transformative capacity of 'travel, displacement, mobility, and flow' (Yegenoglu 2005: 120). She is critical of the work of Clifford (1992, 1997) and others for focusing upon diasporas located in the first world rather than considering the plight of the marginalised and often displaced poor in 'homelands' of the developing world. She writes:

> One is struck by the similarity between Clifford's and Hardt and Negri's positions here, as they all attribute a necessary transformative capacity to the

mobility of migrants and the hybrid cultural forms that emanate from such movements ... my concern is to highlight how attributing a transformative and resistive power to migrancy, mobility, and hybridity has become something of a structural and structuring feature of a certain type of intellectual discourse in the Anglo-American academy. (Yegenoglu 2005: 123)

Others have also argued against a romanticised conceptualisation of transnationality (Fabricant 1998). In opposition to writers such as Portes who argue that transnationalism from 'below' weakens 'a fundamental premise of the hegemony of corporate economic elites and domestic ruling classes ... that labour and subordinate classes remain local while dominant elites are able to range global' (Portes 1997: 18), Fabricant urges us to consider the differences between elites benefiting from 'globe trotting' and marginalised poor migrants seeking work on any terms, and to question if it is sensible to imply that we are 'all in the same boat' (Fabricant 1998). Favell similarly distinguishes between 'elite' and 'ethnic' migrants arguing for nuanced understandings of each while, in an unexpected twist, suggesting that 'elite' migrants should not universally be characterised as having it 'easy as foreigners' while 'ethnic' migrants are cast as having 'no social impact, or access to goods and forms of social power' (Favell 2003: 423). Mindful of this, one might nevertheless think to question, for example, in whose interests migrant groupings might 'maintain a role as movers for social change' (Goodman 1997: 457) and, in sympathy with Yegenoglu's arguments, what positive impact this might have, or might not have, on the 'slum' dwellers of many world cities? As Christiansen highlights:

How positive the involvement of migrants actually is can of course be questioned. As reported by scholars researching the Mexican case it may not lead to development at all, instead it can become a means of securing and carrying out the interests of the migrants from the village, perhaps at the cost of the non-migrant inhabitants who live in the village permanently. (Christiansen 2008: 89)

What the idea of 'structured space' alerts us to is the need to focus not only on the networks, and the practices and behaviours of individuals and groups (the focus of much of the literature on transnationality), but on the social structures enveloping and constraining, or conversely, enabling migrants and potential transnationals. Furthermore, it is not only the 'receiving spaces' that need to be considered here. Authors engaged in discussions of transnationality similarly need to be interested in the structure of spaces in 'sending societies' too.

In the course of history, millions of people have migrated from one place to another in search of better living conditions and/or work. In fact one of the salient, and now classic, texts of modern sociology *The Polish peasant* (Thomas and Znaniecki 1958) dealt with this issue as a central feature of contemporary society. Such movements have wrought change not only in the places, villages, towns and countries which people have chosen to leave but also in those places where they have resettled (Ballard 1987). Thus, Rotterdam may be said to have been altered as much as Manila, or a village in Cebu, as a result of the influx/outflow of Filipino seafarers into its confines.

The main determinants of the size and timing of migrations have been described as patterns of economic transformation, and importantly, the actions of individual states (Eades 1987). From time to time states, such as South Africa, have a vested political interest in sustaining migratory work patterns (ibid.). However in the post-war period the importance of remittances to the economies of migrants' 'home' societies has become increasingly apparent and some states have been motivated by such economic considerations to encourage outward migration and contract work. In Pakistan in the 1980s, migrants provided 50 per cent of the country's foreign exchange and fuelled local economic 'booms', at least initially, in areas such as Mirpur (Ballard 1987). In Hong Kong the importance of remittances sent back to impoverished mainland Chinese families was a feature of Shenzhen life long before the region was returned to Chinese governance and before China began to promote migration and the return of remittances as an act of patriotism (Landolt and Da 2005). O'Donnell reports this memorably in her article on the urbanisation of Shenzhen when she explains:

> For these residents Hong Kong was always a resource. In fact, Uncle Liao, an elderly fisherman went so far as to assert that opening the local economy to Hong Kong wasn't even an original idea. I smiled at his vehemence.
> 'Don't laugh'. He shook a finger at me emphasising his point. 'What was the so-called "eighty cents economy"? Whenever things were too difficult here, we wrote a letter to a Hong Kong relative asking for help. It cost eighty cents to mail'. (O'Donnell 2001: 421–2)

The importance of remittances has led administrations to consider the usefulness of protecting the social glue which binds migrants and contract workers to their 'homelands' and efforts have been made to enhance such 'stickiness'. A strong example of efforts to maximise the benefits accruing in the 'home' state as a consequence of migration is found in the Philippines. Here, as in other states, efforts have been made to positively benefit from the absences of Filipino migrant workers, maximising the positive impact of migration upon local towns and villages. However, the Philippines can be said to have gone beyond this in actively encouraging and supporting an exodus (and return) of migrant workers, including seafarers.

In the year 2000, Filipino seafarers alone were estimated to earn $3bn annually in foreign exchange (Almazan 2000). Such large influxes of dollars were recognised by the Marcos administration as essential to the viability of the Philippines' economy. Marcos himself is credited with introducing the term 'Balik Bayan' (literally meaning 'return country' or more manageably 'homecomer') into the national language. He is said to have used it in a speech imploring Filipinos to visit their 'home' country at least once a year during holidays (Basch, Glick Schiller, Szanton-Blanc 1995). This request was supported with legislation to facilitate their return, and to allow them to bring two boxes of duty-free, foreign-bought goods into the country every year. Today such practices have been institutionalised. Providing they can produce a supporting airline ticket, 'Balik Bayans' can visit a duty-free shop in Manila and purchase goods up to seventy-two hours after their return from overseas employment.

As well as encouraging Filipinos, and Filipinas, to migrate in search of lucrative work the government has also sought to regulate such migration and maximise the benefits which can be accrued by the Philippines' Economy. Seafarers' employment is thus regulated (along with that of other overseas workers) by the Philippines Overseas Employment Agency (POEA) and all seafarers are required to remit a minimum of 80 per cent of their basic earnings aboard foreign vessels to a Philippines bank account. The POEA also exercises more general control over seafarers' employment terms and conditions setting, for example, the levels of compensation due with varying forms of disability associated with injuries sustained in the conduct of work.

Thus, government legislation (with regard to rights, taxes, investments and so forth) is important in determining the 'stickiness' of 'homelands' and the extent to which migrants are likely to retain multi-stranded relationships across national borders: Space is structured in 'sending' countries not only in 'receiving' nations.

That the Philippines, and other state administrations, encourage seafarers, amongst others, to work overseas is undeniable. In the Philippines the state's success in promoting the 'migration' of seafarers ensures that Filipino seafarers are one of the major groups constituting the contemporary 'ethnoscape' as envisaged by Appadurai (1990). What is less clear from an examination of state practices and a consideration of the structure of space in both home and host societies, however, is what impact living and working abroad, and aboard, has on Filipino and other seafarers and their families, and on the communities they bisect. As a migrant labour-force constantly moving across borders, both to search for work and to undertake it, are they a part of a transnational 'community' and/or do they lead transnational lives? Are they like some migrants located on the 'edges' or 'margins' of societies and are the spaces they occupy spaces of oppression, resistance, or harmony (hooks 1990)? What are the links between the societies they span, and where do such seafarers feel they 'belong'? Does their identity remain constant or is it subject to a process of transformation over time? These questions can only be addressed by a detailed consideration of the practices and behaviours of individuals and groups of transmigrants and the contexts of such practices. Thus a detailed consideration of transnationality needs to focus upon the *spaces accessible to potential transnationals and the kinds of interaction these facilitate*, alongside the networks, attitudes and activities of groups of potential transnationals. Given the current interest in transnational capital and transnational communities, it is worth examining the extent to which seafarers ashore in countries such as Germany, and afloat aboard internationally flagged ships, occupy hyperspaces and/or constitute 'deterritorialized', 'transnational', or 'cosmopolitan' communities (Kearney 1995, Werbner 1999). It is similarly worth considering the extent to which the families of migrant seafarers are affected by their exposure to transnational spaces and practices. We might consider, for example, whether the idea of transnationalism can be stretched at least as far as the immediate family of transnational workers, or whether this is taking the idea of transnationality too far? Such questions are considered in some detail in the chapters that follow.

3

Changes in the shipping industry and their consequences for contemporary seafarers

'Sea Fever'

I must go down to the seas again,
to the lonely sea and the sky,
And all I ask is a tall ship
and a star to steer her by,
And the wheel's kick and the wind's song
and the white sail's shaking,
And a grey mist on the sea's face
and a grey dawn breaking.

I must go down to the seas again,
for the call of the running tide
Is a wild call and a clear call
that may not be denied;
And all I ask is a windy day
with the white clouds flying,
And the flung spray and the blown spume,
and the sea-gulls crying.

I must go down to the seas again
to the vagrant gypsy life,
To the gull's way and the whale's way
where the wind's like a whetted knife;
And all I ask is a merry yarn
from a laughing fellow rover,
And quiet sleep and a sweet dream
when the long trick's over.

John Masefield, 1902

The globalisation of the shipping industry

While some elements of seafarer life have remained immutable – crying seagulls, grey dawns, salt spray – shipping has changed a great deal from the days of sail, and seafaring, too, has been transformed to differ from Masefield's characterisation of a 'vagrant gypsy life' in his poem 'Sea Fever' (Masefield 1902) – albeit not 100 per cent. This way of life, that has so enthralled writers, painters and poets over the centuries, has traditionally been overlooked in the work of social scientists[1] and to some extent it remains under-explored even in the twenty-first century.[2]

Aboard ship, life is isolated. Sometimes, in the peace of a sunset, watching a school of spinner dolphins on the horizon, such isolation can be welcome. Traversing empty expanses of ocean there are some magical experiences to be had, whether these include watching the Southern Cross high above you set against dark velvet skies, or looking in wonder at streams of phosphorescent algae lighting up the water as it is broken by the ship's bow. More often than not, however, life aboard a merchant cargo vessel is noisy, lonely and dangerous. Seafarers are vulnerable workers. They work on very long, generally temporary, contracts and can be hired and fired at will. Union activism is often punished with blacklisting and in general seafarers recognise that putting up with 'their lot' is part of the life. They consider that the work and the life are something to be 'endured'.

In order to understand the background to the creation of the environments and contexts discussed throughout this text it is first necessary to appreciate the changes that have taken place within the shipping industry and how these have affected the global labour market for seafarers. Primarily these can be understood in relation to the processes that have come to be termed 'processes of globalisation'.

Globalisation, in contrast to shipping, might be argued to have been rather over-engaged with across the social sciences. However, this reflects the centrality of the range of concepts represented by the term 'globalisation' in understanding contemporary social transformations. There is considerable disagreement amongst theorists interested in globalisation as to its definition, the time of its 'birth', its trajectory, and its likely risks and benefits. Writings on globalisation reflect this plethoric diversity and emanate from a variety of disciplines some of which cloud (Schirato and Webb 2003) and some of which clarify (Newton 2004, Scholte 2000) the debate about what globalisation is and what effects it may, or may not, be having on workers and on society.

Hirst and Thompson's influential work in the 1990s suggests that globalisation 'in its radical sense should be taken to mean the development of a new economic structure, and not just conjunctoral change towards greater international trade and investment within an existing set of economic relations' (Hirst and Thompson 1999: 7). Implicit in their critique of those arguing that globalisation is a current feature of contemporary society is a suggestion that definitions of globalisation equate with internationalisation. Others see globalisation as relating more explicitly to flows of trade, investments, technologies and tastes (Radice 1999), while yet others, as Kellner (2005) has argued, see it as synonymous with westernisation and/or modernity (Giddens 1990), or a new epoch – a 'global age' (Albrow 1996).

In his influential, and helpful, text Scholte (2000) offers five categories into which present definitions of globalisation can be seen to fall. In the case of four of these definitions the term arguably fails to describe any new phenomenon and this begs the question as to whether a new term is required at all. Scholte suggests that internationalisation is synonymous with globalisation in the definition of authors such as Hirst and Thompson, liberalisation is framed as globalisation in the work of some such as Sander (1996), universalism is seen to equate with globalisation in some of the earliest writing on the topic (see Reiser and Davies 1944), and it is synonymous with, westernisation, or alternatively modernisation and colonisation, in the writing of authors such as Spybey (1996), Taylor (2000), Khor (1996). The fifth definition mentioned by Scholte is deterritorialisation and it is in this body of work that the term has been used to denote what is arguably a new process.

Work on deterritorialisation considers that transborder activities and relations are central to the definition of globalisation (Held, McGrew, Goldblatt *et al.* 1999). In this conceptualisation it is important to argue that globalisation is a process and not an event, an outcome, or a distribution. While questions of universalism and internationalisation are of interest they may, in some cases, be described as outcomes of globalising processes but are not synonymous with globalisation itself. Questions about the extent to which we can talk of a 'global culture, space, world', etc. are also of value but they are separate and discrete. The processes of globalisation, where the term is used to denote something 'new', entail cultural, political, or economic leaps beyond the boundaries of nation states: a 'stretching of social, political, and economic activities across frontiers' (Held and McGrew 2001).

The argument that the shipping industry has been subject to extensive economic globalisation is founded upon two central and associated 'planks': the relationship between the locations of vessel ownership and the places of ship registration, and secondly the extent to which companies scour the world 'in search of cheap but efficient production locations', a phenomenon that Hirst and Thompson suggest is indicative of 'real' globalisation (Hirst and Thompson 1999: 67). In the case of shipping, where 'plant' is mobile, the re-flagging of vessels (moving the place of ship registration) can be seen as equivalent to relocation of factories from one country to another. Such moves are associated with a search for cheap labour on the global labour market and/or the introduction of cheap, migrant labour into existing manufacturing locations (Kahveci and Nichols 2006). It is this – the search for such labour on an international scale – which has produced the rich ethnic mixes which can be found on contemporary cargo ships and has created the contexts in which transnationality aboard ship is worth exploring. In this process, the relationships between vessel ownership, management and registration are key, as all of these factors impact upon the environment that is found on board a ship and in which seafarers are obliged to work. Before outlining the various elements of the transformation of the shipping industry that have impacted upon the lives of seafarers, it is worth briefly describing the functions and roles of 'flag states' in so far as they are apposite in relation to the question of globalisation.

The role of the 'Flag State'

In the shipping industry the vessel is the equivalent to the plant or factory in the manufacturing sector. It is the vessel, and its use, which generates profit for companies and it is, generally, on board the vessel that the majority of the work-force are employed (being supported only by shore-side management functions). Shipping is almost unique in that its 'plant' (vessels) is mobile and thus decisions about the 'location of plant' in relation to labour markets, in particular, do not apply. Similarly shipping companies do not incur major costs when shifting 'production' from one country to another (although it has been argued that multinational corporations rarely incur such costs under the terms of many of their agreements with countries keen to attract foreign direct investment on initial establishment of their plant). In pursuit of cheap labour, while they do not shift the location of their vessels in a spatial sense, however, ship operators/owners do shift the location of their vessels in terms of their registration and this equates with choosing to locate a factory or plant in a specific state. The vessel's registration essentially determines the state whose jurisdiction it operates under. A British-flagged ship, for example, is subject to regulation under British law. Tax is payable under the regime established by the flag state of the vessel, i.e. British-flagged ships would normally be due to pay tax to the UK inland revenue; collective bargaining agreements are reached with the trade unions of the state of registration, where these exist, and so forth.

In the post-war period, and particularly following the world downturn in trade of 1973–76, ship operators and owners increasingly looked towards shifting the location of their vessels' registration in pursuit of competitive advantage (Bergantino and Marlow 1997). Such advantage accrued as a result of the different tax regimes being operated by different flag states, different employment regulations pertaining to vessels flagged with different nations and, importantly, the different regulatory regimes operated by different flags. The growth in the numbers of vessels 'moving' across borders via a change of registration post-dated the growth of the land-based multinational. Such multinational corporations (generally of US origin) had a firm grip on production in specific European markets by the 1970s. They arguably contributed to the economic instability and turbulence which resulted in the de-coupling of the dollar from gold (the suspension of dollar–gold convertibility) under the Nixon administration of 1971; the world recession that followed on from this; and the oil price hikes of 1973 (Newton 2004). It was this world recession, in particular, that encouraged ship operators to 'flag out' to open registers (often termed Flags of Convenience or FOCs) in far greater numbers than had previously been seen (Selkou and Roe 2004) and with 'flagging out' came 'crewing out' and the development of a genuinely globalised labour market for seafarers.

The right of open registers to set their own terms and conditions for registration was enshrined in the United Nations Convention on the Law of the Sea (UNCLOS 1982). Article 91 of this convention states that:

> Every state shall fix the conditions for the grant of its nationality to ships, for the registration of ships in its territory, and for the right to fly its flag. (UNCLOS 1982)

The convention elaborates, stating that states can exercise 'jurisdiction and control in administrative, technical and social matters' (*ibid.*) in relation to all vessels flying their flag. While one may expect that in these circumstances the flag of the vessel would impact significantly upon a ship's character, this is not at all the case in practice. In reality the exercise of 'jurisdiction' equates with effectively none at all being exercised by some registries (flag states) for which the main aim, in operating, is commercial gain. Even where regulation is stronger, the impact of a flag upon a vessel is likely to be in relation to influences on technical standards. In terms of the social environment on board very little effect is noticeable. The exception to this, however, relates to the nationality composition of those found on board and, in this very narrow respect, flag might be said to be of considerable significance to the social spaces which constitute the on board environments of ships.

Vessel ownership and vessel registration: the impact on crew composition

At the dawning of the twentieth century it was relatively commonplace for vessels to be registered locally, i.e. in the countries where vessel owners located their head offices and where shipowning companies were themselves registered. By the beginning of the twenty-first century, however, such practice was far less prevalent and the relationship between the location of vessel ownership and the flag of a vessel was far less predictable. It is worth outlining the development of 'open' and 'second' registers internationally before considering the ways in which their proliferation facilitated the employment of multinational crews and the concurrent globalisation of the seafarer labour market.

'Flagging out' in the twentieth century was facilitated by an increase in the numbers of open registers willing to accept onto their books tonnage owned/operated by companies located in any nation. These registers were set up for commercial gain and were frequently owned, part-owned or franchised by national governments. Often such registers have little appetite for regulation and exercise no control over working conditions on board their ships. Indeed many seek to maximise competitive advantage, vis-à-vis other open registers, via the conscious pursuit of a lack of regulation (Alderton, Bloor, Kahveci *et al.* 2004). Kahveci and Nichols illustrate this in an imaginative way by linking the results of a published 'audit' of flag states (Winchester and Alderton 2003) to the GDP of states with ship registers. They conclude that the poorest states, presumably with the greatest motivation to operate a register for 'profit', are the weakest in relation to regulatory capacity, i.e. that the poorest states 'interfere' least with the way in which ship operators run their vessels:

> As is confirmed by the mean GDP per capita data … the weakest regulatory flags tend to be located in the poorest countries. In short, uneven development rules: the richer countries are likely to flag out more; and the best 'deals' to be got

by shipowners (in the sense of the least regulation and the worst protection for seafarers) are from the poorest countries. (Kahveci and Nichols 2006: 23–4)

By 2008, 'flags of convenience' accounted for more than 54 per cent of the world fleet in terms of deadweight tonnage (UNCTAD 2008). As such they posed a genuine threat to national registers and their growth represented considerable 'capital flight' from OECD countries.

Prior to this, in an effort to retain some of their vessels, protect local labour markets, and retain the financial benefits of industries related to shipping (e.g. financial services, insurance, etc.) traditional maritime nations began to set up what are known as second registers. Looking back on the establishment of the Norwegian second register, State Secretary Oluf Ulseth outlined to a shipping conference in 2002 the reasons for setting up the Norwegian International Shipping Register (NIS). He told his audience:

> The year 1987 marked a turning point in Norwegian shipping policy. A new international shipping register was established – the Norwegian International Shipping Register – better known as the NIS. I am therefore pleased to say that it will be celebrating its 15th anniversary this year, and its prospects for the future look good. At present there are registered approximately 780 vessels at 19.2 million tonnes. These numbers have remained moderately stable during the last ten years.
>
> The NIS allows the employment of non-Norwegian seafarers on ships registered in the NIS at local salary levels. When establishing the NIS we had two major goals: firstly, to ensure that the operation of Norwegian ships in international trade under Norwegian flag could be competitive; and secondly, it was clear from the onset that the NIS was to be a register for quality tonnage. The key lies in maintaining the long-established 'stamp of quality' on all our shipping services. We have taken great care in ensuring that the vessels are fully operated in line with our international obligations, most notably under IMO and ILO regulations. In addition, NIS ships are subject to Norwegian law. Perhaps most importantly to emphasize here is that the safety requirements are exactly the same as for ships in our other and more local register – the NOR, or 'Norwegian Ordinary Register'. (Ulseth 2002)

However it was not a desire for quality that primarily lay behind the decisions to set up second registers but a desperate desire to retain and perhaps attract (back) tonnage to traditional maritime nations. In setting up the Danish International Register, the motives were, perhaps more openly, stated by the Danish Maritime Administration to be as follows:

> The Danish International Register of Shipping was launched in 1988 as a supplement to the ordinary Danish Register of Shipping to improve the international competitiveness of the Danish merchant fleet in international trade.[3]

Such considerations were, arguably, the primary motivation in the establishment of most second registers.

Some second registers, in maintaining 'competitiveness', allowed standards to fall and were denoted as nothing more than flags of convenience by the International Transport Workers' Federation (ITF) who consistently designate the German second register (GIS), for example, as a flag of convenience. However, others have retained a reputation for reasonable standards and, partly as a result (they were less likely to be targeted for inspection by port state control officers than flag of convenience vessels), second registers increased in popularity amongst ship owners in the late 1980s (Selkou and Roe 2004). Such registers were attractive in that they were designed to be more commercially competitive than their corresponding national registers. They offer more flexibility in terms of the minimum numbers of seafarers required to be employed aboard specific ships, and the nationalities of those seafarers (Selkou and Roe 2004, Winchester, Sampson and Shelly 2006), and also in relation to wage agreements which are often not negotiated with the unions of the flag state but rather with the home nations of employed seafarers (Selkou and Roe 2004). However, such registers, while attracting increased tonnage, have not unsettled the dominant position of flags of convenience (see Table 1). Their inability to wrest tonnage away from open registers is perhaps explained by the fact that while they tend to be less restrictive than national registers they generally maintain some regulatory standards and in some cases nationality stipulations (e.g. the Danish International Register retains the specification that vessel captains be of Danish nationality). They are better placed therefore to attract tonnage from national registers, perhaps slowing the exodus to open registers, than to compete effectively with flags of convenience/open registers.

Table 1: Total tonnage of open and second registers (thousands of deadweight tonnes)

	2004	*2005*	*2006*
Open registers	357,845	364,833	391,174
International (second) registers	151,900	172,735	184,821

Source: Adapted from UNCTAD 2006, Table 18, p. 36. Data excludes vessels of less than 1,000 gross tonnes (grt).

The combined impact of open and second registers has been to globalise the labour market for seafarers. Freed from compliance with national labour agreements on salaries, contracts, and conditions, ship operators flagging their vessels with open, and to a great extent second registers, are able to 'scour the world' for cheaper labour in an effort to reduce variable costs. They have done so, and this is now apparent when studying the crew composition of very many ocean-going cargo vessels (Ellis and Sampson 2008). Whereas once, officers were generally recruited locally (even if ratings were of more mixed provenance), today a pick-and-mix approach to crewing has produced considerable diversity amongst officers in particular. This pattern is not peculiar to open and second register vessels, however, as many national registers have followed in their footsteps and considerably relaxed (if not completely abolished) their nationality requirements for fear that locally registered ship owners would otherwise 'flag out'. This has produced something of a labour market 'free for all' where employers chase down the cheapest labour sources and seek to establish competitive advantage via control over variable costs. Interview material collected from ship operators and owners offers a clear and detailed picture of the kinds of influences acting upon their decisions about ship registration and crewing and illustrates the impact of these issues in practice.

Choosing a flag, choosing a crew: decisions by ship operators

In the search for labour, the picture is a little more complex than that which would be produced by a simple 'dash for cash'. Ship owners, and managers, do not simply recruit the very cheapest labour available on the labour market and, indeed, they are not always 'free' to do so. Similarly, while the decision about the flag of a ship is most often a freely made choice this is not always the case. Ship operators may base their decisions about employment upon the stipulations made by particular flag states, rather than cost, and some of their decisions about 'flag' are related to trading areas (where ships operate) rather than regulation and taxation.

Where operators choose to register with a particular national flag state they may be constrained in relation to the nationality of the seafarers they employ. National registers may impose restrictions on the proportions of crews who can be drawn from countries beyond state boundaries, as with the Thai flag discussed in the following interview:

> Thai flag has the restriction on the nationality – 75% must be Thai, only 25% can be foreigners. (John – an employee of a ship operator)

In such cases, choice of register determines, to some extent, the choice of the nationality of employed seafarers. The decision of where to flag may, in turn, be contingent upon where a vessel trades or it may be determined by ship financiers. Vivek explained, for example, that:

> Some of the contracts that we have in the Norwegian sector, then we need Norwegian flag. [With] The Spanish ... vessels, the loan companies specify certain flags. Australia to ... work on that coast, you've gotta have Australian flag ... (Vivek – an employee of a ship operator)

However, while such restrictions do determine flag choice in some circumstances, where ship operators are free to flag wherever they prefer, it is evident that cost-effective crewing remains a major driver behind the decision to 'flag out'. This is illustrated in the comments made by the majority of human resource managers. They repeatedly explained the importance of cost in their decision-making processes. The following example is illustrative:

> *Ned:* We're currently looking at India as a potential source of officers, but we haven't made a decision yet.
> *Helen:* What sort of decisions come into play when you're thinking about that?
> *Ned:* A large part is cost. We are under pressure, like all owners, to reduce costs.
>
> (Ned – an employee of a ship operator)

This process is ongoing as exemplified by the announcement of tanker company 'Jo Tankers' that it was to transfer the registration of four vessels from Holland to Singapore making fifty Dutch officers redundant in the process (Tanker Operator 2009). The search for the cheapest flags appears enduring within companies even in the first decade of the new millennium. Having taken the decision to flag out, companies continue to shift between registers in order to minimise costs and maximise profits.

> *David:* We had Liberia before and the reason they changed the flag to Bermuda [was] to save the, save the cost.
> *Helen:* Cheaper?
> *David:* Cheaper.
>
> (David – an employee of a ship operator)

Such cost reductions relate to tax savings as well as crew costs, but crew costs constitute a very significant proportion of total variable costs for ship operators and it is frequently issues over crew costs that cause companies to initiate an exploration of re-flagging. Steven put it like this:

> I think the upside [of re-flagging] is clearly ... there are a number of upsides. First one of course, why did we do it in the first place – cost. So certainly, reduced manning costs. (Steven – an employee of a ship operator)

In tight markets, competitively priced crews may be critical to the continued operation of vessels and decisions to re-flag are taken in preference to the breaking up of a ship as the following example illustrates:

> Well, it was either scrap the ship, because of the freight rates in the bulk carrier markets, or we had to find another way of crewing. By switching to PRC [People's Republic of China – flag] we could cut the crew costs by 50 per cent. (Gary – an employee of a ship operator)

Once a decision has been made to re-flag, companies choose between flag states on other grounds including rates of taxation, ship detention rates, and so forth. In terms of crew selection, they select on the basis of cost and their perception of the competence and knowledge (the 'quality') of seafarers. In doing so, many go to considerable effort to keep their knowledge of a rapidly changing labour market up to date. Mike reported that:

> We have an internal report we do which compares all the nationalities, and we do this bi-annually, but we do an assessment of all the likely seafaring nationalities, what the current wages are, what the current conditions are, how big the pool is, what the training facilities are. (Mike – an employee of a ship operator)

Essentially, companies are constantly on the lookout for new sources of labour that give them a competitive edge. Following new developments in the labour market or intelligence gathered from talking with other vessel operators many managers 'try out' cheaper crew compositions, in terms of nationality or combinations of nationalities, to see whether they can operate vessels to a required standard at a reduced cost. Operators are also under pressure to access new sources of labour at the same cost as existing sources due to concerns about imminent shortages of officers on the global labour market, predicted recurrently in labour force surveys (e.g. BIMCO/ISF 2005). If an experiment with the employment of a particular nationality of seafarers 'works' companies generally switch to recruiting more and more of the nationality concerned, moving out of one part of the labour market and buying into another. As Craig put it:

> Well I am free to crew them any way that I like within certain parameters. The parameters are primarily an ability to speak English, that is vital, followed closely by economics. Basically our crew are Filipinos. The company does encourage me to look elsewhere and try to experiment but the cost of the other crew should be on a par, if not slightly less, slightly more than Filipino, but not too much more, which is why I actually have one vessel which is fully manned by Ukrainians, I just recently started this, to try them out as a complete unit, meaning from Chief mate, Second Engineer and below right up to Cook. They are all Ukrainians. The captain and Chief Engineer are Dutch and they are people who are from [company's name]. I'm asked to look at others as well so I am also looking at Burmese and people like that. (Craig – an employee of a ship operator)

Others questioned the notion of a threat of labour shortages however, suggesting that seafarers were available but emphasising that the issue was price. Steven suggested:

> It's not difficult to recruit officers providing you offer them the correct terms of conditions, the officers are there if you like, not that we're requiring huge numbers of them, and I think maybe if you're manning a fleet from the start you might find it quite difficult, but in the intake that we might be looking for I don't think there's any difficulty. I think the difficulty is perhaps a financial one rather than anything else, it's contingent upon cost and quality. (Steven – an employee of a ship operator)

Certainly this view would be supported by evidence relating to the example of the UK. In the UK the state has encouraged the training of new cadets and colleges report running at full capacity. There is a strong indication, however, that companies are unwilling to pay the price of British junior officers, preferring to recruit cheaper junior officers from elsewhere. Thus the overall numbers of UK officers in work have not risen dramatically (Gekara 2007).

However, it is not just fear of labour shortages that keep employers on the lookout for new labour supply countries. There also seems to be a growing awareness amongst ship operators that labour supply nations themselves could upset profitability by setting local terms and conditions for the employment of seafarers that would render those companies that were over-reliant upon them at a disadvantage relative to their competitors. The Philippines is widely acknowledged to be the single largest supplier of seafarers to the global seafarer labour market (see Table 2) and as such potentially holds a degree of influence, and power, in relation to employment terms and conditions as experienced on the global seafarer labour market.

Table 2: Estimation of active seafarers by selected nationality based upon crew list data collected by the Seafarers International Research Centre in 2003 at selected major ports

Rank	Nationality	No.	% of total
1	Philippines	141,698	22.4
2	Ukraine	45,607	7.2
3	Russia	44,101	7.0
4	Indonesia	43,592	6.9
5	China	32,379	5.1
6	India	26,335	4.2
7	Turkey	23,810	3.8
8	Poland	20.057	3.2
9	Greece	15,952	2.5
10	Myanmar	12,519	2.0
	The rest of the world	225,217	35.7
World total – active seafarers (snapshot)		631,267	100

These data exclude personnel working on ferries, cruise and other passenger vessels.
Source: Ellis and Sampson 2008.

Such dominance of the labour market by a small number of nations is unsettling to ship operators. As Craig explained:

> We could also have a situation where a particular country, let's say the Philippines, decides to throw in some legislation that really makes it difficult for us to get the crew. That could have a very damaging effect … so if you rely on one nationality that could be a serious problem. So it's good to have a few. (Craig – an employee of a ship operator)

Fearful of this, some actively seek to utilise a range of nationalities when crewing their vessels, all paid at different rates and generally hired under different terms and conditions (in relation to hours of work for example, or length of on board contract).

Sectoral differences and the impact on the globalisation of the seafarer labour market

Managers' requirements for 'quality' (often specified as a need by crewing managers) is generally adjusted according to the type of ship being operated. Tankers and chemical carriers are associated with high pollution risks and the financial penalties attached to spills from these types of vessels are catastrophic for companies in many cases. The loss of a tanker such as the *Erika*, or the *Prestige*, may result in a company (or their insurers) paying out millions of dollars. The loss of a bulk carrier such as the *Christopher*, lost with all twenty-seven 'hands' in December 2001 costs relatively little in 'dollar terms'. Such assessments of financial risk are an integral part of the decision-making process with regard to crewing. John explained his thinking about crewing his vessels as follows:

> Okay, based on the types of ship and the training. Let's say I'm at sea, [I put] the Chinese crew, mainly on the smaller types of ships, the bulkers [because they] are easier to handle. I say 'handymax' [this term relates to vessel size] from 45,000 tons to any size, the bulkers. So this crew [the Chinese seafarers], most of the time, they were on these ships [bulkers] so they're familiar with the ship operation and then for the bigger ships, [ship name], [I] put Indian senior officers and Filipino, and [on] our Chemical tankers, [I put] Indian and Filipino or Indian because they have that experience on chemical tankers whereas [in] China, I don't find any Chinese crew have good experience on chemical tankers and we cannot afford to have any accident, anything wrong on the chemical tankers – it's terrible, the consequence of any accidents. (John – an employee of a ship operator)

Here the notion of 'terrible' does not relate to loss of life, nor to widespread environmental damage, but to the 'dollar' cost to the operator of any accidents resulting in cargo spillage.

Decisions about crewing are invariably framed by human resource managers as involving issues of cost and quality (see also Gekara 2010), however, the balance between these two variables alters, sometimes dramatically, from one company to another. For some employers quality appears to be a central consideration while others seem to be driven by cost. One employer, Danny, was insistent, for example, that the same standards pertained to all their vessels regardless of where they were flagged, or crewed, and that crew competence was their overriding concern. His company owned and managed a tanker fleet:

> *Danny*: We've got the Australian registered vessels, we've got the Bahamas registered vessels, we've got Norwegian registered vessels, we've got Spanish registered vessels, our policy is, it's more commercial, where is it [flagged], you know, where does it make good business sense for our vessels to be left [flagged]. It's, you know, the company standard and I've always said this is something totally devoid of flag or, or legislation, in my book, it's something that, you know, the company has to decide where it wants to be and then, having done that, then of course it's, coming down from the management to, to put the, the right tools in place to be there.
>
> Helen: So what you're saying is that you make a commercial decision, what flag to, say, register certain ships with, but you apply your standard regardless of whether or not the flag state actually has lower standards than yours?
>
> *Danny*: Exactly so. What we're trying to sell is ... what we're saying is that, we have an operational franchise and the way I describe it to everybody is, it's like a Hyatt, you know, if you went, if you went to a Hyatt here, or a Hyatt in Hong Kong, or in Manila, you have a perception in your mind, like, when you get a certain level of service and ninety-nine times out of a hundred, that's the level of service you get ... And, well, that's the same level thing we trying to achieve with our Vizla ships, so when, when a customer er, if you like, joins a Vizla ship, he gets a similar experience no matter what the vessel, the flag, he doesn't care, it's a Vizla vessel in his eyes.
>
> (Danny – an employee of a ship owner-operator)

However, in other cases operators or managers are subject to strong external pressures that militate against the prioritisation of quality. Such pressures are particularly experienced by ship managers and those involved in joint ventures. The pressures come from owners (also known as 'principals') and from controlling interests associated with joint ventures as the following quotes illustrate:

> What you're used to, it's tried and proved, so better the devil you know than the devil you don't just for the sake of change. We change it [the nationalities of crews] if somebody says they want to do something else. Or they turn round and say no, these ships have got to be run on the lowest budget possible, what can we do to match that? And we'll probably go into Burmese or something like that. (Gary – an employee of a ship operator)

> The Joint Ventures – the people running them, they have a greater say in the type of crew they want and they are more bottom-line orientated, so it is difficult to suggest crew who might be more expensive and because they get very wary when they try to do experiments on board their ships because they are afraid you know, they are less flexible in that sense. (Craig – an employee of a ship operator)

Whether employers stated motivation is purely cost or purely quality (or more often a mixture of the two), however, there is little doubt that as a result of their requirements and crewing practices the labour market for seafarers has become thoroughly globalised in recent decades. This has produced changes in the organisation of the labour market and in the terms and conditions offered by operators to many 'outsourced' seafarers who often do not enjoy direct contractual relationships with ship owners or even the fairly prevalent ship managers who constitute a second significant and relatively new element of the labour supply picture.

The rise of ship management companies

Ship management companies are a relatively contemporary (twentieth-century) phenomenon. However, in some respects their functions mimic those of captains in the eighteenth and nineteenth centuries. The earliest 'ship managers' therefore might be said to have been ship captains who in the early days of sailing ships were responsible for running their vessels and all aspects of their management including fixing cargoes, arranging maintenance, crewing and provisioning, and taking and making payments for services provided. This largely occurred, of necessity, at a time when vessels were expected to be absent from their 'home ports' for years at a time and when no practical means of regular, or timely, communication were available. The arrangement was facilitated by the simplicity of the industry at the time, the lack of international regulation, the straightforwardness of labour markets and the non-litigious environment of the day (as compared with the present time). In the present-day environment captains are overwhelmed with demands once in port (by customs and immigration officials, by inspectors and so forth) and it seems inconceivable that all aspects of the management of a vessel could continue to remain in their hands. However, not all owners wish to accept such functions and tasks in the stead of the captains of yesteryear. Furthermore, they may not be competent to undertake them, often having had no prior experience of shipping but entering into shipowning purely for financial gain – a matter of investment. Many such ship owners have therefore turned to emergent 'ship management' companies to fulfil such roles.

Ship management companies have been identified as initially developing in the post-war period, in small numbers, to serve niche markets (Panayides 2001). Their growth in popularity can be traced to the 1960s and 1970s (Spruyt 1994, Panayides 2001) when oil majors invested in their own vessels in order to transport cargoes but lacked the necessary expertise to operate vessels. They therefore required that their ships be placed under the management of shipping experts and became significant clients for the growing ship management sector. The sector further benefited from the downturn in world trade and the crisis this caused in shipping in the early 1970s. At this time many mortgaged ships were repossessed by financiers (again without shipping expertise) following the bankruptcy of owner-operators. Faced with a decision to sell or scrap repossessed vessels at a time when their value was highly depressed in both markets (sales and scrap) many creditors decided to maximise the return on their assets by doing neither and entering, instead, into agreements with specialist ship managers to provide for all the operational management needs of the vessel (Alderton *et al.* 2004, Kahveci and Nichols 2006).

Ship management can be defined in various ways. Broadly speaking it represents a kind of contracting out of services. These can relate to commercial aspects of ship operations (securing cargoes/charters, marketing and so forth) and/or may comprise technical management functions such as crewing vessels and taking care of their supply and maintenance (see Spruyt 1994 for a good breakdown of management services). While it is difficult to arrive at accurate statistics in relation to ship management (*ibid.*) it is nevertheless reasonable to identify an ongoing expansion in ship management services for a variety of economic, competitive and practical reasons. Practically speaking, it is suggested that shipping in the modern context is so complex that a single ship owner (i.e. the owner of a one-ship company) is unlikely to be able to resource the many departments and considerable expertise required to ensure the proper, and prosperous, operation of his/her vessel (Spruyt 1994, Panayides 2001).

This constitutes quite a major change in the sector over a relatively short period of time. It was not uncommon for single ship companies to be established in OECD countries, with a maritime tradition, even as recently as the 1960s. However in the course of that decade it became more and more apparent that the days of the owner-operated 'one-ship company' were rapidly passing.

Outsourced labour: crewing agents and the distance between seafarers and vessel operators

The industry has been transformed by the phenomenon of flagging out and the rise of ship management companies. In relation to the recruitment of labour, such changes have been accompanied by the rise of third-party crewing agencies which have transformed the recruitment processes underpinning the global seafarer labour market. Third-party crew agents, generally located in non-OECD countries, commonly enter into agreements to supply locally sourced labour to globally located ship managers and ship owners. The direct recruitment of seafarers, and recruitment based upon personal recommendations, is increasingly unusual in the shipping industry which is now dominated by outsourced labour. It is this transformation of the labour market that has impacted so dramatically on what might be termed transmigrant seafarers based in European hub port cities such as those considered in Chapter 4.

The historical account offered by P.M. Heaton of David Lindsay Street, a ship owner-operator of the 1960s, provides a useful example with which to contrast the day-to-day practices of most ship operators in the twenty-first century.

In the 1960s in South Wales, a local man, born in Penarth and given the name of David Lindsay Street bought a former refrigerated cargo ship (reefer) from an established shipping company and refitted her as a dry cargo deep-sea tramp.[4] In order to operate his single ship, in 1961 he set up a private limited company and he operated her for four years, at some points single-handedly fixing cargoes, hiring officers, planning voyages and dealing with issues of finance. Perhaps a sign of the times and an indication of the winds of change about to sweep shipping, his venture was short-lived and the vessel went into receivership following the collapse of the merchant bank with which he had always dealt. Unable to raise loans elsewhere, and following a spell of poor luck, the vessel, the *Redbrook* was sold by its reluctant owner. In reconstructing its history in the period 1961 to 1964 the author P.M. Heaton makes the following remarks:

> It is one thing to operate an ageing ship profitably under a convenience flag, and the Greeks are very adept at doing this. However, it is a far different story to operate such a ship under a British flag and this fact had not gone unnoticed in the shipping industry, where a certain amount of admiration was felt for Lindsay Street, particularly as he had kept the ship well out of the reach of the receiver for eight months after the crash of the bank, *and had had to undertake every aspect of the business on his own for that period* [my emphasis]. (Heaton 1981: 62)

The story of the *Redbrook*, under the ownership of Lindsay Street, serves as an example of the changes afoot in the industry in the 1960s. Changes associated with globalisation (including the proliferation of supranational regulation) meant it was increasingly impractical, and economically unviable, in the latter part of the twentieth century, for single ship owners to operate without the use of ship management companies, and for any ship operators to function without recourse to outsourced labour, and changes of flag (flagging-out). Such changes had important implications for workers and again the *Redbrook* serves as an illustrative example.

In 1961, the vessel *Redbrook* set sail with a crew of Welsh officers, Arab firemen and Malay ratings. Heaton reports that the captain was recommended to Lindsay Street (the Welsh owner) by friends and the remaining crew were organised by the Shipping Federation at Cardiff. The international make-up of the crew highlights the extent to which multinational crews are not a new feature of shipping; the manner of their recruitment, however, contrasts sharply with the contemporary organisation and operation of the global seafarer labour market. Similarly, so too does their relationship with the vessel owner/operator and the commitment made from one to the other which worked both ways; from crew to owner and owner to crew. In an early part of the ship's 'adventures' *Redbrook* was remarkably prone to losing anchors which were extremely costly to replace and which placed a huge strain on operating profits. The crew evidently felt this keenly and Heaton reports that:

> On his return to Cardiff Captain Rees who was a teetotal, non-smoking Welsh master of the old school related to Lindsay Street and his uncle how when he had arrived alongside the ship he had been met by the distressed Malay bosun who had said to him 'Captain Rees, why is God doing this to our anchors?' (Heaton 1981: 25)

Commitment to their vessel is still found amongst seafarers today and cannot be thought remarkable. In the case of the *Redbrook*, the owner's appreciation of this and desire to ensure just treatment of the crew when the vessel was put into receivership seems to contrast dramatically, however, with the commitment displayed by many, or perhaps most, ship operators in relation to their crews in the twenty-first century. In a remarkable account Heaton describes how Lindsay Street, presumably much preoccupied with his own financial affairs and disappointments, at the time of his vessel's final voyage under his ownership, took steps to ensure that the crew were paid their due wages before signing off (something which the receiver was not planning to attend to). He reports that:

> While the *Redbrook* was discharging at Bremen Lindsay Street contacted her Master –Captain Maloney to find out the exact amount required to pay off the crew on their return to the United Kingdom from her handing over port, Antwerp. A figure of £34,000 was needed and in consequence he notified the receiver Mr. Duncan McKellor. To his great surprise he was advised that the crew would have to look elsewhere for their money ... The ship had been away from the United Kingdom for fifteen months at this time and Lindsay Street felt a deep obligation to ensure that his loyal crew did not lose their hard earned cash. While the ship was in Bremen the receiver held all the aces, but having sailed and being on passage to Antwerp the position changed for a short while, in which time Lindsay Street held all the trump cards. While underway the Master of the *Redbrook* would take his instructions from his owner and Lindsay Street knew that if he instructed Captain Maloney to arrest the ship on arrival at Antwerp, this would have the effect of holding up the sale of the ship to the Greeks, something which would have horrified the receiver. The first claim on a ship is that of her crew and their interests had to be safeguarded at all costs. So while the ship was on passage between Bremen and Antwerp Lindsay Street contacted the receiver and informed him that if he did not give his word that the crew would be paid he would send a telegram to the Master to instruct him to arrest the *Redbrook* on arrival at Antwerp on behalf of the crew ... the receiver relented ... and subsequently on their return to the United Kingdom by sea and by train they were all met at Victoria Station by a representative of the receiver who took them to the bank and handed them their money. (Heaton 1981: 61)

This surprising account of the end of his days as owner of the *Redbrook* could hardly contrast more with the tales of the treatment of modern-day seafarers who are frequently left unpaid and abandoned when a ship operator gets into financial trouble and a ship enters receivership or is arrested pending legal proceedings. A detailed illustration of the common realities faced by contemporary seafarers when their companies get into financial difficulties is offered by Kahveci (Kahveci 2005) in detailing the experiences of Turkish seafarers stranded, and unpaid, aboard the arrested vessel *Obo Basak* in a French port in 1997. While the account demonstrates some loyalty from seafarers towards the company involved, it is devoid of any sense of loyalty on the part of the company towards its workers. Kahveci's account contains the following extract from an interview with one of the seafarers involved:

> When I spoke to my wife from Dunkirk she told me that the cheque that Marti [the company] gave me to join the ship was bounced on the 6th of June and

she has been to the company every day since then only to receive abusive treatment and there was nothing to eat at home. (Interview by EK, 15 October 1998,
Istanbul). (Kahveci 2005: 36).

This kind of experience is not uncommon. For example, eighty-nine cases
of abandonment were recorded by the ITF in just the first six months of 2002
involving 1,780 crew members (Kahveci 2005). The figure was smaller in 2004
with twenty-two vessels listed on the ILO website detailing reported abandon-
ments[5] and it declined further as the industry entered a period of booming freight
rates and trade. Nevertheless, details of the cases presented in such forums overwhelmingly indicate the lack of concern for crew members demonstrated by vessel owners, and operators, in the globalised industry of today. As a result of the
complex and opaque links between labour suppliers and vessel owner/operators
it is often not even possible for seafarers, or other interested parties, to determine
with whom ownership, and with it responsibility for a vessel, lies. Given that crew
agencies, who generally supply labour to today's vessels, are only responsible for
recruitment of seafarers on behalf of operators and not for the management or
technical operation of a vessel, this is tantamount to seafarers not knowing who
their employers are. An illustrative example is provided by the following comments posted in connection with the case of a vessel originally listed as the *Dauria*
on the ILO website detailing cases of abandonment. Under a heading of comments and observations the following text appears:

> This vessel changed its name to *Balcar* on 31 March 2007. Flag now seems to be
> Bolivian. The vessel has been operating in the Black Sea since the beginning of
> 2006. In September this year the ITF received a call from one of the current crew
> complaining of unpaid wages of the 11 Ukrainian seafarers on board, no food,
> little water. Ship manager claimed that crew would be repatriated and that food
> and water problems would be resolved, however it was not possible to verify this
> due to loss of contact with the crew. The ship manager and operator is Petunia
> Shipping Srl, Italy, the DOC company is GM Trading and Chartering and the
> registered owner is Aileen Corporation, Panama … Crew were effectively de-
> ported, wages not paid, unclear as to whether vessel is still owned by the same
> company.[6]

In a briefer entry referring to a vessel (*Sri Lakshmi*) which actually sank without loss of life the following text is telling:

> Ship sank off the coast of Bahrain, 11 Indian crew rescued by Bahraini Coast
> guard. Owner nowhere to be found. Local Embassy and Dept of Shipping are
> not able to fund the repatriation, nor are the flag state.[7]

Finally, one further example is worth quoting to illustrate the commonalities
which can often be identified in such cases. In this case a small vessel with six
Georgian and one Turkish seafarer on board was abandoned in 2006. The circumstances are described on the website as follows:

Ship and crew abandoned, no contract on board, crew starving and requesting repatriation. The ship is substandard in all aspects, having main engine and hull deficiencies, inadequate fire fighting equipment and unacceptable working and living conditions. The ship is under arrest by the Port State Control following the discovery of false documents. The apparent flag State of Cambodia denies any knowledge of the vessel in its register. The ship was originally abandoned at anchorage, but on 01 June was moved to a berth. The ITF inspector, together with the local seamen's club have been supplying food to the crew. In the absence of an owner, the authorities were unable to embark upon legal proceedings against the vessel, however the court did eventually accept the case pleaded by a lawyer on behalf of the crew. The first hearing took place on 21 June, but no decision was taken. On July 4th a hearing found in favour of the crew and the vessel is expected to be sold next month. [...] 5 crew members are owed 4 months wages, 2 are owed [sic] 7 months wages, currently amounting to a total of US$30.400 [...] According to the Equasis database the Ship Manager is listed as PLD Shipping, Pissau Industrial Estate, Miri, Malaysia and the registered owner is given as Bermuda Transacts, Malaysia. (last updated 20 November 2006). Local information however suggests that the owner is based in Bulgaria.[8]

While these cases are extreme (though not rare), personal contact between owners and their crews is, nevertheless, virtually non-existent in the modern shipping industry and many companies display contempt towards the welfare needs of their crew in practice if not in policy (Kahveci 2007). The out-sourcing of labour supply as a response to the globalisation of the industry and the labour market has had a manifestly negative impact upon the terms and conditions of employment for seafarers and has further distanced them from employers facilitating neglect of welfare, of health and safety, and even in some circumstances of training and competence (Sampson and Bloor 2007, Bloor and Sampson 2009).

Thus, in many ways the globalisation of the industry, while bringing opportunities to would-be seafarers in developing countries, has brought an overall deterioration in the working and living conditions at sea. Seafarers are regarded, somewhat, as 'commodities' rather than 'people'. There is often little concern for their welfare, little commitment to their long term futures, and a very market-oriented approach to their recruitment, retention and training. In an environment where seafarers are recruited from countries where local employment possibilities are severely limited many people are unwilling to complain about poor living and working conditions on board and will only resort to appeals to trade unions in very extreme circumstances (for example after a long period of unpaid wages and/or when a vessel is abandoned). They are a highly exploited workforce with limited 'muscle' in terms of industrial relations with their employers.

The globalisation of shipping and the associated search for new sources of labour on the global labour market has resulted in a prevalence of multinational crews. The process has been driven by employer desires to recruit the cheapest possible labour, of the quality required, in order to maximise competitive advantage. At various points in the last four decades, pressures to cut costs within the shipping industry have been immense and flagging out, and crewing out, have accelerated. The outsourcing of labour has been facilitated by the emergence of hundreds of crewing agents in new labour supply countries. Such agents supply crews to owner/operators but also to third-party crew managers, the emergence of which have also played a significant role in altering the context of contemporary seafaring.

As ship operators have gone 'belly up' in times of fierce competition, high operating costs, and low freight rates, ships have fallen into the hands of banks and finance houses that have often been reluctant to sell them at scrap rates and yet have been unequal to the task of running them. This has created a large part of the market for ship management services. Such services have also been in demand from small companies unable to resource all of the expertise required in the modern, complex and increasingly regulated industry. The outsourcing of labour facilitated by flagging out and driven by the demand for cheap labour, combined with the rise of ship management companies, has served to transform the world in which seafarers work.

In the modern context, seafarers work alongside those of other nationalities in environments which are relatively independent of national character possessing neither the cultural identity of the flag state (which is largely irrelevant to life on board) nor the owner. Ship owners contracting with ship managers are likely to have few direct links with seafarers, and the crewing companies that hire them. Even in times of severe anxiety, as when a company gets into financial difficulty and withholds wages from its workforce, there is often little direct contact between seafarers and ship owners.

Thus the flag state, the ship owner, and even the vessel operator, are unlikely to impose a nationally embedded culture on board internationally trading cargo ships. As a result, vessels sailing international waters with little embedded national culture constitute remarkable spaces in which large numbers of seafarers live and work in mixed nationality groups. The nature of the arrangements that arise under such circumstances is of fundamental interest in the following chapters.

Notes

1   For some exceptions see Schrank 1983, Lane 1986, Kahveci and Nichols 2006.
2   There is however an interesting literature on the fishing industry.
3   http://soefart.inforce.dk/sw306.asp, accessed 5 November 2005.
4   A vessel which does not follow a fixed route but is engaged to load and discharge cargoes as markets allow.
5   www.ILO.org/dyn/seafarers, accessed 17 September 2008.
6   *Ibid.*
7   *Ibid.*
8   *Ibid.*

4

Transmigrant seafarers in Germany

There is a restaurant in Hamburg where you can look out at the ships coming in and out of port while an announcer informs you, over a loudspeaker, of the ship type, its flag, its cargo etc. As they snack on their appetisers, customers have been known to place bets between themselves on what kinds of vessels the ships they can see might turn out to be: such is the enthusiasm for shipping in this city.

Hamburg and some other notable towns in North Germany have always been important centres for shipping. Some major companies are located there. Famous names in shipping such as Hapag-Lloyd can be found emblazoned on some of the largest and most prestigious of Hamburg's buildings. Other companies, less visible to the passing visitor, remain nevertheless a significant presence in the industry. Yet seafarers are not a dominant part of the modern-day city and are largely invisible, in terms of impact, even in the areas where seafarer services, mostly in the form of charitable support, are located.

Prior to the globalisation of the industry, Hamburg was a very different kind of port where seafarers came in their droves to search for work aboard German-flagged vessels. Down near the water's edge a large building, which is now a hotel, was once the port labour office (labour exchange). Transmigrant seafarers could arrive from their country of domicile and be away aboard a new vessel, with a new company, within a week. Even men, for these were invariably men, with no previous experience of any kind aboard a seagoing craft could find a job with relative ease. Once established, their experiences encouraged family members, or friends, to try their luck and brothers would show brothers the ropes[1] in terms of getting work, cousins would help cousins, and even newly formed acquaintance-ships could yield job opportunities for the garrulous. Such workers could be char-acterised as transmigrants as they came to Germany for indeterminate periods of time staying ashore only until they found work. They transited or passed through Germany as regularly returning migrant workers from Ghana, from Cape Verde, from the Philippines, and they worked under German law as a consequence of boarding German vessels.

North Germany was not the only site where transmigrant seafarers could be found in the 1960s and 1970s. However, German ships were popular amongst would-be seafarers because of the favourable conditions that had been established in relation to work on board. Furthermore, the German fleet was sizeable and work was not difficult to come by. Travelling abroad in search of work was a challenge, and a risk, for would-be seafarers. Yet people kept coming to Europe, motivated by financial desperation, lack of opportunity in their homelands, and sometimes, as the following examples demonstrate, by political/military considerations, to pack up and 'travel North' in search of work. This was something that had impacted particularly on seafarers originating in Cape Verde who fled to Germany to search for work at sea in order to avoid conscription and civil unrest. Mostly they were successful as plenty of work was around. Joe explained:

> There weren't many jobs [at home] and some of my friends went to sea to escape the military service. At that time Portugal was at war in Africa [Angola]. (Joe – Cape Verdean seafarer)

Tony, another seafarer from Cape Verde, told of how:

> It wasn't really my intention to become a seafarer. I'm from Cape Verde. I didn't even know that seafaring exists to such an extent. Of course, there are ships between the islands in Cape Verde, I knew that. But apart from that I didn't know much more about it. Cape Verde was a Portuguese colony but many wanted the independence. And in 1975 they became independent. A short time before that the atmosphere was unbearable for me. I had just finished with school and for me there was nothing ... I wanted to go to university ... But due to all this unrest the situation wasn't easy for me. And then I flew to Lisbon and tried to start a life there, get into university. But that was really difficult. The Portuguese didn't want to see the Cape Verdeans anymore. It got worse and worse until I finally had the idea to go and see my [older] brother in Germany ... My brother ... had already been in Germany for five or six years ... At that time it wasn't as difficult as today ... I had a Portuguese passport then. And then I came here [Hamburg]. And my first place to stay was here in the seafarers' hotel. They know me well here. The only thing I could do was to find a job on a ship ... we are three brothers and were all seamen ... My brother ... registered me with the Heuerstelle [Labour exchange]. And I didn't even wait one whole month [for a job]. (Tony – Cape Verdean seafarer)

Sometimes the people who travelled to North Europe looking for work had little knowledge of the labour market opportunities that existed. They became seafarers, and transmigrants, by virtue of the fact that their compatriot connections were engaged in seafaring, not because of any innate desire to go to sea. Some of them travelled to Germany thinking that they would work ashore and live in Germany. It didn't cross their minds that their friends and relatives were actually working aboard German-flagged ships and barely setting foot on German soil itself. The following example illustrates one such case:

> I should have known, or maybe not, that all these guys here knew about was seafaring. They didn't know anything else. But I didn't know before. I only knew that they are working in Germany but that was about it. But when I came here I realised that none of them really lived here. They are here for two or three days and then they leave again. (Leo – Cape Verdean seafarer)

In this somewhat haphazard way, networks began to be established and extended beyond Germany across northern Europe. In the seafaring web that emerged, Rotterdam and Hamburg were strongly connected. Antwerp constituted an important link, and Scandinavian and Southern European countries (Italy, Greece, Spain) also featured. It was not uncommon for people to move between cities and countries in search of work and some seafarers who initially found work in Holland later became established in Germany as a consequence of finding regular work aboard German-flagged vessels. The following account was not untypical:

> [I have worked] Since 1976 on German ships ... Before I sailed on Dutch ships. For six months. From Holland I came to Germany. I was eighteen years old and I went from Cabo Verde to Holland via Lisbon. Because then we were a Portuguese colony. From Cabo Verde to Lisbon and from Lisbon I went to Holland. To look for a ship. To look for a job. And there I stayed for a year. Because then it was a little bad [difficult] to get a ship ... Then I got a ship ... and was six months onboard. Then I paid off and then I went six months again [without work]. There was no other opportunity ... Then a colleague [fellow countryman] had a job for me. A German ship ... so I sailed without a seamen's book [for] sixteen months ... Afterwards the captain – from Brake – helped me to get a seamen's book. From then on until now I always sail on German ships. (Otis – Cape Verdean seafarer)

In Brake, a small town to the west of Hamburg on the river Weser, an agency brought seafarers from Cape Verde to work aboard the smaller numbers of vessels registered there and in these ways parts of North Germany became accustomed to the comings and goings of seafarers, as well as of ships. Companies often favoured family members and who you knew, or who you were related to, could impact enormously on your employment prospects and the ease with which you could find an initial job at sea. The following example provides a strong illustration:

> I had four brothers who were already in Germany here at the shipping company *Finto* in Brake ... one of them had stayed there already for twelve years. I was the youngest brother and then when I finished the military service and I directly got a contract and I went directly from Cape Verde to Germany to the shipping company Finto. There I worked for a few years. (Theyer – Cape Verdean seafarer)

In the 1960s and 1970s such networks were reported to have been very effective in enabling people to move about and to find work both ashore (where regulations allowed and sometimes even where they didn't) and aboard. In Rotterdam, for example, a large group of Filipino seafarers (or would-be seafarers) was established combining with a longer standing group of Filipina nurses to form what might be described as a coherent, shore-based, Filipino community (Sampson 2003). In Hamburg the situation was different. Different immigration regulations and more restricted access to work permits for shore-based work kept seafarers from Ghana, Cape Verde, and the Philippines, either at sea or 'on benefits'. There were few opportunities to find shore-based work and integrate into shore-based communities although some Filipino seafarers, like their compatriots in Holland, formed relationships with Filipina domestic workers, and carers, and sometimes married German women, remaining ashore in Germany for longer periods of time. Nevertheless, transmigration was a marked feature of the German labour market and the seafarer workforce was highly transient in nature as seafarers moved in and out of Germany rapidly, on their way to a new job or, to a lesser extent, on their return home.

Globalisation hit such seafarers hard. In the latter half of the twentieth century, as processes of globalisation in the shipping industry accelerated, the German fleet 'flagged out', and such transmigrant seafarers were increasingly left stranded and trapped in Germany looking for work. If they accepted a contract aboard a foreign-flagged vessel they lost their entitlement to social security payments during their next, largely inevitable, period of unemployment. If they remained ashore they were prevented from working or restricted in terms of the hours they could work and the pay they could receive. If they went back to their homeland they risked losing all benefits and would additionally risk losing access to their full pensions.

In the late 1990s and early part of the twentieth century there were few migrant seafarers in North Germany, where once, in the 1960 and 1970s, a population of up to 15,000 were estimated to have resided. Bars and restaurants that once catered for the throughput of Cape Verdean and Filipino seafarers had closed down altogether or were surviving on meagre pickings as their clientele vanished. As a field note records:

> There is a Bar Pinoy run by a young Filipina who is half German ... she said she doesn't have much contact with Filipinos which suggests that there may not be many about ... She hasn't been to the Philippines for eight years ... She told us about another bar just one door down called La Ilonga that is closed and is/was more of a seafarers' bar ... On the Reeperbahn itself there is a [Filipino] restaurant which she also mentioned called Cebu Pacific. I went there and it is a Filipino restaurant in the heart of the Reeperbahn district [but] nevertheless it was empty. This is all indicative of a small Filipino community here and this seems to be related to work permits ... [later] ... We went ... to the bar and met three Filipinos who are working on a ferry ... Every week they have one day, which I think is called 'a layover', in Hamburg where they are put up at the hotel. They said there was no Filipino community in Hamburg, which reinforces the impression I had. (Sampson field note 2001)

That there was once a thriving population of Portuguese speakers in, and around, the seamen's hostels in Hamburg is obvious to the modern-day visitor. Portuguese restaurants, bakeries and bars are located in close proximity to the hostel where seafarers (employed and joining/leaving a vessel) stay. Some of these establishments used to accept vouchers from seafarers (provided by companies) for meals. They are, however, no longer frequented by the resident Cape Verdean seafarers (who are mostly long-term unemployed) and the voucher scheme has fallen into disuse. The decline of trade in this area is an indication of the declining numbers of seafarers passing through Hamburg looking for work. Those seafarers who are about, appear to fall into one of two categories, the 'unemployed and impoverished' (who can't afford to eat in restaurants), and the 'employed but rushed' who spend hours, rather than days, in the area just prior to joining a ship and occasionally on leaving one.

While in 2002 it was still possible to gain a job aboard a vessel in Hamburg via informal networks, the organisation of the international seafarer labour market had become highly structured by the turn of the century and 'foreign' seafarers were generally hired via crewing agencies located in major labour supply countries (e.g. the Philippines) using official channels. As this process kicked in, and labour market intelligence was passed back to 'homelands', the numbers of seafarers travelling to Hamburg in the hope of finding work fell. However, a number of Ghanaian seafarers remain prepared to travel to Hamburg to await the few remaining opportunities for work on German-flagged ships while a dwindling population of older seafarers who had once travelled to Germany for this purpose continue to live as long-stay residents in some of the hostels. These older seafarers have all previously been employed aboard German-flagged vessels for long periods of time (often more than twenty years) but have latterly found it increasingly difficult to find work and have 'semi-retired' into what would more accurately be described as 'long-term unemployment'. They are from different parts of the world but the biggest group is from Cape Verde and can be further differentiated into two significant groups: those with Portuguese passports and those without.

The beneficial conditions established for transmigrant labour aboard German-flagged ships had the unforeseen and unintended consequence of trapping people into lives of unemployment, poverty, boredom and loneliness once the process of globalisation got under way. Having worked in the German fleet for decades, they found themselves collectively disenfranchised and demoralised. Residing in hostels and poor bed and breakfast accommodation, in the 1990s and the early years of the twenty-first century a few can still be found 'sitting out their time', waiting to draw their pensions or hoping, largely in vain, that a ship will turn up for them. As such, they are located within Germany and resident there for most of the year yet they are, nevertheless, largely absent from German society. Poverty means that they do not have a presence as consumers (not even in local cafes or restaurants where they cannot afford to eat) and they suffer the kind of marginalisation experienced by the poor in any city. Immigration laws mean that most cannot function as workers and consequently cannot escape their poverty nor integrate with other German workers. Language barriers prevent some from communicating with local residents and cultural chasms mean that these seafarers are not just unable to integrate in German society but are often rather disinterested in doing so. Experiences of discrimination and prejudice minimise access to public spaces and many older, more vulnerable seafarers only leave the safe environment of their rented accommodation and its immediate surrounds on rare occasions.

However, within this broad context, what emerged in talking to different groups of transmigrant seafarers in Hamburg and Brake was the extent to which the general common experience of working in the German fleet, and subsequently struggling to find work, was mediated by a number of factors. Some of these may be regarded as 'structural' and some might be seen to be an element of the variable distribution of 'capital' – human, social and economic. The experiences of different groups of nationals demonstrated some variation attributable to their capacity to speak different languages, to their culture, or to their legal status within Germany. In short their access to social space was differentially experienced. The social space available to them was structured by the socio-legal, cultural and economic framework governing their specific circumstances. Concurrently their capacity to inhabit the limited space available was a function of the social, human and financial capital accessible by particular individuals. Their experiences illustrate the way in which all social space is structured, and differentially so, and the ways in which migrants (be they workers, asylum seekers, or refugees) are not completely free to determine their own degree of embeddedness in 'host' societies but indeed may find they are somewhat constrained in attempting to do so. Societies themselves display various degrees of 'porosity' and some are distinctly impermeable to particular groups at particular moments in history. In Germany, the rules and regulations associated with permission to work and with pension entitlement affected transmigrant seafarers of different nationalities in different ways.

Making out: Ghanaian transmigrants in North Germany

In the late 1970s, a group of Ghanaians were amongst the seafarers who came to Hamburg to look for work aboard a ship. Some came in small groups and initially travelled to southern Europe as a result of its relative proximity to West Africa before subsequently deciding to head for Hamburg. The choice of Hamburg was primarily because of the reputed (better) conditions to be found aboard German vessels. Some of the seafarers had experienced what they considered to be the inferior conditions offered by other employers, in other countries, and actively sought out a life, and a future, in Germany, aboard German vessels. As Gilroy with a group of friends explained to me:

> We know each other from childhood ... we met up and went to Italy and then Greece ... because Italy is much easier to get to than Greece. So we went to Italy and worked a little bit more and got money ... [and went to Greece once we had saved enough] ... After seeing Greek company we decided that we have a future here [in Germany]. In Greece we don't have a future. (Gilroy – Ghanaian seafarer)

A major attraction of working aboard vessels with the German flag was the requirement for workers to make social security contributions (the equivalent of National Insurance in the UK) and crucially for employers to also make contributions which would count toward pension entitlement. Hailing from a nation where no such social security system, or welfare state, operated this benefit was worth accepting a lower salary for. Charlie, who was originally from Ghana, explained it as follows:

I started working on a German ship. But the money wasn't good, I got more money from the foreign ship. But I think it was because of the [social] security [that I took the job] … On the foreign [flagged] ship there was no social security, you don't pay annuity insurance, but on a German [flagged] ship you have to pay for it. And they told me this money I would get in the future when I'm old. The company told me that, because they knew that I was a new person and that they had to explain that to me … I saw my pay slip and saw all the deductions. So I went to the captain and the captain told me everything. 'This is when you are sick, if you have to go to hospital, this money is for when you are old.' (Charlie – Ghanaian seafarer)

Access to social security benefits enabled nationals from Ghana (and from Cape Verde) to live in Germany at the end of a contract, or period of leave, and search for another vessel. In the 1970s such waits were not excessively long but in the 1980s and 1990s as the German fleet 'flagged-out' employment possibilities became increasingly restricted and periods of unemployment stretched for months and sometimes years. Transmigrants became increasingly like unemployed overseas contract workers and were forced to spend more and more time in Germany and less back in their 'homelands' or countries of origin.

In terms of finding work, the experience of Ghanaian and Cape Verdean transmigrant seafarers differed. It seemed that despite a shortage of vacancies aboard German-flagged vessels, some Ghanaians were still reasonably successful at finding work at sea. They reported waits of up to six months as opposed to the years of waiting reported by some Cape Verdean seafarers. However, while some did seem to remain active in the seafarer labour market it seemed they were also successful in finding work ashore. In Bremen they reported that they were legally entitled to work, in between jobs on board ship, and this was significant in maintaining the morale and prosperity of the group overall. In Hamburg the situation was different however, and Ghanaian seafarers reported that they were not allowed to work for wages ashore. In Hamburg it nevertheless seemed as if transmigrant Ghanaian seafarers did work in between contracts although what kind of work they did was not precisely clear. While, the nature of this work was not specified it was apparent that they were in touch with the world of the informal economy and could readily identify many jobs that could be done 'for cash'. It was evident from their lifestyles and appearance that they were not impoverished in the manner of the Cape Verdean nationals. They were well dressed in expensive coats, well 'adorned' with the very latest mobile phones and generally gave the appearance of being terribly busy and constantly having somewhere to get off to.

The inability to work legally between shipboard contracts was a constant source of frustration to the Ghanaians living in Hamburg, however, and some appeared to volunteer to take part in interviews primarily to air this grievance. They were angry at being forced into long periods of unemployment or alternatively employment in the informal sector. They wanted permission to work ashore in between sea jobs so that they could do so officially and 'above board'.

This separation from society at the level of employment and employment rights was also reflected in terms of the social lives of Ghanaian transmigrants.

While one or two suggested that they had German 'friends' these were sometimes economic relationships where odd jobs were done in return for cash, or assistance was provided in getting work aboard a ship. Most generally there was a sense that despite sometimes getting on quite well with German seafarers on board, few maintained friendships with German people ashore. As Josef talking with me in a group of friends explained:

> Sometimes it may be that you work with them on the ship but the moment when you sign off from the ship then they are no more friends ... Germans, sometimes you can talk with them but ... .[Josef – Ghanaian seafarer]

Many of the Ghanaian transmigrant seafarers knew each other and/or came from the same part of Ghana, facilitating the development of a strong sense of solidarity between Ghanaians in the face of isolation from German society. Simon explained how his group acted almost as an 'offshoot' of their home society. The individual comings and goings of group members operated as a regular conduit of communication and transportation between Ghana and the small satellite seafarer group resident in Hamburg. He explained:

> Yes, we live the same style as we do at home [in Ghana]. In close proximity ... when I finish this here for example I will go to a friend and we are going to talk and to laugh to forget about everything. Do you understand me? If one of my friends goes home, I say 'please, take this here for my wife' and he will go and deliver it to my wife. (Simon – Ghanaian seafarer)

It was clear however that the Ghanaians who were interviewed did not regard all Ghanaians as a homogenous group of potential 'friends'. Regional differences were regarded as significant and groups appeared to be constructed along lines mirroring local distributions of Ghanaians in their homeland. This highlights the ways in which migrants from particular nation states cannot be seen as homogenous groups ready to bond and to integrate with one another – something which is perhaps under-emphasised in some of the literature on transnational communities.

While differences amongst migrants are important however, those between migrants and host communities can be difficult to bridge and this is particularly the case for transmigrants. Ghanaian transmigrants perceived major differences in the ways in which their society and European society functioned. They experienced a cultural chasm between themselves and the German communities around them and they indicated that there was no connection between themselves and their German neighbours and little prospect of such connections developing. Ghanaian society was experienced by them as far more communal than European society and they found the latter unattractively unfriendly and 'cold' by comparison. As Charlie explained:

> You see, Ghana is not like Hamburg or Germany. [In Ghana] We know each other if we live in the same community ... Here in Hamburg, I may live in St Pauli and you too and we've seen each other many times but we never talk to each other ... For me [living in a community] means, in my country Ghana, we

love ourselves. We have a feeling for ourselves. But here in Europe it's not like
that at all. Sometimes here in Germany people are not friendly, I'm sorry to say
that. Like my neighbour, he comes from work, he opens his door and goes to his
room. In Africa, we don't live that way! That's why in this country for example it
can happen that somebody dies in his room and for one year nobody even no-
tices. It's because people are not friendly! We Africans are not like that. We live
like brothers, sisters and neighbours. (Charlie – Ghanaian seafarer)

The Ghanaians and Cape Verdeans did not mix particularly despite being
aware of each other's presence. The Ghanaians suggested that this was because
the Cape Verdeans regarded themselves as more 'European' while the Ghanaians
ascribed to an 'African' identity. Clive explained:

They [the Cape Verdeans] always look more Portuguese and have Portuguese
passports sometimes. You don't know the difference, they seem Portuguese. It
is not easy to make them speak English although we talk together … we do …
things together, not all the time, as we are not close … I'm Ghanaian. We are
black … We haven't [become European]. (Clive – Ghanaian seafarer)

While they didn't mix very frequently there were very strong common elements to the experiences of the Ghanaian and Cape Verdean seafarer groups.
Their sense of discrimination in the realm of employment inevitably impacted on
the broader perceptions of both the Cape Verdean and Ghanaian seafarer groups
in relation to their place in German society. The feeling amongst transmigrant
seafarers of a lack of rights, of marginality and exclusion, often resulted from a
strong sense of their host society being fundamentally unwelcoming, or bluntly
put, racist. Marco, who was clearly at pains not to cause offence nevertheless tried
to explain his feelings. He suggested:

Things are like that because I'm black … You are white, and I am black and
that makes all the difference. So why don't they give a passport to other people?
What they produce they sell outside the country, in Ghana there are BMWs.
Why don't they just keep it in their country? If you go to Ghana, you can see
German people there. And if they go to an authority there, nobody will tell you
that they've been discriminated. Nobody will do anything to you just because
you are a foreigner. They have to welcome you in a nice way. (Marco – Ghanaian
seafarer)

Despite such experiences of exclusion, racism, and lack of access to work, Ghanaian seafarers were clearly making out. That is to say they had somehow carved
out a niche for themselves as a group within the context they found themselves
in. Their social capital, their links into the African community and their greater
access to the limited work available aboard German-flagged vessels all appeared to
contribute to their relative success. By contrast Cape Verdean transmigrants fared
poorly, seemingly less able to overcome the social, legal, cultural and economic
barriers confronting them.

Waiting it out: Cape Verdean transmigrants trapped ashore

The flagging out of the German fleet impacted on all migrant seafarers who had been building up pension and social security entitlements regardless of where they were from. Thus Cape Verdean nationals found it increasingly difficult to find work at sea at the same time as Ghanaian citizens. They needed to find work aboard German-flagged ships to preserve pensions that they had been building for many years. It seemed that the regulations regarding pensions meant that two eligibility criteria had to be met by foreign seafarers in order to claim their pensions. Firstly, they had to have accumulated twenty years of sea time aboard German-flagged ships where employers had not 'opted them out' of the contributions scheme. Secondly, as Lucas, an official from the Seafarers Professional Association explained, they had to work 50 per cent of the time in their previous eighteen years, prior to claiming a pension, aboard German flagged vessels. As he put it:

> Premises [for pension entitlement] are easy: you must have worked 20 years under German flag, pure times on board, OK including paid holidays of course. Every time that compulsory insurance contribution was paid due to compulsory insurance employment on a German ship. The second point, that is relevant for a number of people who have worked on foreign ships: they must have worked mainly on German ships in the last eighteen years. That means if you are fifty-seven in the year 2000 and you want to retire, then from 1982 on you must have spent at least 50 per cent, i.e. nine years and one month, on a German ship. (Lucas – German Seafarers Professional Association)

This meant that for some seafarers working aboard foreign-flagged ships might nullify contributions previously made. The pension requirements effectively trapped them into unemployment at a time when German vessels existed in small numbers and seafarers' jobs aboard them were hard to come by. This situation had gradually got worse over time as fleet personnel managers increasingly hired crews via overseas crewing agents. The following experiences were typical:

> Today ... it is not better [to find work in Brake than Hamburg]. I mean I am registered there, too. Four months – nothing happened. Here in ... [Hamburg] ... too. They try to help me, too. Because I am always going there and checking. But there is nothing in sight yet. Neither in Brake. In Brake it became bad. [It has been bad for] a few years. Two or three years. Because in Brake – I have many colleagues who live in Brake, because [before] one could get a ship quickly – but today that doesn't work any more. [It is] very bad ... Hamburg is big [and in the past] one might get a job quickly. And that was a fact. But today this is not [the case] any more. We only wait for the Heuerstelle – if they have something. I mean I know many companies here in Hamburg, but nowadays you go there and ask whether they have something – I mean they still have ships, many ships, but they hire cheap men. With German tariff, we get no job. (Otis – Cape Verde seafarer)

Even those regularly employed by the same company found their waiting periods had increased. Angus explained:

> I always had to wait a few days [to get work] … But now things are different, because I have already been waiting here for two weeks and I still don't know when I will be able to go on board … I have to wait [in Hamburg] to go on the ship. It would be really bad if they [his regular employer] called me to go on board and I wasn't there. (Angus – Cape Verde seafarer)

While Otis elaborated on the situation, describing how:

> I came from Cabo Verde four months ago and I am still waiting for a job. I am unemployed. I have to pay my rent here, send money home, I have to eat. There is nothing left … But we cannot help it … The situation became so bad. Hopefully it gets better. But it doesn't look very bright. (Otis – Cape Verde seafarer)

Another seafarer, Flynn, described how people working for a company in Brake were left out of work for years in the current employment climate. He explained:

> Some people from Cape Verde used to [all] work for the same shipping company. But nowadays with all those problems, we are unemployed for maybe two years and they always talk about sending us back home. (Flynn – Cape Verde seafarer)

Just as the Ghanaians were frustrated by regulations preventing them from accepting land-based work, so too were the Cape Verdean nationals some of whom had been in Germany on and off for more than twenty years. Otis again explained:

> No, I am not allowed [to work ashore]. For the German law I came a little too late to Germany. '76 I came. Many of us who came before '73. Then you have a chance to work ashore … I have tried to work ashore. But I couldn't make it. I had a firm and got a contract. I then went to the immigration authorities but they said, I am sorry, we can't do it. I would have liked very much to do it because it is very bad with seafaring, now [in terms of finding work]. I wanted to work ashore in order to continue making a living … That hurts me. I mean I am working for twenty-three years, now. All my early years I worked here. Now, I am unemployed. I will get one year unemployment benefit. If it stops, they have to send me home. And that hurts. I am here for twenty-three years. Now, when they send me home, I don't know what to do to provide a living for my family. I have no other option. I am still young. Not too old. Half and half [laughs]. But what am I supposed to do there [back home] There is no firms who would take me … I have no record. I never had difficulties here in Germany. Yet, why don't they give me another chance? Give me the right to work ashore. But they don't do it. I've tried but it didn't work. (Otis – Cape Verdean seafarer)

Some seafarers had even experienced problems with getting permission to work aboard ships (not just ashore) when they applied to undertake specific jobs (such as those in catering) as the following account from Cary indicates:

This man called me and said 'We are happy about your papers. And I want to work with you, please send your passport pictures and your account number etc to our address.' So I sent everything to them and he asked me 'Have you got a working permission?'And I said that I didn't have one … I was very happy that I got a good company and I sent a letter to my agent at the labour department [responsible for finding jobs for the unemployed] and told him that I had managed to find myself a job and that the company sent me a working permission. And that I have to send this to the labour department to get it stamped … [and I was told] … that I had to go to the boss and he said 'No, I can't stamp it, you must send it to the department in Cologne because the company is in Cologne!' And I said 'Even though the company is in Cologne, my labour department is here in Hamburg.' If I'm working on the ship I will never be in Cologne so why do you refuse to stamp this for me? Because I'm black or what? This man didn't like me … So I became very very sad. I went back to my unemployment agent and he told me that he couldn't do anything if that other man didn't help me. But he told me that if I was working as a sailor I wouldn't need a working permission. But [because] I wanted to go as a cook I needed a working permission. And I said to him 'Listen, I've been here for almost eighteen years, I've never got any bad record. I've always paid for my taxes, social insurance, everything … I'm here for work!' And also, the government wants everybody to work and not be dependent on unemployment money or support, and I'm here with my own job! Why can you not help me? Do you want me to commit suicide or what? I have a family! If I don't work, how can my family live? (Cary – Cape Verdean seafarer)

It seemed that other restrictions were also applied to Cape Verdean nationals with regard to work at sea. Some faced restrictions relating to permanent work and could only accept jobs at sea that were officially temporary in nature. One seafarer in this situation described being prevented from accepting a 'permanent' contract because his visa was restricted to two years.

Notwithstanding the restrictions on jobs at sea, seafarers more commonly reported feeling restricted as to the shore-side work they could legitimately engage in. This had the effect of segregating unemployed transmigrants with time on their hands, from workers without, and compounded the divisions between transmigrants and German society and their sense of isolation. Freeman, explained that he never met people and on being asked if this was because he didn't know many people, he described how:

Well, I do know a lot of people. But most people never have time, because they are too busy with their work. They do not have time to talk … (Freeman – Cape Verdean seafarer)

Aside from the sense of isolation associated with unemployment (which is not uncommon and has been documented elsewhere) there was also a strong sense in both 'communities' (Ghanaians and Cape Verdeans) that one of the barriers to integration in German society was the lack of rights. Often these were tied to employment rights, as discussed previously, but they extended beyond this to a more general feeling of disenfranchisement including a frustration at being disallowed from engaging in commercial enterprise. Jim and Pete, a pair of Cape Verdean ex-seafarers explained it thus:

> That all is very difficult here in Germany, because the laws don't give us any kind of rights. I've been here since 1975 ...
>
> Definitely, those laws are awful. I believe that this is catastrophic. In Holland for instance they don't have these problems, because all the Cape Verde people there have the same rights as the Dutch people. Here in Germany it is not like that. And we people from Cape Verdean are good workers. We don't want to live from the unemployment money, but are willing to work very hard ... A person from Cape Verde with a Cape Verdean passport will never ever be able to open a shop here. (Jim and Pete – Cape Verdean seafarers)

Jim went on to say that it was particularly difficult for unemployed seafarers:

> I hope you don't misunderstand us, because the Cape Verdean people don't talk badly about Germany in general. They are not satisfied with the laws here and that's all. We realised soon that the government doesn't care about us little people. I believe that the government could have helped us at least a little bit and could have supported the seamen who have been working so hard a little bit more. I used to see my family only once every year. Can you imagine that after thirty years of marriage I have seen my wife only thirty times ...
>
> The only thing we know as people from Cape Verdean is that if you have been working here for thirty years, you don't have any rights at all. You have to be very careful here with what you say, especially when you have been unemployed for already two years. (Jim – Cape Verdean seafarer)

Feelings of exclusion were exacerbated by the awareness amongst Cape Verdean seafarers that work permits were only given out to non-Europeans in labour markets where no Europeans could be identified as available (a similar system to that operating in the UK). This led Cape Verdeans to feel they were regarded as a 'third class' by many Germans, as Freddie, who held a Cape Verdean passport, explained:

> It is indeed very difficult to get a job on land, because I know that there are a lot of German people, who are unemployed, too. At the administrative body the people told me that the first person who gets a job is a German person. The second person who would be able to receive the job is a European person and at the third position are we people from Cape Verde. Of course you can talk a lot about equal rights, but most people don't behave in that way. They treat us like people from a third class. (Freddie – Cape Verdean seafarer)

Not being allowed to get a job ashore left people depressed as well as impoverished. Living in the cheap accommodation provided by seafarers' hostels had the advantage of preventing them from becoming completely isolated but it also resulted in a cloud of desolation descending on these places during 'hard times'. Seafarers were absent from society as political and economic actors but they were also excluded as social and cultural actors in a climate of unemployment and depression. As Bogdan explained:

> In the past the [seafarers' bed and breakfast] was better. Now it is 'tote Hose' ['dead trousers' – German expression meaning boring] ... There were many people. And when there was work, the people were in good mood. If there is no work the people are down ... Many Cape Verdeans have left for home already ... For example from Brake, many people have left ... [before] it was full ... more than twenty people. And the seamen's hotel was full, too. Now there may be four men ... There aren't many people left ... Those who are close to retirement age have left. They don't want any more: to sit here for one year ... That's not a life! (Bogdan – Cape Verdean seafarer)

In a seafarers' hostel in Hamburg, many were disinclined to go out at all, living very isolated and institutionalised lives. This was partly a consequence of poverty and seemed partly a consequence of a feeling of difference and separation from wider German society. Karel, a regular Cape Verdean visitor to the seafarers' centre was asked if he sometimes met Cape Verdeans outside the Centre. He replied:

> Not really. The people from here [seafarers' centre] do seldomly go out. Only four or five people go into town every day. Most people stay here all the time, playing cards and so on. (Karel – Cape Verdean seafarer)

This idea that people had gradually become largely 'house-bound' was supported by a description of a change in the rules at the hostel. This had occurred following the recognition of foreign seafarers' impoverished status. In dire economic straits, seafarers could not afford accommodation that did not make provision for self-catering and as a result the hostel reversed its prohibition on cooking. In an interview, Fabian commented that:

> Yes we can [cook for ourselves]. We have to. We have a kitchen up there for everybody who wants to cook. We got this two years ago. Before it was prohibited to cook in the house. But now they allow us. Because they, too know: we are out of jobs. We cannot go to the cheap restaurants. They are too expensive. Here we can buy things ourselves and cook ourselves. (Fabian – Cape Verdean seafarer)

The degree of institutionalisation, which appeared to result in part from their impoverished status, was marked amongst unemployed seafarers residing at the seafarers' hostel. It led Jerome to describe the hostel, rather than Germany as his second home although when pressed he altered his definition of 'second home' to include Germany as well. As he put it:

> The second home [laughs]. Yes [name of hostel] is the second home. Yes I only came to here, to no other place ... (Jerome – Cape Verdean seafarer)

Others described the hostel as being 'not what it should be' but suggested they had little option but to accept it the way it was and patiently wait to leave for a job or for retirement:

> We are in a foreign country, we have no house, so we are here. We have to accept what we have [laughs]. If you don't feel to stay, nobody will stop you to stay [go].

So, that's the life. You have to accept it even if it is not good. I don't going to rent a house for three or five months and then give it back. So, here, we have to stay and then you have to support it [the hostel]. All of us we have to accept that. So I have not much things to say against. I know what atmosphere here. So … I do good to everybody and everybody do good to me. We respect one another, so … we hold the time until we go home to stay. (George – Cape Verdean seafarer)

Living apart from their families while unemployed was experienced by some as particularly difficult. One man, Alan, who for nineteen years had been in a relationship with a woman living in Rotterdam identified his passport status as a key cause of his unhappiness. He explained how:

I want to leave, but I can't. If I had a European passport, I could go to Rotterdam, to Portugal, to Denmark, no problem then. But with a Cape Verdean passport I need a visa for example to go to Rotterdam. You have to pay for it as well … But I can't do anything about it. I'm on my own here. And I prefer living with my wife. But if I leave, I won't get any money. My wife works only four hours, that's not enough. When I can retire, I can go abroad and work there and earn more. But now, if I went abroad, I would lose everything. (Alan – Cape Verde seafarer)

Other issues faced them too. Being forced to rely on benefits had additional consequences for these transmigrant seafarers in as much as they were often unable to pay for flights home at short notice. In the event of a family emergency or a decision that they wished to return permanently seafarers could be effectively stranded. One employed seafarer, Alfred, explained that for his unemployed compatriots life could be very hard. He described how:

Sometimes someone has no money and is homesick, but just has to wait until a job comes up. Without money one cannot get home. Sometimes there are people who want to go home, but they don't have the money for the flight. (Alfred – Cape Verdean seafarer)

It was notable that none of the seafarer groups, regardless of their ethnic origin or passport status, considered themselves to be integrated into Brake, Bremen, or Hamburg society. When asked if he belonged to two different countries Peter exclaimed:

No, I don't belong both sides! I belong to my house [in Cape Verde], but … I have to come. I have to work. I can say I belong to work and to my house but I don't belong to another country … I didn't have a feeling at all … but well, I am here because I have to stay here and not because I have the feeling to stay here … It's a cheaper place than a normal hotel. If I go to a normal hotel, the money never lasts. That's why we are here. But we don't have any feeling. No one living here has a feeling to stay here. So the situation forces us to stay here. Not that we like to stay here. We come here to look for work, not to stay here. It's no job, so this is our waiting place for the job. (Peter – Cape Verdean seafarer)

It emerged that in as far as contact with German people was concerned, some could only conceive as having contact with German women, perhaps sex workers, in their constricted worlds. German men hardly featured at all in their social land-scape or imaginings. Illustrating this point, when Blake was asked if he had any German 'friends here in Hamburg?', he instantly responded 'No! I have no inter-est. I am married … my wife! I am not interested in other women … .OK in the past … '(Blake – Cape Verdean seafarer). Another put it succinctly when he stated 'As regards [German] friends here in Hamburg or Germany, I have none' (Jonty – Cape Verdean seafarer). Thus their sense of community was generally confined to the small group of compatriots they spent time with. It did not include German men and rarely German women. These friends were regarded as their 'community' and were defined as such because of the regularity of meetings amongst them and an almost total absence of other social contact. Otis described his circle of contacts as follows:

> Yes, I would say that we are a community. Here in Bremen there are maybe seven or eight people from Cape Verde, who meet on a regular basis. We aren't many people. (Otis – Cape Verde seafarer)

Another, Miles, replied to a question as to whether he saw the seafarer hostel resi-dents as a 'community' as follows:

> Yes, sometimes yes. Sometimes we meet and play the guitar and sing. So. Also this Thursday. There is no mass this Thursday. With many people and also peo-ple coming from the Caritas we go to Harburg [area in Hamburg] and we will party and eat. Normally I go to mass here on Thursday and on Sundays I got to the Caritas, too, where the Portuguese meet. There is nothing to do while I stay here. So, I go to church. (Miles – Cape Verdean seafarer)

As with the Ghanaian transmigrants, the strongest groups comprised people from the same locality rather than simply from the same nation state. Stan, for example, described meeting regularly with just two friends in Hamburg:

> No … I have only two [friends] here. Directly from my village in Cabo Verde. I see them every Saturday. I might stay a few hours say from 1pm and then leave again at say 7p.m. We watch sport or we talk about it. If there is nothing in the Portuguese channels we might watch the Spanish channels. Football is what I am really interested in. (Stan – Cape Verdean seafarer)

However looser groupings were also formed on the basis of new friendships made in Germany between individuals of common nationality who had not been previously known to each other. As Dylan explained:

> We all come from different islands. I met a lot of my colleagues here in Germany. We used to work together on a board and that's how I met them … There are a lot of people who know each other just from Germany … I always do my activi-ties with people that I know. I know some of my colleagues from Cape Verde (from before), but most of the people I got to know them here in Germany. (Dylan – Cape Verdean seafarer)

Another described how a seafarer helped him when he first arrived in Hamburg, putting him up in his house, and helping him to find work. These men came from different islands far apart from each other but nevertheless the Cape Verde connection was sufficient to elicit the offer of assistance. Billy recounted:

> The first three days I used to live with a colleague ... During those days I realised that the living standard here was far too high for me. Hamburg is a very expensive city and I knew that if I wanted to stay here in the future I had to be economical ... I lived at a friend's house ... He was from Cape Verde. He had also a Portuguese colleague with whom we went to eat in a restaurant. I slept those three days at his house ... I only knew him from Germany, because this colleague actually comes from an island which is very far away from my island. We got to know each other much better here in Germany than in our home country. Everybody lives on his/her island and it is really difficult to meet the people there and therefore you can't know everybody there. But here in Germany, I had the chance to meet more people from my own country. (Billy – Cape Verdean seafarer)

In the past seafarers often came into contact with fellow compatriots in the seafarers' houses, aboard ships, and through frequenting shops, bars, or restaurants carrying their national identity. As Sanley explained:

> There was a Portuguese restaurant, where we met. You always prefer [the company of] your relatives [meaning fellow nationals] When you go to a foreign country and you see somebody from Portugal [you want to talk with them]. (Sanley – Cape Verdean seafarer)

While such activities were rare in the contemporary context, once established these groups, although fluid (seafarers came and went to join ship/return home for vacation, etc.), seemed to be enduring. Within them it seemed some of the social conditions of 'home' could be recreated.

It was evident from the lifestyles of the Cape Verdean seafarers that most did not access informal labour markets ashore and did not engage in illegal work. There was a tangible difference in the atmosphere surrounding the Cape Verdean and Ghanaian seafarer groups. The Ghanaians had an air of enterprise and energy about them, a sense of purpose and activity as well as visible signs of affluence. This related in part to the permission that some had to officially work in Bremen but it seemed to be a more general phenomenon than this would imply. By contrast the Cape Verdeans were a disconsolate group with the appearance of deprivation and an atmosphere of sadness and suffering surrounding them.

Breaking out: Cape Verdean seafarers holding Portuguese passports

However for one group of Cape Verdean transmigrants the situation in North Germany was very different. Some Cape Verdean seafarers had acquired the legal right to work in land-based jobs in Germany by virtue of acquiring Portuguese and, more unusually, German passports. For many this meant that they suffered less deprivation than their fellow countrymen. They were able to work in restaurants, in fish farms and in a variety of lesser skilled occupations. As Henty explained:

> I used to work on sea for fifteen years. And since 1995 I learned how to become a cook and now I'm working in a restaurant. Since that time I'm living on land.
> (Henty – Cape Verdean seafarer with Portuguese passport)

Another, James, contrasted the situation of Cape Verdeans with Portuguese passports and that of those without. While appreciating the entitlements which Portuguese nationality allowed he nevertheless described how he and others in his privileged situation became embroiled in the troubles and, by association, the pain and frustrations of Cape Verdean nationals. He explained:

> For example the colleague from yesterday. He came in November and is still looking for a job ... The stamp from the immigration authorities. They need a job in order to get a new stamp from the immigration authorities. The Portuguese don't have this particular problem. But there are too many problems. There is a new law, under which many people from Cabo Verde are not eligible for Arbeitslosenhilfe [the second step of unemployment benefits, formerly payable after twelve to thirty-six months of Arbeitslosengeld. Arbeitslosenhilfe is about 53 per cent of the last net income]. There are many problems and many people who are afraid. They don't get any help. What can they do: they have to go home soon. They cannot stay here. That sometimes is much too heavy for us to bear. (James – Cape Verdean seafarer with Portuguese passport)

This undoubtedly impacted upon transmigrants resident in North Germany, many of whom retained some connections with the seafarers' hostel and thus with non-resident transmigrant seafarers from Cape Verde and to a lesser extent Ghana.

Not only did the right to work create evident differences between the lives of Portuguese passport-holding Cape Verdean transmigrants, and those from Cape Verde without a Portuguese passport, but the ability to have their families living with them was hugely significant. There were examples of transmigrants who had eventually settled in parts of Germany, with their families, and described being happy in their current circumstances:

> Well, it's [Brake] my first place in Germany when I came, and I like it. And my family came also, they like it, I'd rather live in Brake than in Bremen or Bremerhaven, or Hamburg, it's too big, I don't like the big cities. Small town, quiet, clean. (Claud – Cape Verdean seafarer with Portuguese passport)

To suggest that all Cape Verdean seafarers with Portuguese passports were happily settled in Germany would, however, be a great over-simplification. Sometimes, even seafarers legally entitled to work were unemployed. Occasionally, this seemed to be due to their age but many also complained of the low wages available to non-German workers; wages that they felt were being depressed by workers from the former East German republic and from other areas of Eastern Europe, notably Poland. The following descriptions, from Harry and Oscar, of wages and wage dynamics were given:

> There are also a lot of people from the former DDR, who work for only seven DMs an hour. They abuse the people as workers to construct their roads ... They use them, because they are very cheap. It is very difficult here. (Harry – Cape Verdean former seafarer with Portuguese passport)

> Yes, I have a Portuguese passport. I can [work ashore]. Ashore they pay, eight Marks, nine Marks per hour. That's no money, that is! I have to find a flat – that doesn't work. Now, with all the Poles and Russians, the firms pay three Marks or four Marks per hour for these people ... Ashore! Three Marks or four Marks for the Poles and Russians! (Oscar – Cape Verdean seafarer with Portuguese passport)

The spaces that could be occupied by transmigrants were not just structured by employment rights as enshrined by law, therefore, and the example of the Cape Verdean seafarers with European passports, and a right to work, clearly demonstrated this. Not only did economic factors limit employment prospects but the experiences of the Portuguese passport-holding Cape Verdeans taught them that the right to work legally did not guarantee socio-cultural acceptance on the part of employers, and Cape Verdeans perceived discriminatory action in relation to getting jobs and integrating into society. Harry suggested:

> The German people don't really look at our passport but at our culture, which they obviously don't like. The rich German people make us a lot of problems to integrate ourselves here in Germany. (Harry – Cape Verdean seafarer with Portuguese passport)

Some Cape Verdean ex-seafarers residing and working ashore on Portuguese passports felt that there was a pressure for 'foreigners' in Hamburg and Brake to abandon their culture and fully assimilate dominant German cultural values and practices. They felt they were actively discouraged from asserting or displaying cultural 'difference'. The creation of spaces where such differences are welcome has been described as important for migrants in coming to feel at home. Flores, for example, argues in relation to Latinos in the United States that such space is key to the concept of cultural citizenship, suggesting that:

> A key aspect of the concept is the struggle for a distinct social space in which members of the marginalised group are free to express themselves and feel at home. (Flores 2003: 89)

The feeling that transmigrant seafarers in Northern Germany had of being unwelcome, culturally speaking, led to particular resentment when combined with an awareness that there was a strong place in the German labour market for migrant workers to undertake poorly paid and low-skilled work. One ex-seafarer explained how:

> We would like to open a little cultural centre, where all people from Cape Verde could meet together, but the government doesn't support us to do that. (Marlon – Cape Verdean ex-seafarer with Portuguese passport)

His friend, Tango, angrily added:

> Here in Germany there is clear system. All the culture that come from Europe is treated nicely, but we people from Cape Verde aren't treated like that at all. When the Germans need us to do their dirty work we are good enough for them, but when we show them that we would like to represent our own culture they ignore us totally. (Tango – Cape Verdean ex-seafarer with Portuguese passport).

While another, Ollie, implied that Cape Verdean/Portuguese nationals had a raw deal in Germany as their inability to integrate was not really compensated for in terms of economic success. It seemed the promised land of 'milk and honey' had, for him, turned sour:

> I tell you that you get annoyed when you think that you have been working and living here for so many years, without really having achieved anything … . My colleague for instance, he has been working here almost thirty, thirty-six, no forty years. I guess I could never ever, not even in my nicest dreams achieve the things I wanted to when I first came to Germany. Even if I had been working in Germany for one-hundred years, I still wouldn't get what belongs to me. (Ollie – Cape Verdean with Portuguese passport)

The sense that transmigrant groups had, of being required to fit into German society, appeared to be validated by the attitudes of some of the people with whom they had direct dealings. For example, the chaplain at one of the seafarer houses commented that it was very difficult to get the seafarers interested in anything German, clearly viewing this as reprehensible. A field note recorded that:

> He [the chaplain] said if he suggested they [the Cape Verdean seafarers] go to a German museum or tried to get them interested in German music they weren't interested at all. When the chaplain left I quietly asked one of the [Cape Verdean] guys if he liked German music and he just laughed … I asked him if he liked German food and he said it was OK but that he preferred Portuguese food and said that was much better. (Sampson field note 2002)

While the German chaplain noted the disinclination of the transmigrants to wholeheartedly embrace German culture, it seemed that both the Ghanaians and the Cape Verdeans felt that they, and their cultures and traditions, were not valued by German nationals. This sense appeared to contribute, to a major extent, to their sense of separation from German society and the alienation they appeared to experience while resident in the cities of Brake, Bremen and Hamburg.

Even those apparently content to have settled in Germany often described having few German friends, or indeed friends of any nationality. As Jack put it when asked if he spent time with German people:

No, only, with other people, if there's time, we get together, there's not that many, last time in the seaman's home, and sometimes everybody is gone, and we have four families we have contact to. My family is good enough when we are together. If together with other people, it's OK, but I'm happy with my family. (Jack – Cape Verdean with Portuguese passport)

The lack of integration impacted on the future plans of those with a right to live and work in Germany and a number intended to return to Portugal or to Cape Verde once they were able to draw their pensions. Ray, a former seafarer still looking for work aboard vessels explained that in the not too distant future (he was fifty) he would return home to live with his family as a retired man. He explained:

In ten years time I would receive my pension, I would be with my family. In ten years I am sixty years old. With fifty-seven years you can start receiving your pension. (Ray – Cape Verdean seafarer with Portuguese passport)

Links 'back home'

The experience of transnationality is not only determined by the extent to which migrants or transmigrants are embedded into 'host' societies. It is critical to also consider the extent to which they are connected to 'home' societies in order to gain a sense of the extent to which they can be said to reside dually, across borders. In Germany, there was a strong sense amongst transmigrant seafarers that they were merely marking time. Few had put down 'roots' and most envisaged returning 'home' to the Philippines, Cape Verde, Portugal, or Ghana, at a point in the foreseeable future. They maintained regular contact by telephone with family members and sometimes letters (not email however) and they kept in touch with local news via the comings and goings of others returning home perhaps once a year. Ralph explained:

I wanted to work at sea until the age of forty-five. Then I wanted to go home [i.e. to Cape Verde] and do something else. Because, I am already at sea for more than twenty years. There are times when I am really fed up with that. I want to leave in three years time but it doesn't look as if I can actually do it. It doesn't look bright. I wanted to stay home and do a business together with my family. (Ralph – Cape Verdean seafarer)

In this aspect, many of the transmigrants in Hamburg differed from their counterparts in Rotterdam (Sampson 2003) who despite living on the margins of Dutch society were nevertheless more strongly glued into it than Cape Verdean or Ghanaian transmigrants were bonded into North German society.

Most Cape Verdean nationals described having little interest in politics but some did describe a strong set of political connections between expatriate Cape Verdean nationals and had been involved in national politics while temporarily residing in Germany. Philo explained that:

> We have a political aim, which can be seen by our political attitude. Of course
> we try to be diplomatic but as I already said we do have a political aim. When
> somebody receives his salary in a foreign country this is already a political signal
> ... At the moment Cape Verde is a democracy, but only because of these embas-
> sies from the other foreign countries. The government controls everything for
> the people who live in Cape Verde ... It was governed by this [one] party for
> fifteen years. Almost half of the bread [money] comes from a foreign country.
> We had those political interests, because our family lives there ... Now we are a
> big community from Cape Verde and we are trying to change something about
> this situation. There are indeed twice as many people from Cape Verde living in
> a foreign country than in Cape Verde. People from Cape Verde live all around
> the world. They live in places like America and South America in countries
> such as Brazil and Argentina ... For this reason, the political interests from the
> Cape Verdean people living in a foreign country are very influential and we do
> indeed have a lot of power ... There were two men, one in Cape Verde and an-
> other one in America, who founded the party. They were especially concerned
> to represent the interests of the Cape Verdean people living in foreign countries
> ... Since than a lot of things have changed. People started to rebel against this
> single party. Also the Cape Verdean people who were living abroad, were always
> watching the political situation in Cape Verde ... The party informed us via
> leaflets ... Yes, they existed everywhere, where people from Cape Verde were
> living. There was always a person, who found one of those leaflets and therefore
> the others were able to read it as well ... We did photocopies of it. (Philo – Cape
> Verdean national)

In Germany most people sent regular remittances home and had dependents relying upon them and their financial support. Unlike their counterparts in Holland few had dependents residing with them (in Hamburg, Bremen, or Brake) although some Cape Verdeans holding Portuguese passports were in this position. For almost all of them family ties remained in their country of origin and this impacted significantly on their sense of identity and 'home'. The situation described here is fairly typical:

> Every month I have to send 500 DM to my wife. That's for living and school etc.
> And I also have to send money to my mother, because my father is dead so I'm
> the one taking care of my mother. And she is very old and I have to give her 200
> DM every month. She needs a lot of the money for the doctor, you know old
> people have to go and see the doctor all the time. And that's in Africa, not in
> Europe, we don't have social insurance or anything like that. If you are sick, you
> have to care for yourself. (Tim – Cape Verdean seafarer)

The contributions that transmigrants could make to the finances of those back home were curtailed during periods of unemployment however. As a result many of the long-term unemployed were simply waiting for the right to leave the country with full pension entitlement. While they sat out the months and years required to meet the criteria for pension entitlement, they sent small amounts of money home and spent the barest minimum on their own needs. This wait was depressing and difficult for many, as the following comment illustrates:

> I thought about having it paid up [his pension], but these two years [waiting
> out his time until he is entitled to a full pension] are too long ... Yes, two years.
> It's too long ... And I am away from home for such a long time. I'd prefer to go
> home. But I don't know yet. I must think about it ... Six months were OK. Two
> years are too long (Hugo – Cape Verdean seafarer).

The longing to go home and the requirement to make money were things that
many men seemed to be constantly weighing up. As they got older they became
more conscious of their own limitations upon returning home in terms of the
work they would be capable of and this often led them to decide that they must
hang on in Germany until they gained their full pension entitlement. Edward explained:

> I just would like to go home to live with my family again. But then I wouldn't be
> able to work that much any more, because I'm already an old man. The children
> will be already grown-up by then, except maybe one child. I will have to make
> money for that child ... (Edward – Cape Verdean seafarer)

Home and homeland thus seemed to be a greater reality for the transmigrants
of North Germany than it was for those living in Rotterdam. In Rotterdam homelands were more imagined than real. Communities of transmigrants had become
more separate from their original social groups as they had been able to establish
themselves more firmly in Dutch society (Sampson 2003). In Germany transmigrants lived such a marginal existence that their sense of transience seemed ever
present. Many had bought small houses in Cape Verde or Ghana and their entire
focus was on return. Despite dividing their time between living in Germany (with
far more time spent in Germany) and their homelands they could not be described
as transnationals as such. Their existence in Germany was almost spectral in character. Their presence was barely noticed by wider German society while they, in
turn, were barely touched by it. None expressed any regret at the idea of leaving a
country in which they had spent so many months and years. For many, Germany
which had once offered so much had simply become a prison. Their focus, their
dreams, their aspirations were all elsewhere.

Transnationality amongst seafarer transmigrants in Germany

Reflecting on the situation of transmigrant seafarers in Germany it is evident that
their foothold in German society is very tentative and precarious. They are a long
way from being embedded in this host society. Despite long absences from their
homelands their focus and their hearts remain there and they merely wait out
their time in Germany as ghostly presences on the fringes of society. As such, they
may not be regarded as archetypically transnational.

In Germany the experience of transmigrant seafarers was greatly affected by
the legal framework governing their employment and residence. On the one hand

laws regulating conditions of employment worked to their benefit while aboard German-flagged vessels, but on the other they worked very much against them during periods of unemployment when German law prevented most from seeking alternative work ashore. Social benefits such as pension entitlement and unemployment benefit were clearly materially advantageous in the short term and yet in combination with restrictive immigration and employment laws these too worked against transmigrant seafarers to the extent that they encouraged, and sometimes more or less forced them to remain in Germany even when work at sea was impossible to find.

The situation for one group of transmigrants was materially different. Cape Verdeans with European passports had integrated better into German society at the level of the workplace where they communicated with and developed connections amongst fellow workers. They were sometimes living in Germany with their families which brought them into contact with the education system and sometimes the health system and other social services. These seafarers nevertheless described a strong cultural gulf between their own societies and German society and they felt that German culture was somewhat resistant to adaptation, or to newcomers with different cultural practices. As their bonds with their homelands became weakened, for example, so too did they become increasingly 'spectral' in nature, neither present in their traditional 'homes' nor strongly embedded in their new ones. While the structure of space and access to various kinds of capital mediated the experiences of transmigrant seafarers, therefore, it was nevertheless the case that none really met the criteria for transnationality.

Notes

1   Showing someone the ropes, the phrase meaning 'teaching people how things are', derives from seafaring. In the days of sailing ships new seafarers had to learn the names and functions of countless different ropes aboard and 'experienced hands' thus had the task of 'showing them the ropes'.

Figure 2 (above): Welding over side while underway
Figure 3 (below): Baking bread in the galley

Figure 4 (above): On deck with the mooring crew
Figure 5 (below): Fire drill on board container ship

Figure 6 (above): Heaving a mooring line
Figure 7 (below): Painting the ship's name

Figure 8 (above): Securing a mooring line
Figure 9 (below): Cleaning up after cargo tank inspection

5

Life on board: ships, hierarchy and workloads

> Well Captain's a wicked man
> He gets drunk any time he can
> And he don't give a damn for grandpappy
> No, nor me
> He kicks us around
> And he knocks us about
> Well I feel so broke up, I
> I wanna go home[1]

Amongst serving seafarers today, there is perhaps more 'I wanna go home', than there is 'sea fever' of the kind that John Masefield describes, in his poem of that title (see Chapter 3). The 'call of the running tide' is an urge described by few. For most, the sea is not the main reason they return, contract after contract, to their jobs on board. Seafaring nevertheless remains a popular occupation in many parts of the world for those who are willing to sacrifice life ashore and travel the world in search of adventure or, perhaps more often in today's environment where much adventure has gone out of the seafaring 'gypsy life' (John Masefield), in return for 'hard cash'.

In contrast to the transmigrants searching for work in hub port cities such as Hamburg, most seafarers are today recruited through crewing agencies, based in their homelands, on a short-term basis (i.e. employed on a per voyage contract). Many people who go to sea initially have high hopes of a good and prosperous life. They are seduced by the idea of travel and exploration. However, they are all too often disappointed in this, finding modern-day seafaring to be different to the world they had imagined: that which has been immortalised so frequently in song, poem, book and film (see Gould 2010).

Despite the fascination that the sea holds for the arts and the extent to which it features in popular film and literature, the world of the real modern-day seafarer is in many respects a remote one. Cargo ships are not generally accessed by members of the public who, if they think of them at all, tend to think of them as sets of twinkling lights on the distant night horizon, or, less attractively, as sources of potential pollution. Even where a vessel fetches up close to the shore, like the MV *Napoli* which grounded off the Dorset coast in 2007, it is quickly reduced to a metal hulk and a source of 'booty' for beachcombers; the life aboard invisible to the curious eyes of onlookers. This 'invisibility' and inaccessibility has also tended to mean that as occupational workplaces and multinational living spaces cargo ships[2] have often been overlooked as potential sites of social science research (but see Schrank 1983 and Lane 1986). There has, however, been increased international interest with the waning of the twentieth century and beginning of the twenty-first (see for example Knudsen 2004) reflecting, perhaps, the fact that ships are complex settings which constitute potentially fascinating and revealing social microcosms.

Shipboard 'society' is unique in some respects but shares sufficient similarity with that of other social groups, such as particular categories of migrant worker, people living transnational lives, and specific occupational groups, to make the study of the seafarer a rewarding one. In the post-war period the shipping industry has become increasingly globalised in its structure and organisation. Ship ownership and management are concentrated in OECD countries but as a result of a process of 'flagging out' labour is increasingly supplied by the nations of the developing world. Aboard many deep-sea (internationally trading) vessels this process (described in more detail in Chapter 3) has resulted in the establishment of 'fluid' multinational crews. Such crews are only weakly unionised and solidarity aboard (across ranks and across nationalities) is often difficult to foster. Seafarers from many parts of the world come together aboard internationally trading cargo ships to live and work in a confined and very restrictive and institutionalised space for periods as long as twelve months and usually no shorter than two.[3] They are generally employed on different terms and conditions (according to both nationality and rank) and they are a vulnerable work group subject to the constant threat of instant dismissal by senior officers on board and the potential for subsequent 'blacklisting' by crewing agents in their homelands. A crew on a specific vessel may never work together again, or in some cases individuals may return after a period of leave to see some familiar faces on board. Either way, the crew of a merchant cargo vessel is characterised by constant comings and goings, as crew members join a vessel with a long stretch ahead of them, or leave with a spring in their step.[4]

Several factors facilitate this fluid movement of workers who when they leave a ship may never return to her again. The first critical organisational factor is that the shipping industry has adopted one language (English) as the international language of the sea and this is generally utilised as the working language for multinational vessels. The second factor is that ships are fairly standardised in terms of both layout and operation and this allows seafarers to transfer their skills and knowledge from one vessel to another with only short requisite periods of familiarisation. While this is not a result of globalisation (such standardisation pre-dates the phenomenon of flagging-out which is the fundamental characteristic of the globalised, as opposed to the merely international, status of the industry) it does sustain the employment and training practices which underpin the successful operation of the globalised seafarer labour market. Training was once concentrated in ship-owning nations and there were close links between owners, cadet trainees and the vessels they would ultimately be employed upon. Today, by contrast, the relationship between owners and cadet trainees has been largely severed. This is often because cadets, if recruited at all by ship operators, are likely to come from developing regions of the world[5] and on joining the ranks of qualified seafarers may work on temporary contracts for a series of employers aboard a variety of vessels.[6] That they are able to make transitions between ships, and between employers, is largely due to the standardisation of training and of work. This facilitates the operation of a global labour market whereby seafarers can be recruited from any nation, by any operator, from any part of the world, to work aboard any vessel under any flag.[7] It also rather fortuitously facilitates description by social scientists. Although every ship has its own unique character most also share a number of fundamental qualities. Perhaps the most important of these are organisational hierarchy, the exercise of power, and the overwhelming dominance of work on board. In order to consider the extent to which seafarers are embedded in the life on board ship, and therefore to explore the extent to which they can be considered as transnationals, these important influences on shipboard life need to be understood and taken into consideration.

Hierarchy at sea

At a conference, in Cardiff, organised by a group of postgraduate students, I was surprised to find that they seemed to have recruited one of their friends to wear a military-style uniform in order to lead us all down to the lecture theatre. As it turned out this impression was quite misleading. The 'usher' was in fact a member of the coastguard in a South American country and one of the conference speakers! The mistake is easier to understand if you have ever visited a cadet training centre in the Philippines or in Eastern Europe. Many of these bear the hallmarks of military training institutions and involve parades and 'drilling' as well as uniforms and strong discipline. It is hard to think of another (non-military) occupation where trainees are required to be up and on a parade ground at five in the morning in the course of their studies or are required to move around the buildings in crocodile formation saluting staff as they pass. However, seafaring is a unique occupation in some respects and it remains an extremely hierarchical one, not only at particular colleges, but also at sea.

Ships' workforces are made up of officers and ratings, with officers divided into seniors and juniors. Aboard larger vessels, most modern fleet personnel managers distinguish between the 'top four' senior officers (captain, chief engineer, chief officer and first engineer)[8] and the others (see Table 3).On some larger ships a distinction is also made between officers (more senior) and petty officers (less skilled and more junior covering functions such as chief steward).

Table 3: Typical hierarchy of jobs on board

Senior officers	Junior officers	Petty officers	Ratings
captain	second officer	bosun	AB[9]
chief engineer	third officer	pumpman	OS[10]
chief officer	cadet	chief steward	oiler/motorman
first/second engineer	second engineer (where a first engineer is on board)	electrician	wiper
	third engineer	reefer engineer[11]	second cook
	fourth engineer	carpenter	messman
		fitter	
Direction of descending seniority →			

This occupational hierarchy is extremely influential not just in relation to working relationships on board but to social ones as well and it seems that the introduction of mixed-nationality crews has strengthened rather than challenged it. Many officers consider that mixed-nationality crews are much easier to manage than single-nationality crews whose members might prove to be resistant to instructions and/or 'bolshie'. Some suggest that being in single-nationality crews allows for occupational rank to become blurred by friendships and makes professional behaviour more difficult to maintain on board. Generally speaking, there is a view that life on board, which consists mainly of work, is much easier aboard mixed-nationality ships where everyone is more aware of their 'place' and more inclined to 'keep to it'. One Croatian officer expressed this general sentiment as follows:

> I think … the worse ship I have [was] with all Croatians. Even now if somebody put me on all Croatian ship I would not accept it … Because with single nationality you have one very, very famous problem we are all human beings, we all trying to associate with one another and then when you are coming from the same country it's always the way the people try to go around and you always have to think twice when you invite somebody for beer or when you talk somebody friendly way because you never know when he's going to use this. Here we are professional we know exactly where is the line. When you are with your own people I believe in any other kind of work people … misuse your friendship and it's very difficult to maintain a professional distance … I do the same things you know and also if I have British chief engineer or Croatian chief engineer I know I would have hard time with Croatian chief engineer cause of these things you know. With British we will respect each other he may you know he may ask me for something I don't think it's good or you know acceptable but this is part of my job and I don't have to question. But the Croatian will always try to go different and you end up on the wrong side. (First engineer, *Norwegian Imp*)

Thus it seems that in the contemporary context, and with the operation of a highly globalised labour market, nationality and occupational rank work together to buttress the hierarchical relationships found in merchant shipping and increase the professional and social distances between officers and subordinates.

Power and authority: captain is king

Workers employed to labour in the premises of most transnational corporations are land-based. They go home at night to interact with a land-based community which may be of a different nationality but is nevertheless a presence. They are constrained by local laws relating to every aspect of their lives but they do not have to live cheek by jowl with their supervisors or 'bosses'. In the case of migrants and transmigrants local laws constrain their rights to employment, to political and cultural participation, and to social benefits and rights. Aboard vessels however, seafarers do not 'go home' and there is little such governance. Paradoxically, however, this does not produce a less restricted social environment but one in which they are never, or very rarely, free from their managers. A highly institutionalised workforce, they live, as they work, under the ever present surveillance of their 'superiors'.

Ships are technically bound by the laws and regulations of the states in which they are registered, or flagged. As such living and working conditions and health and safety are regulated by flag states. With the development of open registers, in practice, such regulation may be of little consequence, if it exists at all, as enforcement undertaken by flag states is negligible in some cases (see Sampson and Bloor 2007 for a fuller account of the regulation of ships by flag and port states in the context of globalisation). Even where the regulation of safety standards is more rigorous, there is very little interference in the social organisation of life on board vessels either on the part of flag or port states or even owner-operators/companies. The control of on board social arrangements is largely left to the captain, therefore, who may take a greater or lesser role in 'social regulation' as he, or she, pleases. The captain, and the power vested in the captain (which is vast while the vessel is at sea but also while it is alongside), impact enormously on the 'structure' of space on board. While ploughing the oceans remote from the land any jurisdiction of a flag state is fairly irrelevant to most seafarers on board. Similarly a berthed vessel is subject to much inspection and auditing in relation to technical matters and shipping law but no efforts to control much of what constitutes the life on board. The experience of seafarers is largely that it is captains, and to a much lesser extent companies (where they are interested), that structure the social space on board.

Captains occupy a dominant position on ships not unlike that traditionally epitomised in historical novels and film. On board, the captain is still 'king' and controls not only the work aboard the vessel but the living arrangements, and to a great extent, the out of work activities of all the crew. Individual captains I sailed with impacted on crew members' 'spare' time in the following ways: one refused to allow any food to be cooked after 5p.m.; they generally controlled access to alcohol on board (where it was permitted by the company); they controlled leisure activities; they determined if swimming pools were to be used, when, and by whom; they controlled shore-leave; they controlled access to email; they controlled catering; they controlled the use of launderette facilities; they controlled use of public spaces; they controlled expenditure of the 'welfare fund'; they controlled the issue of cash advances; they controlled the maintenance of cabin spaces; they controlled cleanliness; they controlled access to medicine; they controlled access to health care; and they controlled the organisation of events such as competitions and parties. Generally speaking, therefore, nothing of a public nature occurs aboard ship without the captain's consent and ships are spaces where little of a private nature can occur at all. Solitary drinking, drugs consumption and sexual activity between seafarers may initially be private. In general, however, most things become public knowledge and open to intervention from the captain. As such, the notion of 'captains' as 'kings' is a very understandable one, even to a casual observer.

Captains are overwhelmingly dominant aboard ships despite the fact that vessels also carry chief engineers who have the same number of 'stripes' on their epaulettes and occupy a position of equal rank (but not equal responsibility). The presence of chief engineers aboard vessels seems, in general terms, to differ markedly from captains and chief engineers tend to occupy a very different social role on board. They seem to consciously bow out of any kind of *non-work*-related leadership except occasionally in relation to the social activities of the engineering team. Perhaps they do this consciously in order to avoid any misunderstanding about who retains ultimate authority on board as disagreements between captains and chief engineers have the potential to cause significant rupture. Mostly, chief engineers seem to strive to get along with captains respecting the difficulties inherent in their position and accepting the established social order. There are times however when they resent the interference of captains. A field note records one such situation as follows:

> I was out on deck and the captain and chief engineer started to walk up and down (taking their usual exercise together). The captain shouted to me that I would have to be given a safety belt if I wanted to sit in my position on the forecastle (he was joking). I then saw the two of them walk back up the deck and start to examine the gantry crane. Then the chief engineer hurried off as though he were about to do something. The captain did a couple of deck lengths at a run and the chief engineer did not return. Later I learned that the chief engineer had got very annoyed with the captain who was trying to persuade him to get the engineers to do overtime. The chief engineer does not believe it is necessary and resents the captain treading on his toes. He said he didn't know why he is so irritable (perhaps because he is coming to the end of his contract) but he lost his temper and told the captain 'you take your exercise' and stormed off. (Sampson field notes, *Santos Sunset*)

In general such irritations were suppressed as captains and chief engineers strove to get along and one effect of this was for chief engineers to take a very back seat with regard to control over seafarers' non-work lives on board. As a result, they were at greater liberty to enjoy friendly social relations with other crew members. Chief engineers socialised more freely with the crew than captains, and were often observed to share a joke or a drink with them. By contrast captains were frequently avoided by crew members and treated with considerable care when avoidance could not be achieved. One seafarer's response to being asked if there was anyone on board that he avoided was telling. He replied:

> Only the captain! I am very scared of the captain. Maybe I did things [wrong] I did not notice...I don't want to make the captain unhappy with something ... (able bodied seaman [AB], *Santos Sunset*)

It seems that several factors determine the exercise of power and the style of leadership on board. The personal style of individuals is one crucial factor. Natural authority, size of ship, company style, and charisma, are others. Between the different departments (deck, engine and galley) different styles are also apparent. Engineers resemble *teams* of workers much more closely than deck officers. As a result relationships appear much warmer and more personal amongst engine crews. In the galley, the team is always a small one with the chief cook generally in close control. Again the galley tends to be a place where cordial working relationships dominate, although this is not invariably the case.

The huge authority and power vested in the captain can produce a chasm between the officers and ratings, particularly where the crew is divided between officers of one nationality and ratings of another. Similarly however the authority and power of the captain also allow him (most captains are male although a small number of female captains are employed in the cargo shipping sector) to do a great deal to foster an undivided team-like crew which both works, and even occasionally 'plays' together. Aboard the vessels I have joined there has been a fairly even spread of 'tyrannical-type', 'team-working-type', and 'disinterested-type' captains.

Aboard one ship, for example, the captain was a terrible bully of whom the crew were universally afraid. This vessel demonstrated the extent to which all social life on board can be determined by the attitude of the captain. In a field note I recorded that:

> I asked if they didn't drink beer on the ship and commented that I had not seen anyone drinking in the recreation rooms etc. They said that they did drink but in their cabins and indicated that this was out of sight of the officers or more specifically the captain ... Parties are obviously not considered OK. In the course of the conversation the messman indicated that the Germans stayed separate and the Spanish stayed separate. He used the word German not officer so I assume that he did mean a national split rather than an occupational one. (Sampson field notes, *Qui Auora*)

Aboard the same vessel the captain's influence dominated not only social activity but all work activities including food and provisioning. The chief cook talked 'secretly' with me and prompted the following note:

> He said the captain is 'no good' because he is too controlling and he used the phrase 'too much control' and gestured with a closed fist. He said the other

> captain was all right ... He tried to explain something about meat ... I think
> he was saying that the captain would not allow him to buy the meat and veg
> he wanted to cook or to cook what he wanted ... (Sampson field notes, *Qui
> Auora*)

Later the messman further described the grip the captain had on the ship. A field
note records:

> The messman also said that everyone is afraid of the captain, including all the
> officers, because he constantly threatens them with instant dismissal. (Sampson
> field notes, *Qui Auora*)

This power, while most overtly and unpleasantly exercised aboard this particular vessel is present aboard all merchant ships and summary dismissals are
not particularly unusual. On the very first vessel I ever joined, for example, an
engineer who failed to start a lifeboat engine during a drill (not appreciating that it
was in neutral) was sent home. In this case the seafarer was repatriated as a direct
consequence of what was regarded as extreme incompetence (he had endangered
the lives of all of us who were in the lifeboat with him as it had drifted beneath the
hull of the vessel in quite a strong swell and came very close to being smashed by
the waves on the ship's underside) and the seafarers on board felt that the decision
to terminate his employment was the right one. However, regardless of the moral
questions involved, the example serves to illustrate the extent to which a captain
at sea is able to exercise power over employees facilitating their instant dismissal
with little concern for employment 'rights' or 'due process'.

On another vessel with an unpopular captain, I recorded numerous comments
about his behaviour. These ranged from the timing of social events to the atmosphere aboard the ship. The following notes made over a period of several weeks
are illustrative:

> The crew are a little displeased as the captain has arranged the barbecue for
> today and they would have liked to have it yesterday (Saturday) because they
> finish earlier on a Sunday and therefore have a little time to recover ...
>
> It is curious how the captain is able to exert control in so many subtle (and
> not so subtle) ways. The slop chest [the bond from which sundry items can be
> purchased on board] is a good example as it is run on the whim of the cap-
> tain rather than to any routine. There aren't any regular times when you can go
> and purchase goods, you have to approach the captain and ask when he is next
> opening the store. He also personally oversees what you purchase and visibly
> approves or disapproves ...
>
> Both Faro and Lund had talked last night about how the other captain had
> organised all sorts of events for the crew and put up prizes etc but that this one
> does not like to do it. They believed that it was much better to have things going
> on to keep the crew happy ...
>
> The atmosphere on the bridge is electric whenever the pilot and the captain
> are on the bridge. The captain is enormously tense and everyone seems to be
> holding their breath awaiting and fearing an outburst. On this occasion Faro
> and Lund were very obviously subdued and Arnie and Lenard (Filipinos) were

likewise silent. Once the captain was off the bridge Faro (Swedish) was very friendly with Lenard (Filipino) talking to him with his arm around his shoulder and joking etc ...

The next evening Faro told me how the captain's nickname is 'Captain Satan' and he talked a lot about his moods and bad behaviour. (Sampson field notes, *Eclipse*)

As a consequence of a remarkably strong hierarchy, combined with the traditions of the sea, captains have the capacity, and the power, to perpetrate systematic abuses against seafarers aboard. This capacity in some ways relates to the vacuum in social regulation aboard and the congruent absence of the rule of law (for example laws in place in many OECD countries, such as equal opportunities laws, have no influence over shipboard practices) but to some extent it can simply be seen as a result of the isolation of the ship, the captain's lack of on board accountability, and his right to 'fire at will' (i.e. dismiss people rather than shoot at them!) As one officer reflected:

> ... And I don't know, people, when they have money, they can leave, they can stay at home, but they don't. Some power is there, which they won't get at home. Some captains, they have so much money, they can stay at home. But most of the time they spend at sea ... I saw some other captain's family, the daughters do not obey his orders. The wife, if you say something to the wife ... back something. Finally they are fed up with the family. But they can't throw them out. And when they come on board ship, the captain, if somebody says something and he doesn't like, he becomes very angry, because his mentality – his family is no longer obeying him, so he is always crazy. I have seen this on many ships. Sometimes I have become close to them and asked, and finally found it is correct, they don't want to live at home because – they have money to leave, but with a small vacation they are fed up with home. They are running away from their home ... So those people are very dangerous on board ship, because unfortunately they fire others. At home they can't fire daughter, they can't fire son, they can't fire wife, and those people come on board ship with the power and sometimes they harass people, it's very bad. In my ... sometimes I go to party and I talk with them, and finally found that this is the problem ... They are crazy always. If you disobey, they try to kill you. What they can't do at home. (Officer, *Santos Sunset*)

This influence and dominance means that many seafarers identify captains as key to their sea experiences, be they good or bad. One rating, asked about his favourite ship, did not hesitate in identifying, unprompted, the influence of a captain in relation to his experiences. He said:

> My favourite ship is *Candy*. Because for me, I liked the captain there, the captain was very good. (Ordinary seaman [OS], *Santos Sunset*)

The same sentiment has been expressed to me in different ways with seafarers either stressing the potential captains have had to have a negative, or a positive effect. One for example made a point of saying that:

I've been on mixed nationality rigs before, the master if he takes a little bit of initiative the Filipino's love bingo, they love their horse racing, so do we all. If the master takes a little bit of this and says Saturday party, everyone happy. Here we haven't had a party in like years, and bingo and horse racing we already have the horse racing, with the tables for the bingo and everything then. Just because the master not interested in it it's not happening and well in my last company we had this thing where every Sunday all the officers got together and we had a bar lunch and we all sat and we chatted. Here it's a very exclusive thing, you know, we talk formally and sit for two hours at the dinner table, the junior officers should not be around, I've never had that before. Always before we all off us sticking together. It depends entirely on the master, not even the [other] individuals I think it's the master. The master takes a little bit of interest then everyone else is active ... Here there is not interest and no encouragement and everyone is disappointed that we are not having generally as much of a social life as we generally do on most of the other ships. (Third officer, *Norwegian Imp*)

Aboard some other vessels, captains exert a very positive influence. Some see it as their responsibility to try to get to know their crew a little and talk of the benefits that this can bring in relation to work as well as non-work activities. While some captains remain aloof in an effort to bolster their power, a more paternalistic and benevolent attitude can also serve to enhance their authority. On one ship the captain was well-liked and highly respected. Exercising a great deal of control over the crew, as his counterparts on other vessels did, he nevertheless had a positive impact upon the atmosphere and the experiences of the crew. He allowed parties on board, encouraged social and sports activities and generally exuded a benign but nevertheless very dominant spirit. While broadly beneficial in terms of the quality of life, and quality of work, on board this captain also exemplified the authority vested in the position. Indeed his very popularity and the esteem with which he was regarded enhanced rather than diminished his power, making subordinates particularly reluctant to do anything that might meet with disapproval, and also rather unlikely to be critical of him or to complain despite the fact that he was demanding at times and quite a strong presence on board with his own very particular ways of wanting things done. While an inspector was on board and the crew were under some pressure, for example, the captain had to disturb several officers in their 'off time'. Although this was clearly legitimate it is quite likely that a less popular captain would have been subject to at least minor moans and groans in the same circumstances. However, on this occasion, despite interrupting seafarers watching a film no grumbles were expressed.

Naturally captains do not only embody the paternalistic or the tyrannical stereotype as portrayed by the examples given thus far. Some occupy a middle ground where they concern themselves mostly in the operation of the ship and are rather neutral or disinterested in the non-work aspects of shipboard life. They have power but they choose not to exercise it in some areas, so long as this presents no particular challenge to them or to the operation of the vessel. However, this can leave something of an unwelcome vacuum. Seafarers used to following the captain's direction, or will, may not 'occupy' space that is left to them by disinterested or disengaged captains. They may not make suggestions for changes in social activities, the use of space, or in any significant dimension of social life on board. Thus, in many respects disengagement produces very similar results to disapproval but without the associated social tensions.

The influence of other ranks

Despite their overwhelming authority, and impact, it is not only captains that make a significant difference to life aboard ship. There are a number of other key roles which involve a management/supervisory function and thus carry with them a degree of particular authority. In this context it is worth considering the role of the chief engineer, the chief officer, the first engineer, and the bosun.

Chief engineers are normally responsible for the maintenance and safe operation of the engine and of a variety of mechanical devices aboard (cranes for example). They are required to manage the team of engineers and to be responsible for functions such as budgeting and planned maintenance in relation to the engine. They carry with them a considerable amount of authority and although technically of equal status to the captain they mostly confine themselves to the engine room and play no visible part in the control of the social life on board. In periods where they are 'off duty' they seem to be experienced by crew members as far less intimidating than captains and generally occupy somewhat more benevolent and paternalistic roles.

First engineers and chief officers play significant parts on board ship in relation to management and supervision. These roles are highly circumscribed and vary little from ship to ship. For example, chief officers are usually responsible for overseeing cargo operations and in this context sometimes supervise second or third officers on board. On a more full-time basis, they are responsible for the management of the maintenance activities of the deck crew and they generally meet daily with bosuns to provide instructions regarding which work is to be carried out. First engineers have responsibility for the daily supervision of the engine room staff and answer directly to the chief engineer who is largely remote from the engine room itself except in some cases. One first engineer described his normal working day as follows:

> As the first engineer I go into a different room to the other people to check everything, I have to know everything. At 8 o'clock my crew comes and I take them round and tell them what needs to be done. This is why I get a good response from my crew because I go around and I am working too and also my behaviour is good with them ... A good first engineer must know his crew mentality, every man has a different mentality, everybody works but you take work with other men, this is the first engineers first job. I know that the second engineer's mentality is to come and have a coffee and then refreshes and goes to work. And some when you say go and do this job they say 'No I don't have time', so instead you say to him 'When you have time after you have relaxed you can do this job for me. If you go and have a rest then can you do this favour for me,

and if you are tired go and take a rest'. So the first engineer must know all these men's mentalities and that is how he can do a good job … maintenance reports and all things like that I do on the computer … Normally everyday doing nine to ten hours, because I go to engine room and let everybody go and then half an hour after they go I have to check, but mostly I am mostly eight, nine to ten hours … this is my duty after they have done their work I have to check this work is good or not and whether people completed their work. (First engineer, *Norwegian Imp*)

Finally the bosun is responsible for the supervision of the deck crew and assigns work to individuals in his team. He also monitors and supervises them. Bosuns generally play a very important mediation role in relation to the ratings and the chief officer and the relationship between the bosun and the chief officer can be a tense one. The following quote is illustrative:

He's good [the chief mate] but sometimes he has some niggles, niggles with them, he'll shout, shout at the boys and then over a small, small job he's always shouting and swearing. The boys always panic, they don't know what they do, they don't know what to do. If they can do these things chief mate shout and if they leave their things and go to another one the chief mate also shout and swear … I'm always the one who they turn to, cause they make submissions to. (Bosun, *Norwegian Imp*)

While he must develop a good working relationship with the chief officer, if a bosun is seen not to defend his team properly, from unrealistic expectations and demands, he generally comes under pressure from his crew. A strong bosun is important to crew members and a weak, or scared, bosun is seen as a bit of a liability. A third officer described a situation he had experienced in his past when, as just an AB, he took his bosun to task for not looking after the safety of the crew properly.

I had a bosun who was an old man, and the ship would be rolling, and he tried to [make us] work. I was the one [who complained] … not to be aggressive, but I was defending my colleagues also. It is dangerous – the swell. You only have one life. (Third officer, *Eclipse*)

It is apparent, therefore, that while different people (with different styles) occupy these roles on board, the jobs in themselves confer authority upon the individuals which they exercise in different ways and to differing degrees. There are also other loci of authority on board and these may relate to age, seniority and charisma. Older seafarers, and those with greater seniority, 'old hands', are often respected either as a result of their greater sea experience and possession of traditional skills and 'know-how' or because within the specific cultures represented on board, age is respected and regarded as a blessing or an achievement rather than as something of a hindrance or 'curse'. On board ship the issue of age has to be dealt with carefully as in some cases older seafarers, from cultures where older people are respected and deferred to (at least publicly), are outranked by young 'stripling' officers who are required to exercise authority and control. Seniority and charisma are less challenging than age to the shipboard social order but also play a role with regard to influence and status which sometimes mediates and sometimes reinforces existing hierarchical arrangements.

The dominance of work

Seafarers on some ships have little time for anything other than work and even captains (who sometimes appear at greater leisure while in deep sea stages of a voyage) can be thoroughly preoccupied by work both when in port and at sea. Generally, they accept this as part of their role without question. On some occasions, they are not even aware of the hours they have worked until asked to reflect upon them, as the following example demonstrates:

> *Helen:* I was told you worked very long hours going into Hickory?
> *Capt:* I worked very long hours? I didn't realise. I can look at my records.
> *Helen:* Did you work all through the night then?
> *Capt:* When we sailed – of course, I worked the whole day. And in the evening I slept for maybe two hours, when the lifeboat thing was going on. Then I signed the papers for this guy at 11. Then midnight finish, then we sailed. I was still busy till 6 o'clock in the morning. So that's six hours, plus six is twelve, plus the day, let's say another 6 hours, so that's eighteen, minus two somewhere for rest. But that is manageable, again, you know. Hickory [said in some surprise], I don't see it any more. We went the whole day of course, and the evening, but then you have two hours rest. And I was off the bridge. I invited [name of officer] to take his rest and think about his previous watch. So I was there until midnight, and then 3 o'clock in the morning we were in sight, so I went up to the bridge again. You wake up. The time you set yourself, without an alarm clock. Then finally 5 o'clock – then the whole day. Yes, it was very long! Twenty hours or so. (*Norwegian Imp* captain)

While this vessel was a well-maintained middle-aged and middle-sized ship, vessels which typify such situations are often small ones, or those with many port calls and 'at sea' periods of short duration. Old, poorly maintained vessels, and vessels operating in difficult weather conditions, also result in tired and poorly rested seafarers whose remaining energies are entirely directed at getting the job done and getting through the next shift/watch.

Work, working conditions and weather conditions thus play a major role in the quality of seafarers' lives. Aboard all vessels some positions carry with them a heavy workload which verges on the intolerable. Chief officers regularly work exceptional hours in port and frequently follow these with the maintenance of a navigational watch once a vessel puts to sea. Aboard one vessel the following field notes were made documenting the duty of the chief officer on board while the vessel was in port:

> We arrived at Buenos Aires at about 5p.m. The chief officer had started work at 4a.m. and had a break from 13.00 until 16.00. Then he worked through from 16.00 to 05.00 the next morning and was once again unable to go ashore ... at

07.00 in the morning he was already working in the deck office again ... the C.O.
told me that [later] in the afternoon the captain had been furious with him for
going back to bed for a couple of hours at around 10.00–12.00. (Sampson field
notes, *Eclipse*)

The pattern of chief officers working very long hours seems a common one
across the industry. However, a variety of specific factors, other than rank, also
impact upon length of hours worked including the age and condition of ships.
Aboard one old bulk carrier I sailed with, the gantry cranes, utilised for loading
and unloading the cargo, had some problematic electrical wiring which caused
the ship to be frequently delayed in port, at considerable cost. On arrival in a UK
port, the team of engineers worked solidly on the cranes and the chief engineer
was awake for a period of thirty-six hours.

It is difficult to overstate the impact of work, and work schedules, on the lives
of seafarers on board cargo vessels. The work of the ship is prioritised above all
else. If something needs doing on board a way is found to get it done. There are
no holidays, no concessions to sea sickness or minor ailments, little concession
to weather conditions and no account at all of the time of day or night when a
ship enters port. This has been the norm on all the ships I have sailed with. Work
dominates all experiences of life at sea. However, it is apparent that captains can
choose to do a great deal to impact upon the workload of individuals and of the
crew as a whole. Generally their actions can be divided into those that do not
attract the attention of shore-side staff and those that do. In relation to activities
invisible to shore-side staff these can include encouraging social activities aboard
to relieve seafarer stress and tension, paying attention to the upkeep of accommodation spaces and resources (for example washing machines, furnishings and
so forth), relieving juniors of specific duties from time to time to ensure that they
are rested (for example taking a watch for the chief officer), slowing a vessel or
altering course in heavy weather at night in order to reduce motion and allow
greater possibilities for crew members to sleep, and a similar array of activities.
Only rarely do captains directly resist the shore-side pressures which drive the
vessel, and in turn the seafarers, onwards. On occasion such resistance does occur
but it is covert illustrating the difficulties that captains have in preventing fatigue
and the prevalence of dangerous working conditions aboard despite the fact that
at sea they carry responsibility for the vessel's safe operation. On one ship that I
joined, for example, seafarers were very tired having been involved in manoeu-
vrings, cargo and bunker loadings, and berth/anchorage/berth shifting, for several days. Once at sea the captain sought to delay the arrival of his vessel at the
next port by turning mid-ocean in very large circles while maintaining speed. He
described how this was the only thing he could do without an argument with the
'office' and that he couldn't simply drop his speed as this could be monitored from
the shore and the charterers would object to such action.[12] The charterers and the
commercial operation of the particular ships they work on are much in the mind
of many seafarers who often express a feeling that their jobs depend upon their
vessels making money. Occasionally however, resentment is also expressed, as the
following field note records:

The chief officer said the pilot was due at 04.00 but I could see that nothing was going on so I went to get a coffee and went through to the crew mess to drink it. The bosun, Rick and Rob (in army fatigues) and a couple of others were there. They complained (gently) that on this route they lose a lot of sleep because of the constant shifting and fast turnarounds. They were aware that the ship was on time charter and was making a lot of money (something confirmed by the agent's earlier description of it to me as a 'goldmine'). Despite all the hours they work they rarely get overtime [i.e. paid] as they have 100 hours fixed overtime in their contracts [per month this means they would have to work more than 100 hours extra in order to be paid anything extra]. (Sampson field notes, *Calmex*)

The relationships that captains enjoy with shore-staff are critical to the operation of the vessel. Where a captain is known to office staff and well-respected he is in a far stronger position to resist shore-side commercial pressures. However, the rise of ship management companies, and crew agencies, has weakened the relationship between many senior officers and shore-side staff. Once it was likely that a ship owner would know the captain of his vessel personally. Today it is more likely that this will not be the case. Indeed, it may rarely be the case. The relationships captains have with crewing agents or ship managers are generally strongly contractual and relatively impersonal. Such companies are likely to be larger than privately owned shipping companies and have a tendency to be very procedurally based having devised 'rules' and procedures for many activities and situations. In this context, the captain aboard a vessel becomes less of an autonomous force and more of an administrator on behalf of the office. Without a personal relationship with an owner, on whose behalf they may feel able to act, vessel captains may abdicate large amounts of their authority and responsibility to shore-side personnel, even asking ship agents in local ports for advice rather than exercising their own judgement. This places them in a weak position to intercede on behalf of seafarers in a vulnerable labour market position. Thus many things aboard vessels, which are in fact a product of decisions and judgements, take on the appearance of immutable situations which nothing can be done about. Seafarers thus accept a range of practices which may impinge not only on the quality of their working and living conditions aboard, but also upon their health and safety.

When considering the question of transnationality at sea it is important to understand the ship as a workplace as well as a place where seafarers live. The lives of all the seafarers involved in the shipboard research were strongly patterned by several enduring features of shipboard work and the most central of these were occupational hierarchy, power and authority, and an overwhelming work ethic which placed the demands of the job before almost every other consideration on board. These elements of the institutionalised life and work on board served to influence (or shape) the space that was available to seafarers both in terms of physical spaces that could be accessed but also social spaces that could be inhabited. Significant exclusion from physical and social spaces militates against a consideration of seafarers as truly embedded into the shipboard community. The extent to which they enjoy inclusion or exclusion from physical and from social space on board ship is therefore a necessary part of the consideration of seafarers' 'transnationality'.

Notes

1 This 'song', which runs to several verses and was popularised by many vocalists, first appeared in a novel by the Liverpool-born author Richard Le Gallienne in 1918. This version, 'I wanna go home', words and music by Van Morrison and Lonnie Donegan © 2010.

2 NB the work on board a cargo ship and the work and its organisation aboard a fishing vessel share few similarities and studies of fishing vessels should be understood as quite separate to studies of merchant cargo vessels.

3 It is not uncommon for seafarers to work for longer periods than twelve months but this is usually because they have chosen to extend their contracts. It is more common for ratings to be employed on contracts of eight to ten months duration.

4 British seafarers have a term ('the channels') for the excitement experienced in contemplating leaving the ship at the end of a contract. The term was coined because seafarers approaching their home port in the UK would become noticeably animated. Despite the fact that seafarers now join and leave vessels all over the world and the notion of a 'home port' has been lost, the term remains in use.

5 Whereas ownership of the international fleet is largely concentrated in OECD countries.

6 Notwithstanding the growing practice of 'bonded labour' whereby employers who sponsor cadets during training demand that they serve a certain period of time with them on qualifying, or repay the costs of their sponsorship.

7 There are some qualifications required for specialist vessels such as tankers.

8 NB on some ships the first engineer is termed the 'second engineer'.

9 Able bodied seaman.

10 Ordinary seaman (lower ranking than able bodied seaman).

11 A refrigeration engineer employed aboard refrigerated cargo ships.

12 Such actions are increasingly circumscribed as shore-side staff have more and more access to information from 'their' ships allowing them to closely monitor vessels.

6

Physical places and social spaces: seafarers at work and rest

Despite the confined nature of a vessel, aboard a ship not all seafarers have access to the same physical or social space. Inevitably their work role on board influences the spaces they occupy during their working time and each of these spaces carries with it a different character which impacts upon social interaction as well as the daily conduct of work-related tasks. Further to the division of space according to work task, however, ships are also divided in relation to the non-working spaces accessible to individuals. As an institutional setting no space on board a ship can be described as truly 'private' and captains have the right of access to any place on board including seafarers' cabins. While no space on board is out of bounds for captains, however, there are many locations which may be regarded as out of bounds for particular seafarers. Furthermore not only is physical space segregated (which clearly impacts on social space), but this chapter will also indicate the ways in which social space is additionally independently constrained by issues such as nationality and hierarchy.

Internationally trading merchant cargo vessels, owned and operated all over the world, share remarkably similar features. From a structural point of view the reasons for such similarities may be obvious, however, it is less evident why they should share such similar organisational and social characteristics.

Structurally, as places, ships share distinctive forms that have sometimes changed, only superficially, over the years (for example in the location of the accommodation spaces on board), and sometimes more dramatically as with the introduction of engines and the phasing out of sail.[1] These changes are primarily led by naval architects, engineers and shipbuilders. Ships are designed first and foremost as cargo-carrying spaces but at brief moments in the history of the shipping industry some attention has been given to the layout of ships as working spaces and as living spaces. In the 1960s Scandinavian shipping lines such as Hoegh gave consideration to the ways in which ships were organised socially and paid some attention to the layout of accommodation blocks and the leisure facilities provided to seafarers on board even, in some cases, going so far as to permit the academic study of life at sea (see for example Schrank 1983). However, such interest has waned and in the twenty-first century ship designers can be seen to be reducing the space available to seafarers (i.e. the non-cargo carrying space) and downgrading the quality of that which is available. The best accommodation spaces on modern ships are generally of a poorer standard than those on the best ships built in the 1980s, for example. Light, and a sense of space, have been reduced by designing smaller portholes (windows), and reducing headroom (lowering ceilings). Cabins and day rooms for senior officers are generally smaller than before, and seafarers often complain of increased noise and vibration as a consequence of the use of thinner steel plating in the overall build of vessels. Where efforts have been made to influence vessel design, modern companies have often focused upon the design of workspaces providing more open-plan office space, integrating the previously separate offices of chief engineers and captains, and moving these down from the accommodation deck (officer workrooms are traditionally attached to their cabins and are known as 'day rooms') to the general workspace deck. In some other respects, however, while standards may have deteriorated at the 'top' end of the scale (aboard the best vessels) the mid range might be said to have improved. It is not uncommon for new ships to be designed with all seafarer accommodation en-suite and this is an improvement for ratings in particular, who have often had to use communal washrooms and lavatories in the past. However, notwithstanding this possible improvement in middle-range vessels, it remains the case that the seafarer today is not regarded as a priority in the design of a vessel, despite the fact that the working and living space of a ship impacts considerably on the social and working relations found on board. This waning interest in the conditions in which seafarers live, and work,[2] has coincided with changes in recruitment practices. Such changes have meant that ship owners have become increasingly distant from their vessels and from their crews. For the most part, the days when senior officers were known to ship owners have passed and crew members are largely 'invisible' to them and may be known only to crewing agents. These agents may deal with many seafarers, crewing many vessels, for a variety of companies. Furthermore, crewing agents are merely suppliers of labour and have no input into standards aboard vessels. Generally speaking, in the twenty-first century, the link between seafarers and ship owners has been broken and with it owners' concerns for seafarers' living arrangements and conditions can be seen to have largely evaporated.

Such changes have been generally accepted by seafarers. The once strongly unionised workforce based within European and OECD countries has been significantly replaced, on board internationally trading vessels, by workers from developing states with weaker representation. Such crew members are not only willing to sacrifice a great deal in pursuit of high dollar salaries, with which there is no comparison for local shore-based jobs, they are also, frequently, recruited from very impoverished backgrounds where living standards, and consequently expectations, are low.

Places and spaces of work

A student who recently returned from undertaking research aboard a vessel for the very first time described in vaguely surprised tones her overall impression of the ship as a location and a space that was 'all about work'. She was right. The ship is a hard-working beast and the seafarers aboard work her around the clock – twenty-four hours per day. Ashore, ship managers regard any time when a ship is idle as money 'going down the drain' and thus where ships' cargoes are not fixed according to a particular route and schedule (in contrast with many container vessels) they place a tremendous store on ships getting to and from ports at maximum speed and particularly upon ships loading and unloading cargoes as quickly as possible. As Sven, a shore-based manager, put it to me when I was undertaking research at a container terminal:

> The main thing … is the vessel … The vessel is the most expensive thing and one of our [particular vessel type] is 3,500 US dollars an hour. So if you keep the vessel idle for ten hours … !! (Sven – shipping line representative)

Not only do vessels have to be navigated, supplied, loaded and unloaded, to meet the objectives of shore-side managers, they also have to be regularly maintained by seafarers. Cargo holds have to be cleaned, emergency repairs have to be undertaken where required, and drills have to be regularly carried out. The ship is therefore about work, and little else is seen to really matter on board most contemporary vessels.

Certainly ashore little thought or consideration is given to other aspects of life aboard cargo ships but seafarers too understand that for the vessel 'turning in a profit' is the 'name of the game' and that their primary role and purpose on board is to contribute to this outcome. Many seafarers consider hard work aboard, and a preoccupation with this, as their side of a bargain with shore-side companies that involves uncomplaining labouring on their part and the payment of relatively lucrative salaries and/or the provision of long leave periods in return (terms and conditions depend on nationality and it is usually European seafarers that enjoy long leave periods).

The standardisation of features of the vessel and the standardisation of training is mirrored (and in the case of training, driven) by the standardisation of work roles and shift patterns on board. It is relatively easy for a seafarer to join a vessel and immediately slot into his, or her, allotted work role after (in the case of officers generally speaking) a short hand-over period when their departing counterpart explains particularly relevant aspects of ongoing work tasks, and may take time to explain new unfamiliar equipment or software and pass on relevant information about personnel (Sampson and Tang 2011). The process is made relatively easy by the adoption of very similar watchkeeping schedules (shift patterns for watchkeepers) aboard vessels which most frequently operate a 'four on eight off' system but may also adopt 'six on and six off' watches where crews and vessels are small. Engine rooms are increasingly 'unmanned' at night although watchkeepers are assigned duty periods on an 'on call' basis and officers may be called out at any time of night to resolve mechanical problems in the engine room or, while in port, with pumps or cranes, or any mechanical/electrical machinery. Aboard a ship at sea, most people are found working in the daytime. However the decks and engine room nevertheless remain relatively unpopulated as crews are small aboard most contemporary ships and personnel have been cut back to what are regarded by most seafarers as minimum levels.

The job of a seafarer determines the particular on-board space where he or she works. Ships can perhaps be divided into four main areas for ease of description: engine rooms, cargo holds, weather decks and accommodation spaces. At the very lowest levels of the ship are the engine room, associated spaces and cargo holds. Above these are the weather deck and accommodation space.

Seafarers with a 'roving brief'

Generally speaking, captains can be found anywhere on the ship, engaged in supervisory activity, but they are extremely unlikely to be found in the engine room which remains the domain of the chief engineer. Both captains and chief engineers have found their jobs to be increasingly dominated by 'paperwork' or more accurately bureaucratic tasks. This generally requires them to be seated in their offices (dayrooms) at computer terminals. They liaise with one another about planned or ongoing work activities and they seek out the other's advice from time to time (and depending upon the relationship between them). Broadly speaking they increasingly work in isolation, however, interacting with others for only short parts of the day to pass on job instructions and information, or to perform management functions.

Captains range in their approach to work with some appearing, to crew members, to do very little when not in port and others taking the trouble to take a regular watch for the incumbent chief officer to allow him more opportunity to rest. The approach to work they select, in terms of when to do what, is largely in their own hands therefore. As one put it:

> For a master? It all depends on the situation. The master does it different. We cannot define our work hours, neither can we define our rest hours. We have to plan ourselves how to take rest and what to do in port. Because a lot of unwanted things happen which you are not expecting. Visitors coming. So no fixed routine. That's it. (Captain, *Santos Sunset*)

Chief engineers are either to be found in their offices located separately from the engine room, and usually several decks above it, or in the engine room itself. Again their individual approaches to work vary but most choose to leave the engine room to the charge of their immediate subordinate (the first engineer in most cases though sometimes termed the second engineer in relation to the same role and responsibility) taking what is known on board as 'a round' – derived one would imagine from the expression 'doing the rounds' – in the morning, and sometimes a second one later in the day. One chief engineer described his working day as follows:

> Every day I wake up at seven. I mean, since I joined the ship I told such and such engineer, everyday they call me at seven o'clock but mostly I mean 60–70 per cent, I always wake up before seven. But maybe I not up ... I mean ... and for

the night person, I already give him instruction everybody ... after midnight, after 12.30, you can call me any time, no problem because I'm not sleeping that time. Another time my door is closed, 11–11.30 but I never sleep before 12.30. But any problem, you always call first engineer, and I told first engineer, any problem that you cannot tackle then you call for me. About 90% of my job is paperwork ... for me, I have a lot to do for all paperworks, besides all engine rooms, all sorts. But thanks God, that engine and other machinery is good. I'm very concerned about going in engine room in morning time and evening time, you just take the round. And whatever the two hour, three hour sitting in the control room but I know each and every machinery there ... what they working and what not working. (Chief engineer, *Calmex*)

Another similarly emphasised the bureaucratic tasks and supervisory rounds and his own autonomy in deciding from day to day what he should/would do:

I don't have a routine. I am working day to day, all depending on the situation. Normal routine is the paperwork which I have to do every day on a regular basis. And morning and afternoon rounds, etc. But there is always something – I would say it is just day by day job, whatever is there to be attended to. (Chief engineer, *Norwegian Imp*)

Aboard some vessels chief engineers take a more active 'hands on' role, than aboard others, and can be found as part of a team engaged in significant jobs such as 'pulling a piston'. Thus captains and chief engineers, and to a lesser degree chief officers and first engineers, can exercise some autonomy with regard to how they choose to execute their responsibilities and have a freedom on board as to where and when they work which is not generally experienced by other crew members. In this respect they can be seen as similar to other managers, for example in factories. However, the remoteness of the vessel from shore-side offices tends to increase their freedom with regard to how and where they carry out their duties.

Other than the top four senior officers, there are also some individuals who on account of their specialist skills are assigned individual roles somewhat parallel with (but not entirely beyond) line management structures. These individuals include, for example, carpenters, refrigeration engineers and electricians. They usually work alone and in isolation and may be found almost anywhere on board with little supervision although occasionally assisted by a rating. Their overall tasks and objectives are invariably agreed with a senior member of staff (often the chief officer or captain) but their latitude in carrying out such tasks can be considerable. Gregor, a carpenter, for example explained that:

Yes, every morning. On the bridge. Some Chief Mates leave you to do what you like. Now, we have plenty jobs below the hatches. But some chief officers, you must go up to every morning. This guy he doesn't ask me to come up every morning ... But there are some guys, every morning you have to come up to the bridge, and he asks what you are doing, what you have done, how far you are. This guy, never. He doesn't ask. Maybe he trusts me. (Gregor – Carpenter, *Eclipse*)

On the bridge

However, for most seafarers work roles are more structured and they are subject to constraints with regard to how they undertake work tasks, and when. They usually exercise no control at all over 'where' or 'with whom' they work.

In some cases this is not experienced as a negative thing, as the location of the work is relatively pleasant and off-duty seafarers may 'pass though' and socialise. For example, navigation officers (often termed deck officers) spend most of their working time at sea on the bridge undertaking two periods of watchkeeping in every twenty-four hours. The bridge can be a wonderful space on a ship. From the bridge you can see over the decks and watch seafarers hard at work undertaking maintenance and cleaning tasks, climbing ladders, taking soundings, descending into ballast or cargo tanks. In calm weather there is always something of interest happening on deck even when the ocean expanses around are empty: devoid of ships or marine life. Occasionally a passing whale or a school of dolphins may be seen from the bridge or clouds of gannets may pass by, diving impressively into the water as the ship ploughs onwards. The bridge is often quiet and peaceful, offering a sense of the vessel's movement, and intent, as her progress is tracked on paper charts or electronic screens. It is the place where you can overhear other seafarers on the VHF radio, where someone out on the remote waters might hail you and ask for information or just seek out some company. It is space therefore which can be relatively pleasurably inhabited. However, it is also a place where watchkeepers can be alternately highly stressed and mind-numbingly bored. Notwithstanding its better qualities, it is nonetheless confined and constrained, potentially monotonous, and frequently very dark.

The primary objective of the navigating officer is to ensure that the vessel maintains as close a course to the planned voyage track as possible, in safety and at a reasonable speed. On the vessels discussed here, this activity generally involved the determination and recording of positions on paper sea charts at regular intervals, observation from the bridge (using binoculars from time to time), operation of radar to track vessels in the vicinity and take evasive action where necessary, communication with other vessels and shore-side stations via VHF radio, the updating of chart information involving the cutting and pasting of updates into the relevant parts of a directory, and the monitoring of weather and radio transmissions (both VHF and GMDSS).[3] Officers also had other tasks assigned to them while deep sea (for example third officers were often responsible for the checking and maintenance of safety appliances and second officers were generally in charge of medical supplies, and the dispensing of them, while chief officers had to organise and supervise the work of the deck crew). In the approaches to port, and in port itself, navigating officers were engaged in other duties such as the supervision of mooring/unmooring, cargo discharging/loading, security and anchor watches and so forth.[4]

While there are regulations and guidelines generally discouraging the practice of solo navigational watchkeeping, particularly in weather conditions producing restricted visibility, and also at night, I found watchkeepers to be frequently alone on the bridge. Paradoxically (in terms of the regulatory requirements) they are more likely to be joined by other seafarers in the daytime when individual officers or cadets might drift up to the bridge to have a chat and to orientate themselves and keep track of the vessel's location and progress in moments of free time. Sometimes navigational watchkeeping officers are joined by a 'watchman' whose task is generally to maintain a good lookout. Many years ago this watchman would be posted on the bridgewing (i.e. outside the bridge subject to the elements) but this is practiced less often today, although it does take place from time to time rendering the navigation officer alone on the bridge while nevertheless accompanied with regard to his main work task (maintaining the safe passage of the vessel). Even where the 'watchman' is posted inside the bridge, interaction between the navigation officer and watchman is usually strongly focused on the task at hand – that is to say on ensuring that all craft and obstacles are identified in sufficient time for the ship to take steps to avoid them where necessary. In coastal waters this task can be very demanding as fishing vessels, pleasure craft, military vessels and other cargo ships sometimes densely populate coastal waters, where fixed structures (such as rigs) and underwater obstacles (natural or man-made) may be expected to be present and add to the navigational hazards to be negotiated. In the course of deep sea passages, by contrast, the sighting of other vessels occurs much less frequently and may surprise a navigation officer used to gazing out at vast expanses of open water.

On entering and leaving ports the bridge of a ship is transformed from a quiet space presided over by a single (more often than not) navigating officer to a tension-filled space populated by a pilot (always on the vessels discussed here but not always on every vessel), a captain, a helmsman, a navigating officer and sometimes a watchman (an AB). The tension on such occasions is palpable as captains negotiate the difficult interaction between themselves and their 'hired' advisers in the form of pilots. Pilots are experienced qualified master mariners (i.e. captains) with expertise regarding local conditions, currents, hazards and so forth. Their presence is often mandatory, being required by local port authorities to guide vessels into anchorages and onto berths, however this is not always the case.

The relationship between pilots and captains is a difficult one. Pilots often talk as if once on board they feel the ship is under their charge. Captains on the other hand take a different view. They understand that their responsibility is never relinquished to a pilot and that part of their duty is to monitor a pilot's actions and resume full command should they believe a pilot to be in error. A pilot sees a variety of vessels and may often be unimpressed with the standards of maintenance on board, the facility of seafarers with the English language and the competence of senior officers. Similarly captains may rightly be suspicious of pilots. After all they generally know nothing of their experience, or record, when they enter the bridge and start to offer 'advice'. This suspicion is fuelled when accidents occur that are clearly attributed to pilot error. In 2007, for example, a pilot notoriously guided a vessel directly into the Bay Bridge in San Francisco.[5] A local newspaper reported the findings from the investigation into the event, clearly laying the blame for events upon both the pilot and (unusually) the company. However it also pointed

to a dereliction of duty on the part of the ship's captain who was deemed to have
'failed' to prevent the pilot taking the vessel out in fog and similarly failed to monitor his activities and intervene as appropriate:

> The ship's pilot Capt. John Cota was sentenced to 10 months in prison last
> month after pleading guilty to misdemeanour charges of polluting the waters
> and killing migratory birds. Cota was navigating the 901-foot *Cosco Busan* when
> it hit a tower of the bridge in thick morning fog Nov. 7, 2007. Oil that poured
> from the ship spread along the 26 miles of shoreline and killed more than 2,400
> birds. The government estimates the cleanup cost at $70 million. In its guilty
> plea Fleet Management admitted that it was partly to blame for the accident
> because it failed to provide adequate training to the ship's new captain and crew
> who allowed Cota, the locally assigned pilot, to leave port in fog and did not
> monitor his navigation … Fleet Management and Cota are also defendants in
> multimillion-dollar lawsuits by government agencies, fishers and others claim-
> ing financial losses from the spill. (*San Francisco Chronicle*, 14 August 2009, pp.
> D1 and D8)

This report highlights both the consequences of accidents and how these may be
very grave for the seafarers involved. A number of captains have been incarcerated
for long periods pending trial following accidents. It highlights the costs for companies of oil spills associated with accidents such as this collision with the bridge,
and it demonstrates the difficult relationship between the local expert provided
by local pilotage services and unknown to the captain (in terms of his experience,
temperament, reliability, etc) and the captain who is required to place a certain
amount of trust in his judgement, while also monitoring his activities and inter-
vening, if necessary, to prevent the kind of incident that occurred in this instance.
To some extent there is contested authority here. Captains talk about pilots as
hired expert advisers seeing their own role as involving the continued oversight
of the vessel and her safety even when pilots are aboard. Pilots talk of taking control of vessels and of frustrations with captains who attempt to intercede in their
directions. In practice aboard the vessels discussed here, captains did appear to
hand over navigational decision-making to pilots while monitoring their activities
closely. That they found this difficult and stressful was evident however. One captain would tremble visibly on the bridge when the pilot was 'in control' and was
prone to sudden outbursts of temper, throwing a stool, which he had tripped over in
the dark, across the bridge on one occasion, as the following field note documents:

> On the bridge later he [the captain] fell over a stool which was in his way (it was
> dark) and he threw it (this is an accurate description not an exaggeration) across
> the bridge towards the deck shouting at the same time. No one said anything to
> him and for a while the stool was left as it was as everyone continued to work in
> tension-filled silence. (Sampson field notes, *Eclipse*)

Thus, at these times, the bridge which is normally a peaceful and somewhat
isolated work space can become a contested space where tensions prevail and seafarers largely work together in silence except in relation to the conduct of their
duties – repeating instructions, giving orders and providing information.

In the galley

Moving down through the interior of the vessel the next workspace where seafarers can regularly be found is the galley. Here a small group of three or four seafarers usually work together.[6] Generally a chief cook is assisted by a second cook and two messmen although increasingly cuts in crew numbers may produce smaller galley teams. The galleys tend to be harmonious workspaces. Here people work together closely as teams, the air filled with banter and chatter. Galley crews bake, fry, stew, poach and roast their way through every day of the year. There are no days off and the hours are exhausting. In rough weather cooking can be hazardous and burns are a routine injury. However these spaces seem very much 'owned' by the workers located in them. Just as there is ashore, there is often a feeling that the 'kitchen' is the domain of the chief cook, and it is he that 'rules' despite the occasional incursions of overly controlling, or enthusiastic, captains.

Crew members take care to interact with galley crews, expressing their appreciation for their work, begging for treats, checking out the menu for the day and generally larking around. Despite the long hours worked and the stress associated with attempting to cater for a variety of different needs these are frequently happy spaces. However, in apparent contradiction of this observation, the number of stories recounted about violent incidents involving galley staff is relatively high, indicating that on some ships, galleys become the site for hostilities and a locus of stress.

The engine room: working up a sweat?

Continuing lower into the vessel one comes to the engine room. The engine of a large merchant cargo ship[7] is an awe-inspiring sight. Generally painted green (for reasons that are unclear to me)[8] it dominates the engine room space by virtue of both its size and its noise. Engine rooms are very hot spaces. They are bisected by levels of metal plating (flooring) joined by, sometimes long, flights of metal steps resembling fixed stepladders such is the steep angle at which they are set. The overall engine room space is reminiscent of a monstrous metal spider's web, the engine located in the centre surrounded with a scaffold of metal steps and platforms. From many of these you can look down upon, or up to, the engine itself. The heat and noise are barely tolerable for workers and visitors alike and one third engineer remembered his first impression of his first ship as follows:

> That's my first time too, to go aboard ship so I am amazed, I am surprised and I gained the engine room, very noisy, dirty, I'm thinking is this it, the engine room? (Third engineer, *Norwegian Imp*)

In this context, the engine control room is a welcome haven of air conditioning and relative (and it really is only relative) quietude. Here seafarers across the ranks (officers and ratings work together in the engine room) may communicate with one and another, undertake routine monitoring, take coffee breaks and maintain logs. The following field note describes the engine room, and the contrast of the engine control room, on one of my days on board:

> I changed my mind and went to the engine room before going on deck. It was very very hot. Three engineers (second, third, fourth) were in the control room where it is cool and they didn't appear to be doing much. They said it was a quiet day. Out in the heat the motorman was painting and the wiper was cutting some hose or other with the help of the fitter. I took some pictures but it was so hot that I didn't like to stay for long. (Sampson field notes, *Santos Sunset*)

Just as with this example, beyond the coolness of the control room, in the heat and noise, seafarers may be found working alone or in small groups of two or three engaged in routine maintenance, in stripping down malfunctioning equipment, in cleaning or lubricating. In some engine rooms there are dedicated spaces where fitters work, fabricating parts which require metal cutting and welding. This could be rewarding and creative work as the following quote demonstrates:

> Sometimes, I'm doing work on a machine, if I put my job on a machine, and how it occurs, how the thing is made ... That I like. You can do any design to your method. (Fitter, *Santos Sunset*)

Despite the noise and the heat and the impossibility of normal communication, engineers on ships seem to enjoy a superficial camaraderie and a working team spirit which is often not evident amongst deck officers whose responsibilities are carried in a far more solitary spirit. The field notes I made aboard the fifth vessel which I sailed with, document this realisation:

> There seems to be a good relationship between the engineers (mostly Pakistani) and the motormen (Filipino). The engineers seem to have a quiet and polite style that contrasts to that of the captain (Croatian) the chief officer (Pakistani) and second and third officers (Filipino). The atmosphere in the engine room reminds me very much of the atmosphere in the engine room of both the *Norwegian Imp* and the *Santos Sunset*. I think there may be a bit of an occupational 'engineering culture' at work. (Sampson field notes, *Calmex*)

This camaraderie was something that engineers seem often to be conscious of and something that senior engineers often deliberately foster. One, for example, explained that:

> I enforce the work. What should be done. And I share myself to all of them. Each and every work around. I have my forms to fill in, my reports. I have my checking, what they have been doing. I go around and test, to see what they are doing. Or they come with questions or ideas. And we work as a team. Not just because I am first engineer, that I want my way. If someone says a thing, I will go with the thing, and we share the idea, how to do things most simply, to see that thing done quite alright. (First engineer, *Eclipse*)

Swabbing the decks?

Out in the open air where the spray and wind might sting your cheeks, the waves might crash around you, or the sun shine benevolently on a mild winter's day, the vessel is a different place altogether. On deck you can feel the elements, see the ever changing ocean, wonder at passing dolphins or whales and marvel at turtles, flying fish and phosphorescence. The decks feel like a small piece of freedom from the confines of the metal accommodation block and the noise and oppressive heat of the engine room. Yet work here is hard too. Painting, chipping, and cleaning (washing deck spaces with salt water and sometimes freshwater hoses) may take place at heights, it may involve relatively heavy hand tools such as jet hammers or sandblasting equipment, and it might be undertaken in extremely cold, or conversely blisteringly hot, conditions. The worst routine work, however, takes place in the cargo holds (dry holds or wet tanks) which must be cleaned when empty in preparation for the next cargo at the next port. Invariably such work takes place at sea and holds are not primarily designed for seafarer safety during the cleaning process. Additionally they are often hot, noisy and full of stagnant air (and sometimes noxious gases which must be removed before seafarers can safely enter). The following field note was made after watching seafarers cleaning the cargo holds of a refrigerated cargo ship:

> The air hose they use to blow all the dirt to one end of the hold is very noisy, and coupled with the noise of the bow crashing down into the troughs of the waves and the heavy motion of the ship, working conditions are not very pleasant ... at all. It was also rather hazardous getting to the hatch as the sea was coming over the decks and it was very windy. Within the cargo bay itself there are (naturally) no rails etc. so when cleaning in these rough seas it must be difficult not to lose balance ... (Sampson field notes, *Eclipse*)

Despite the conditions, or perhaps because of them, seafarers on deck seem to foster a good team spirit. While they might emerge from a tank space covered in cargo residue from head to foot, sweating profusely as a result of the heat and exertion, and visibly exhausted, their tendency to have a joke with one another and raise a smile is marked. Deck crews of ratings are supervised by a bosun and his approach and demeanour impact considerably on the morale of the deck crew. Individual solitary working is as commonplace as group work although for safety reasons some tasks such as tank cleaning can only be carried out by groups of seafarers working together. On entering and leaving ports ratings are joined by deck officers in a supervisory capacity but otherwise their contact with officers (other than cadets who may be assigned to work alongside them) is mediated by the bosun who meets daily with the chief officer to discuss work tasks, progress and planning.

Physical space and social organisation

To some extent the design of ships and the ways in which internal space is laid out, and organised, drives social arrangements on board. There is quite a strong relationship between the ways in which physical space is structured by a vessel and access to social space on board. The occupational culture of seafaring and particularly its hierarchical nature have also impacted upon ship design and therefore this relationship can be seen as a two-way one which militates against change. Seafarers are constrained from instituting dramatic changes in social organisation on board as a result of the design of their vessels, but similarly shipbuilders and naval architects do not have a free hand in developing their ideas of spatial layout and design.

The physical space that constitutes a vessel, and the impact of being on board a floating confined structure, strongly influences the experience of being a seafarer and the ways in which seafarers think about work, socialising and off-duty behaviour. Thus physical space does impact upon social relations aboard (and therefore the possibilities for transnationalism to characterise social relationships) and it additionally impacts upon the 'structure' of social space. While it is argued throughout this text that space is structured by socio-legal, cultural and economic factors it may also be structured by physical space to some extent (constraining and confining individuals in particular sets of relationships) and importantly the organisation of physical space comes to reflect the structure of social space. It is worth, therefore, understanding a little about ships as living, as well as working, environments before moving forward to consider social space and subsequently (in Chapter 7) transnationality.

The general features of ships as living environments

In general, ships are not particularly comfortable living spaces. Some problems are impossible to fully address, for example motion caused by rolling seas. Others require nothing more than the application of effort and resource, yet this is generally not applied, by shipbuilders, designers or operators. Vibration, for example, has been noted by seafarers as a particular problem aboard many new vessels, but it is not a new problem and has also been common to older ships; it is simply a problem that has been allowed to worsen in efforts to reduce the costs of vessel construction. Aboard my fifth ship which was twenty years old I noted:

> The ship is vibrating like nothing I have ever experienced before. It isn't actually a vibration at all but a rather rapid, back and forth juddering. (Sampson field notes, *Calmex*)

Such vibration and the associated noise can be constantly, and oppressively, present for days, as vessels may engage in very lengthy sea passages. Nevertheless, work, as well as attempts to sleep, must continue regardless of the state of the vessel or the sea. To combat the problems of sleeping in conditions causing ships to roll violently seafarers often utilise strategies such as moving their mattresses and wedging themselves into their berths. However there are few strategies that can mitigate the effects of movement and vibration when working.

In such conditions, the parts of the ship that offer respite from the elements, and a degree of comfort for off-duty workers, are of considerable significance.

Good ships are quite often defined as such because of good facilities, as in the following example:

> This one [is my favourite ship so far]. Because my cabin is carpeted, and I have
> my own comfort room [en suite bathroom], and air conditioning is nice. The
> facilities are good. Nice. Also the engine is not too much work. (Oiler, *Eclipse*)

Similarly 'bad ships' may be remembered as such because of poor quality living conditions even where in the end seafarers become 'accustomed' to them as in the following example:

> I joined together with one of my second mate, I was then second [engineer].
> I joined as a third and I was promoted on the ship. And this is the only ship I
> never unpack my suitcase … maybe around midnight ship was just finished dis-
> charging, full of dirt, you come in your cabin filthy, hot. And first in the morning
> he [the second mate who I joined with] come to me and he said 'no I go home I
> cannot stay' I said to him 'come on let's wait. We will see'. Afterwards [later in the
> voyage] I go to his cabin [and say to him] 'I cannot stand this place I go home
> now' and then he said to me 'wait , wait , wait' like this. It was very comical in
> the end but [the] first 15–20 days we were in a pretty bad condition and then
> like anything else later you get used to it, it's amazing what you can get used to,
> amazing … I managed to survive somehow. We have two to three disaster on
> that ship. The air conditioning – disaster, disaster, disaster, but you get used to it
> you know becomes part of your life you know. (First engineer, *Norwegian Imp*)

The living conditions, the standard of accommodation, and the on-board facilities available to seafarers vary considerably. Size of vessel clearly has an impact (vessels of less than 4,000 tonnes have very few facilities and little space) and the age and origin of the vessel, as well as its initial place of ownership and/or operation, also seem to be factors impacting upon accommodation standards. To this day, one of the best vessels[9] in terms of seafarer living space and facilities that I have experienced was the very first I ever boarded. It was a Swedish-operated and Bahamas-flagged reefer (refrigerated cargo vessel) of 15,200 tonnes, which carried a crew of twenty-six men of Swedish and Filipino nationality. The reefer was an old ship but maintained to a high standard and with remarkable facilities as the following field note extracts demonstrate:

> The ship is very comfortable and the super-cargo cabin [occupied prior to my
> arrival by a cadet] consists of a living area with coffee table, desk, sofa, armchair,
> desk chair, set of drawers, and a fridge. There are two large 'windows' overlook-
> ing the stern … The 'bedroom' has a wardrobe, bedside table, bed, and sofa, and
> the bathroom has a good shower … The ship has a crew lounge and an officer
> lounge with a large selection of videos, sauna, swimming pool, gym with table
> tennis, library with dart board. The crew lounge has a card/Mah Jong table set
> up in it and both lounges have a TV and video … [there was also a cinema on
> board that was used infrequently]. (Sampson field notes, *Eclipse*)

Most vessels are not like this however. Aboard an oil tanker trading in US waters high standards were required in terms of structure and technical maintenance, but these were not mirrored in the very poor standards of accommodation on board as the following field note reflects:

> I unpacked, and surveyed the cabin. It is a large room with a settee and two arm chairs and two curtained twin berths that must each be 2ft wide max. There is a desk and chair, and on it a table light and an old fashioned telephone. There is a chest of drawers and a cupboard. There are two sealed (obviously being a tanker) portholes which are also curtained. The curtains and carpets are very old and are marked and, in the case of the carpet, full of holes … The lighting is very dim and the cabin like the rest of the ship is very hot. The bathroom is also in a bit of a state. When I ran the shower the base filled with black water … When the water runs out of the basin some of it runs down the outlet and some just runs onto the floor and your feet … The ship is twenty years old and looks like an old ship. She is pitted with rust spots that have been painted over and is pretty dirty – can hardly see through my 'window' … She was owned by [name of company] until two years ago and when they sold her to this company they stripped out all of her social/welfare gear including all of the videos and TVs [and these have not been replaced] … The officers lounge has a rather sad looking bar (devoid of course of any drinks) … (Sampson field note, *Calmex*)

I found similar conditions aboard a rather old bulk carrier trading in Europe and South America. Here, not only were standards of leisure facilities and recreational spaces poor but so too were cabin areas and facilities for washing:

> The ship is visibly old and my cabin is distinctly grotty. The toilet does not flush very well and on the bridge the toilet has a notice saying 'please pour water after use'. From this I assume it doesn't flush at all. Most senior officers have a dayroom and there is an officer and a crew mess with TV and VCR and dartboard in each … The ship owners are reported by the captain to be disinclined to invest in her refurbishment but he says he does what he can to make the crew comfortable (buying new settees etc). Some Filipinos have cabins with bathrooms (e.g. the bosun) but most do not [and have to use shared facilities]. I think all the officers have en-suite rooms. The launderette is not very well equipped and has a drying room rather than a drier … I have seen dartboards and TVs so far. I am told that senior officers have TVs and VCRs in their dayrooms and that there is a squash 'court' and gym aboard [there is no swimming pool and no satellite telephone] … [some days later] … As a result of the inspection [regular captain's inspection of cabins] a second attempt was made to fix the toilet in my cabin. The spare part needed for the toilet is not on board and some improvisation had to be made […] the toilet next door […] doesn't flush at all! … As well as malfunctioning toilets the ship has insufficient washing machines. For the last four days I have been trying to get to use the [single available] washing machine and have found it in continuous use. (Sampson field notes, *Santos Sunset*)

Thus, there are some vessels with the space for better facilities (like the *Calmex*) where companies do not bother to provide any, and there were some vessels where space constraints make the provision of anything other than rudimentary facilities impossible. The vessel where I experienced the highest standards of accommodation (which differed markedly from most others) was crewed with Swedish senior officers – unionised and accustomed to good living and working conditions ashore.

It is noticeable that in this industry whereas companies may take a pride in providing decent facilities for their shore-based staff, even highly regarded companies may take little interest in the social aspects of life on board their vessels and tend to regard welfare as something that seafarers should take care of for themselves. Wal, a company vice-president I talked with epitomised this attitude as follows:

> We see a lot of individuals who don't seem to feel responsible for their health …
> I think, you know, if people wanna keep fit, they can keep fit, in an – just about
> any environment and, you know, er, but I've, I've exercised nearly every day of
> my life, whether I was at sea, or on a dirty old ship or a, you know, up, right
> until today and so, you know, I think it's a personal obligation and I think there's
> always a way that you can do it, even if there's hardly any facilities there … (Wal
> – vice-president, author interview)

This company is much more pro-active in relation to its shore staff who, in the company head office, are provided with luxurious work spaces, a cafeteria with TV and deluxe coffee machine producing (free) lattes, cappuccinos, espressos and so forth, fresh fruit, light airy offices with comfortable chairs and sweets on all the tables. In addition the company pays an allowance to each land-based employee which can be used to purchase, or go towards the purchase of, any sports activity (e.g. gym or golf club membership). Their seafarers, living in confined and controlled spaces with no access to the shore or to their own homes, seem somewhat neglected in contrast.

Seafarers recognise this phenomenon and it exacerbates the feeling, that they already tend to have, of separation from the land and as an isolated and uncared for working population. This does provide, to some extent, a feeling that they and their colleagues on board are all in the same situation (the 'same boat') and all suffer in common although this feeling is inevitably diluted by the hierarchical arrangements and additionally nationality divisions and prejudices which tend to pervade the industry. It is also the case that poor, noisy, cramped conditions do little to promote the development of social relationships on board and may militate against the formation of friendships just as poorly designed urban public spaces do so ashore.

Hierarchy and space

The established hierarchy, on board, generally plays a great role in the assignation of on-board physical space. Somewhat symbolically, it is commonplace for the most senior officers to occupy the highest altitude decks on board and as you descend to the lower levels of the vessel so does the status of the occupants of the cabins around you. Congruently the most spacious and comfortable accommodation is to be found on the highest decks.

Most ships have two messrooms and sometimes two galleys to service them. One of these is allocated to officers and one is allocated to ratings. A very small number of ships also have a pantry on the officer decks so that officers can help themselves to food prepared by the galley staff and left in the pantries at any time of day. Meals in the officer mess rooms are frequently formal and officers are generally expected, at the very least, to change into clean casual clothing. Aboard some vessels, however, formal dinner dress (normally uniform) is required.

The shipboard hierarchy is frequently, if not always, reflected in a pattern of hierarchical seating for meals. A captain's table or a rigidly hierarchical seating order around a table is not unusual but is generally found, in its most extreme form, in the officer mess rooms. Aboard one vessel I observed in a field note that:

> The Swedes (officers) sit in a very hierarchical fashion. The captain sits at the head of the table with the chief officer and chief engineer either side of him. The second officer sits next to the chief officer and the electrician sits next to him. On the other side the first engineer sits next to the chief engineer and the deck cadet sits next to him. The engine cadet sits at the foot of the table along with me … The Filipinos are not seated in such a hierarchical fashion. The reefer and second engineer sit at one table together but the bosun and third engineer sit mixed in with the others as do the carpenter and fitters. The third officer is on the 12–4 watch so eats lunch with the galley crew but at dinner he also sits with the Reefer and Second engineers (but I think from what he tells me this is out of sympathy with their isolation rather than anything else) (Sampson field note, *Eclipse*)

The contrast between officer and crew mess rooms is generally readily apparent. Very little formality characterises the crew mess rooms frequented by ratings aboard most ships. On some vessels, this lack of formality results in the crew mess also being used by officers not wishing to properly 'scrub up' before their meals. Thus, officers have access to ratings' spaces but on larger ships ratings are invariably excluded from spaces designated for officers. A detailed description of the kinds of differences found between the officer and crew mess rooms is illustrative of the ways in which the hierarchy is frequently symbolically demonstrated in the facilities and the provisions available in respective 'crew' (ratings) and 'officer' mess rooms:

> In the crew mess there are three rectangular tables set alongside one wall. On the other side of the room there are square coffee tables and a hatch/serving area … where meals are laid out. Food is generally presented in a very simple way and without any adornment. By contrast in the officers' mess there are two dining tables … and a coffee table with seating … The coffee table is always laid with white linen and during the day it is also laid with cups, saucers, milk, sugar, and a flask of coffee. This contrasts with the coffee table in the crew mess which is bare and never has coffee on it at all … In the officer mess between the coffee table and the main dining table there is a rectangular table which is laid buffet style at meal times with cheese, fruit, biscuits, desserts, jams etc. In between meals a basket of biscuits is always left out so that the Swedes (officers) … can have a snack should they fancy it. They also have access to a fridge containing the cheeses etc. This is different to the arrangements for the Filipinos [in the

crew mess] who do not have 'free access' to the fridge and are not just able to come down to the kitchen and prepare their own food. (Sampson field notes, *Eclipse*)

Thus occupational hierarchy is ever present in the organisation and use of physical space and the distribution of resources on board. The captain and chief engineer and the senior officers generally exercise the right to priority in the use of the facilities and resources available. Such practices are so embedded that in their daily conduct they are unspoken and invisible to the casual observer. If the captain enters the gym others will leave. If it becomes known that the chief officer uses the gym at a particular time others will regularly avoid it at this time and so on. The crew lounge may be visited and used by any officer but the officer lounge is off limits to ratings. However, as well as rank other factors such as nationality/gender impact upon the use of physical space aboard the ship.

Overall, the key elements underpinning shipboard life include the physical limitations and isolation of vessels; the strong hierarchical relationships which pertain in the modern shipping industry and which tend to be exacerbated rather than diminished by the changes in employment relationships within the industry; the commercial pressures under which vessels operate; the difficult living and working conditions found on-board ships; and the particularly strong authority vested in a single position – that of captain – aboard vessels universally. Only when these fundamental characteristics are understood is it possible to turn to a consideration of issues of nationality and ships as social spaces. Seafarers' experiences of space on board is structured not just by the physical characteristics of the vessel and the environment but crucially by the organisation of work and occupational hierarchy, by employment terms and conditions, and by the nature of work itself. Within the given physical constraints of the vessel, and those relating to the job, captains emerge with enormous power and as individuals they may impact significantly on space and how social space is experienced and constructed on board. The personal characteristics of captains, their leadership qualities, charisma, natural authority and so forth, are highly significant in relation to the quality of life seafarers experience on board but it is vital to recognise the structural arrangements which place captains in this key social role. It is the employment terms and conditions of seafarers, the lack of state regulation of vessels in relation to living arrangements, the influence of company policies or their absence (for example with regard to harassment and to worker appraisal), and similar factors that create the structure of the space on board which is then 'colonised' and 'populated' by individual actors, personalities and characters. Where the structure of the space is altered so too will the experience, and utilisation, of space on board, be reconfigured. It is all too easy to focus upon the dramatic effects of the actions of powerful individuals on-board remote and confined vessels but in order to fully understand life on board it is crucial that we see, recognise and understand the structured nature of social space. This will be considered in further detail in the next chapter with specific reference to the possibilities for transnationalism or 'transborder embeddedness' amongst serving seafarers.

Notes

1   The first steam assisted ship to cross the Atlantic was built in 1819 and by the end of the Second World War screw-propelled and generally diesel-fuelled vessels had replaced sail-assisted merchant trading vessels.

2   NB The ILO Maritime Labour Convention (MLC) is presented by some members of the industry as evidence of a concern to improve living conditions at sea. In reality however the mandatory standards incorporated in the MLC do not represent a significant improvement over the specifications of the many ILO conventions which have been incorporated into it.

3   GMDSS stands for Global Maritime Distress Safety System and VHF for Very High Frequency.

4   The list of navigational duties described here as the activities associated with a navigational watch is not intended to be read as a full job description but as a summary of observed practice on board the vessels included in this research.

5   NB this is not the Golden Gate.

6   Recent cutbacks have hit the galley crews on some vessels and I have recently sailed aboard one, in conjunction with a different study, where only a single cook and a single messman serviced the catering and cleaning needs of the vessel.

7   Here I refer to vessels over 17,000 dwt.

8   I was recently told by a seafarer aboard a container ship that he had known a chief engineer to be sacked for painting 'his' engine room blue. Like me, this seafarer was not aware of the reason for engine rooms to be painted green but he was very clear that this was something of a 'golden rule'.

9   In 2011, I found similarly good facilities aboard another old Swedish-flagged vessel. However these examples really stand out from the poor living conditions seen aboard many ships.

7

Nationality and transnationality at sea

Discussions of transnationalism largely focus on migrants traversing national borders and living lives in more than one community. Modern-day shipping is inherently related to traversing borders and so there is no argument that seafarers are constantly engaged in cross-border travel in a technical sense. In a meaningful sense, however, such border crossings are limited for seafarers. Fast vessel turnaround and rapid port operations which run on a twenty-four hour basis, as well as the distance of many ports from town and city centres, militate against seafarers spending much time ashore even where they are permitted by authorities to do so (Sampson and Wu 2003). As a result they generally do not participate, to any significant extent, in the life of the communities which their ships visit. Thus, seafarers leave their homelands only to exist, in a meaningful way, 'beyond borders' as even when not in international waters they are hardly ashore. Their lives on board their vessels are inevitably, therefore, the focus for an interest in transnationality. More specifically they become the focus of questions relating to transborder embeddedness, and social participation, and the broader issues relating to recurrent migration.

Ships have an official nationality in as much as they come under the legal jurisdiction of their flag state. In practice, however, this may have little significance for the lives of seafarers aboard as there is often little regulation of vessels by flag states. Any oversight that does take place tends to be of a technical nature, focusing upon the structural integrity of ships rather than on social and domestic arrangements on board. There are a small number of vessels where operating companies seek to have some influence over the lives of seafarers on board their ships, attempting for example to implement anti-harassment policies, but these are few and far between and their success is fairly limited. Control by companies tends to be confined to those areas of activity aboard ship that can be monitored, for example the ship's speed, the stores supplied to a vessel, the budgets for victualling and welfare facilities, and so forth. Beyond these areas, where bureaucratic oversight can practically occur, ships operate and run as small worlds, small territories, of their own. To all intents and purposes therefore the structure of space aboard individual vessels is only marginally influenced by the flag of the ship concerned. Nevertheless it might be anticipated that it would be more significantly influenced by the nationality of the seafarers aboard, the occupational culture of seafaring, and the corporate culture of ship management or ship operating companies.

In considering the potential for the lives of seafarers aboard vessels to be transnational in character (if not in every technical detail) it is important to consider two major questions: are seafarers aboard a vessel embedded into the life and the 'community' on board; and are seafarers embedded in a meaningful way into the community and way of life of their homelands despite being away for extremely long periods (typically, for ratings, nine months in every twelve)? These are the fundamental questions that underpin this book and this chapter.

In considering seafarer embeddedness on board ships it is critical to understand the impact of hierarchy and the power relationships which dominate shipboard life (as outlined in the earlier chapters). These are constructed in contractual arrangements made ashore between seafarers and shore-based companies. The occupational culture of seafaring also impacts significantly on life on board. In combination, these factors influence the possibilities for social embeddedness, the kinds of relationships found between seafarers and particularly those of different nationalities, and the extent to which, while they are at sea, seafarers additionally reside in some senses in their homelands (mentally, emotionally, financially, and/or as communicative presences).

The interaction of nationality and hierarchy

Hierarchy is a defining feature of life on board any merchant cargo vessel and it influences not only the working lives of those on board but also the social lives of seafarers. Rank is the most obvious organising principle on board symbolically represented in the habitual referencing of more senior colleagues by rank rather than name; a practice that is widespread at sea. The captain is only ever referenced as 'captain' by the majority of the crew. This also applies to other crew members at petty officer/officer level. For example 'chief' is generally used to address the chief officer or chief engineer or 'sec' for Second Engineer/Officer, 'leccie' for Electrician, or 'bose' for bosun and 'pumpie' for Pumpman. This form of address is applied to petty officers and not ratings (you do not generally, for example, hear of the Messman being addressed as 'messman' or the ABs or OSs being addressed as such either on deck or in equivalent positions (oiler and wiper) in the engine room. Indeed, paradoxically, it would seem rude and a sign of laziness to address a junior ranking crew member in this way. Their 'lowly' status aboard is almost, it seems, hidden in daily conversation in the practice of addressing them by name. Only in higher ranking positions does the mention of rank denote respect. To refer to junior crew members by rank (something most often witnessed in relation to cadets) serves to emphasise their lack of status and is generally avoided unless a show of authority is desired or a careless arrogance employed. The use of a seafarer's name denotes at the very least equality and more usually seniority. It is a privilege afforded to the powerful. So the practice of referring to others on board by rank or by name is not simply about making life easier in the context of regular crew changes, it is also about status, rank and deference, and it is symbolic of the powerful ways in which these mark the life of all seafarers on board.

The importance of hierarchy can be witnessed in many other ways on board commercial cargo ships such as at social events open to all members of the crew. At barbecues and parties senior-ranking and junior-ranking members of the crew are regularly involved in displays of hierarchy as ratings act as hosts to senior officers, plying them with food and drink and deferring to their preferences in terms of the activities that might accompany such events – the playing of music, traditional shipboard games such as 'horse racing' and so forth. The following field note about a birthday party aboard one vessel records an example of this kind of behaviour:

> In the crew lounge the Filipinos were throwing a party for the reefer engineer and Stan [both officers] … When the Swedish guys [officers] arrive the Filipinos make them very welcome by moving so that they can sit down and plying them with beer. They always replace their beer before the one they are drinking is finished and generally make them feel that they want them to stay despite the fact that in the chief engineer and electrician's case they were quite keen that they should leave. (Sampson field notes, *Eclipse*)

Symbolically such social events invariably occur either in spaces which are designated as being for ratings' use or in neutral spaces such as on deck. Ratings are rarely, if ever, invited into the communal spaces allocated to officers. Hierarchy thus defines and constrains the spaces which can be occupied by seafarers aboard in both a physical and a social sense. In this way hierarchy and the occupational culture of seafaring impact upon the potential for crew members to become embedded within the 'society of the ship'. Access to space is also determined by nationality, however, and aboard many vessels nationality and hierarchy come to interact in interesting, if somewhat unhelpful, ways, reconfiguring space aboard and adding to the divisions that may be seen to develop amongst mixed-nationality crews, particularly where just two or three nationalities are present.

On ships carrying two or three nationalities there is a tendency for divisions in nationality to merge with distinctions in rank and to act in a powerful way to reconfigure the traditional social, if not occupational, hierarchies on board. There is normally an overlap between nationality and rank – officers are often of one nationality and ratings are often of another. However, where this overlap is not complete, nationality may 'corrupt' traditional understandings of hierarchy to some extent. Thus on the *Eclipse* (a ship with only Swedish and Filipino seafarers that carried some junior Filipino officers as well as a full complement of Filipino ratings) the Filipino junior officers were clearly excluded from designated communal officer spaces and resided in those allocated to ratings. They never ate in the officers' mess, for example, and rarely spent time in the officers' lounge. Other spaces and facilities were also 'denied' them, which not only impacted upon their living conditions but also, potentially, upon their opportunities for career progression. For example, aboard this vessel Filipino junior officers had no access to computers (denying them use of email) or to on-board training in the use of computers. The following field note describes the situation as perceived at the time:

At 18.00 Bob came to see me and we tried to load the software [his own that he had not been able to use and I had agreed he could try on my laptop]. Eventually we managed to get it running and he was really pleased. I then tried to show him how to start and shut down windows and start up his program so that he could borrow the laptop on his own and play around with it a bit. It became apparent that he really is a complete beginner and it seems ludicrous that he had to come to me for 'training' rather than being able to approach the captain. By this I do not mean that it is ludicrous of him not to approach the captain but that it is a ludicrous situation that exists when junior officers are denied access to computer facilities and training and that those that are keen to learn are not encouraged to do so. The access to the computer terminals on the ship is entirely divided along ethnic lines and does not relate to rank. No Filipinos of any rank have access to a computer terminal of any description. (Sampson field note, *Eclipse*)

Aboard this vessel the boundaries between officers and ratings had been effectively redrawn to reflect the division in nationalities. Thus only Swedish members of the complement were deemed to be officers in the social domain of shipboard life and this even spilled over to some extent to the occupational domain impacting, in this case, on the possibilities for skill development and career progression. This effectively denied the Filipino third officer, the second engineer, the third engineer, and the reefer engineer their proper occupational status as normally recognised and operationalised on board (see Figure 10). It also placed them in a somewhat isolated position as they were regarded differently by ratings of their own nationality as a consequence of their 'lofty' officer status and they were thus

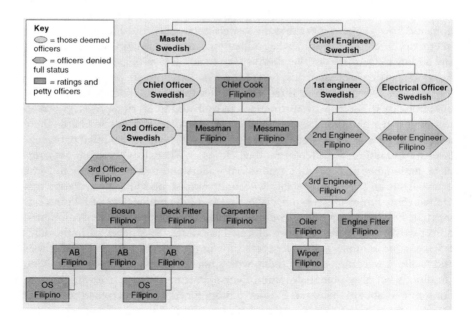

Figure 10: **Nationality and hierarchy aboard the *Eclipse***

a little socially separated from crew members of their own nationality while being concurrently socially excluded by the main body of officers of a different nationality. It was clear that for individuals in this position, occupational rank and nationality, and how these were constructed in relation to physical and social space, worked together to prevent them from become embedded in a meaningful way in the social relations on board.

Aboard another ship, with seafarers of three different nationalities, the lines of hierarchy were again redrawn to correspond with nationality but this time they were redrawn to include more people than there 'should' have been in the officer group. Thus aboard this vessel twelve seafarers were given officer privileges including a fitter (See Figure 11). In this case the fitter seemed to occupy a more comfortable position and was accepted amongst his Indian and Bangladeshi colleagues in the same way that junior officers were accepted.

In comparing these two cases it is interesting to note that aboard the *Eclipse* the individuals occupying the chief cook and engine fitter positions (both Filipino) were deemed to be 'ratings' yet aboard the *Santos Sunset* the individuals in these posts were defined as officers. Additionally four officers aboard the *Eclipse* were recognised by both officers and ratings aboard as 'officers' but were denied their full occupational status with regard to access to space and to facilities. This left them in a particularly uncomfortable social limbo where they were unable to fully integrate with either the officers or the ratings. On these ships with so few nationalities present the intersection between nationality and rank could therefore produce divisions that disrupted the traditional occupational hierarchy, and it is

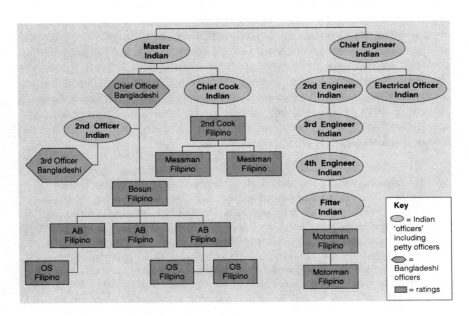

Figure 11: **Nationality and hierarchy aboard the *Santos Sunset***

relevant to note that occupational hierarchy is to some extent deemed functional from a task-oriented perspective. However, not all ships with small numbers of nationalities on board were organised in this way. On some ships nationality was accommodated with regard to some issues, such as food preference, while hierarchy still prevailed as the dominant factor in the organisation of space. Thus on board one vessel the Indian trainee was required to sit with the Filipino crew but was nevertheless allowed to help himself to the (Indian) officers' food. On ships with genuinely multinational crews (generally of four nationalities or more) a very different atmosphere prevailed. Space tended to be divided upon purely traditional occupationally based hierarchical grounds. Officers of all different nationalities, and ratings of different nationality, ate together and socialised together. This facilitated talk about the jobs at hand and a sense of teamwork and it militated against the build-up of resentment.

The social space of two and three-nationality ships was qualitatively different to the social space of more genuinely multinational vessels. Aboard the *Eclipse* there were only two nationalities and on both the *Santos Sunset* and *Qui Auora*, there were three. Divisions and splits in the crew that ran along nationality grounds were apparent in all three cases. Similarly, aboard all three vessels there was a degree of hostility, prejudice and/or stereotyping occasionally displayed against the 'other' nationality/nationalities on board. Hostility was particularly expressed by ratings against officers but typically complaints were not articulated as hierarchically based resentments but as issues of nationality and culture. The resentments often seemed to fester as a result of the separate nationality groups lapsing into their own language and effectively excluding others (an issue which is returned to later). Aboard the *Eclipse* where there was some considerable mixing and socialising between the younger deck officers, cadets and crew, language nevertheless emerged time and again as an issue. However sometimes it was not language but rank that seemed to be the real barrier between nationalities. Resentments over abuses (or perceived abuses) of power rapidly seemed to get translated into grievances about nationality. A relatively trivial incident aboard the *Santos Sunset* is illustrative. Here an action by officers was quickly transformed into an action by 'the Indians' and a falling back onto stereotypes in the hostile reaction that followed. It was recorded in a field note as follows:

> Zed and Bee and the bosun started to criticise Jay (the messman) saying that he wanted to be with the Indians all the time and didn't realise that he was a Filipino. They said that he was grateful to the Indians for his job but they said he didn't realise it was a Filipino agency in Manila which gave him the work. At that particular moment Zed, who had started the conversation, was aggrieved with Jay for refusing to allow him to borrow his karaoke machine. It transpired that the 'Indians' had swapped the VHS system back again yesterday and this also annoyed the Filipinos as it deprived them of karaoke (and I can't see any reason why they have done it). In the discussion following the talk of Jay, Zed was very critical of the Indian officers and Spud in particular whom he does not like…While Zed remained at the gathering he took the mickey out of the officers by saying at the end of each song 'thank you very much' in a perfect

imitation of their style which I cannot begin to explain. (Sampson field notes, *Santos Sunset*).

Aboard vessels with larger crews and few nationalities, stereotypes were frequently reverted to even where social relations were harmonious. A paternalistic approach to ratings was often adopted by officers who frequently voiced stereotyped generalisations about their juniors according them a child-like status. In these cases juniors were generally fully conscious of such, albeit 'well-intentioned', infantilisation. Aboard one vessel, for example, I was told off by the captain for venturing out onto the weather deck in heavy seas. The Filipino third officer who overheard this conversation and thought it might have irritated or upset me sought to reassure by explaining that 'The captain sees us all as his children and he wants to look after us'. This comment indeed reflected the way in which the captain on this vessel, and senior officers on board, characterised their Filipino colleagues describing them as kids who required instruction all the time and lacked initiative or a deep understanding.

In general terms, therefore, social embeddedness on ships is constrained by patterns of nationality and hierarchy. On ships with only two or three nationalities there was a tendency for crews to divide unconstructively according to country of origin. Those vessels with four or more nationalities appeared to be more integrated but remained divided according to rank. On all ships, however, individuals could be identified who crossed 'nationality boundaries'. On the *Eclipse* junior officers and trainee officers (cadets), notably the second officer and the deck and engine cadets mixed more with their Filipino crewmates than with other Swedish officers. They forged more significant friendships with some of the ABs than with officers and discussed a range of topics often regarded as off-limits amongst seafarers illustrating the extent to which these social relationships could be regarded as having depth and strength. A field note records one such example:

> There was also some discussion of girls, love and marriage, and Faro (Swedish officer) said that Quita (a Filipino AB who had sailed on the ship previously) had told him that he would never marry anyone but a virgin and that complete fidelity was expected by Filipinos of their wives (although this does not work the other way round) and that this would be an impossible expectation for the Swedes to have of their 'women'. Lenard (Filipino AB) said that although he had married a virgin he believed that it didn't matter if your wife had been a prostitute in the past if you loved her. The discussion was very friendly and seemed to represent a genuine attempt at understanding each others' national values vis a vis sex and marriage. (Sampson field notes, *Eclipse*)

In the development of cross-nationality friendships it was noticeable, however, that where mixing occurred it could only be at the instigation of officers. Generally officers were free (and seemingly welcome) to enter the spaces of ratings (excluding cabins unless expressly invited or unless undertaking the somewhat archaic practice of 'cabin inspection'). The converse did not apply, and ratings were not permitted to enter the spaces of officers (any spaces, not just cabin spaces) unless expressly invited, or instructed, to do so. It was very rare to find a rating on the floors where officers' accommodation was located unless they were engaged in a work task such as cleaning, conveying a message, or reporting to an officer. By contrast, it was not unusual to find officers in boiler suits eating in crew messrooms, junior officers and cadets socialising in crew recreation rooms, and from time to time whole ship parties occupying the spaces of ratings. Communal facilities could also be controlled by senior officers with regard to usage but this did not tend to happen formally. Where such control was exercised it tended to be exercised by 'consent', whereby a captain's preference to use a facility at a particular time would deter others from attempting to do so without him or her needing to express their desire to have the space to themselves.

In these ways social space was accessed and restricted as a result of the contracted status of seafarers on board. In this, it was strongly structured and constrained by hierarchy but was not predetermined in every particular, being mediated from time to time by powerful individuals. There were contexts in which space became reconfigured upon nationality grounds – largely as a result of the preferences of captains but possibly with wider influences from other senior-ranking crew members at work. The captain ultimately had the power to ordain the pattern and use of space and to reconfigure the patterns of spatial access and usage should he or she see fit. This tended to happen where only two or three nationalities were present on board and where divisions between these nationalities did not directly map onto divisions in occupational rankings. Ultimately of course the captain's capacity to reconfigure space in such ways was no more than a manifestation of the structural conditions governing space on board, i.e. it was a manifestation of his position at the top of the occupational hierarchy and an expression of power linked to his contractual status. Nevertheless the agency of individuals within these positions impacted in significant ways upon the lives of seafarers on board and their access to social space and the associated possibilities for embeddedness.

Seafarer relationships: embeddedness on board

For transnationality to have meaning, transnational migrants need to be embedded in not just one, but two, communities. Social embeddedness for working seafarers depends upon both the relationships between different nationalities and those between different ranks working aboard ships. Where individuals are clearly socially segregated it makes little sense to talk of truly integrated transborder or transnational lives. Rather the focus might be on the marginal existence of many potential transnationals who are not able to fully participate in the life and society in which they find themselves either at home or in their 'from-home' environments. Nationality and rank on board ship clearly militate against social inclusion creating powerful divisions across ships' crews which could nevertheless be occasionally overcome by individuals.

It is not only nationality and rank which create divisions aboard multinationally crewed vessels, however. Language barriers and the occupational culture of seafaring can also be seen to militate against inclusiveness and embeddedness.

Aboard ships English is often the official working language. As a result most work-based communication on board the ships I joined took place in English. However a great deal of day-to-day communication did not occur in the agreed working language of the vessel. Inevitably this use of other languages predominated aboard vessels with the fewest nationalities aboard. In these contexts language could become quite divisive in both work and social settings. Aboard vessels with only two or three nationalities and a clear ethnic division between officers and ratings, suspicion was often generated by the use of the non-shared language in mixed settings. Complaints abounded in these contexts of fears that the groups concerned might be discussing something relevant to the individuals present who did not share the language being used. The following field note reflects on this issue:

> Swedish is generally used on the bridge regardless of who is there (me, third officer, AB, pilot, etc.) and whether or not they can understand. This confirms what Bob (Filipino officer) says and it reminded me of his comment that he felt the officers should speak Swedish on the Bridge. Interestingly the captain has also joked that he thinks he and the chief engineer should learn Tagalog (secretly) so that they can understand what the Filipinos are saying about them. Language barriers therefore seem to cause some uneasiness (bordering on suspicion) amongst the crew and officers. (Sampson field note, *Eclipse*)

Many seafarers confessed to holding a rudimentary knowledge of the languages spoken by their colleagues but kept such knowledge 'secret' allowing them to monitor what was being said in their presence. This practice, based on only a sketchy knowledge of the language concerned, seemed likely to produce misunderstandings and the generation of misinformation. Other complaints around language centred upon the use of the non-working language in work settings (such as on the bridge) where the seafarers present did not all share the same language. Such use of language could render particular members of the team less effective in relation to their on-board role as they were unable to contribute to, or understand, what was taking place as the Filipino third officer aboard *Eclipse* observed:

> Bob complained without any questioning or prompting that the Swedish officers tend not to speak English on the bridge and that this makes it difficult to anticipate the captain or pilot's next instruction, making him (the third officer) appear to be slower and less efficient than he actually is. (Sampson field notes, *Eclipse*)

Additionally poor fluency in a common language could impede work which was identified as having safety implications but also carried more prosaic and frustrating ramifications relating to the everyday tasks involved in the work of seafarers.

While central to work, it seemed that fluency in English was even more vital in social settings. Here personal disclosures, jokes, or sensitive discussions could only safely be conducted if personnel were confident of their grasp of language and/or the friendly intentions of their colleagues. Aboard some vessels individuals joked transparently, if incomprehensibly, with peers and subordinates, and managed to overcome communication problems with clear signals that they were being jocular such as laughter, demeanour and habitual attitude. Others, however, were more dependent upon fluency in English for happy social interaction. Where English was nobody's first language aboard there seemed to be considerable efforts made to transcend linguistic limitations using gestures, body language, and even shared words known amongst the crew but derived from a variety of different languages. Aboard one vessel for example the captain regularly talked of being in 'deep kimshee' (politely understood to substitute for deep trouble). When asked about 'kimshee' (spelt here as it was said) it transpired that this was a kind of pickled spicy vegetable he had come across in Korea. Where he had actually first heard the term (it appears to have some general linguistic currency both as 'deep kimshee' and 'deep kinshee') was never made clear. However, it had been picked up by the whole crew and it spread with him (and no doubt others) as he moved from vessel to vessel in the same company. Thus language could be seen as an impediment to social interaction but it was not necessarily an insurmountable one. Many seafarers spoke very fluent English and even those who didn't could be adept at finding ways of communicating in quite complex ways across language barriers. As such, language per se was not an insurmountable barrier to integration and embeddedness and seemed to exercise less impact, for example, than occupational hierarchy.

In terms of the content of the social interaction between seafarers, this ranged from what might be regarded as fairly 'standard' masculine bar talk (sports, sex, movies, gossip) to more intimate discussions about culture, religion, politics and values. Seafarers had their own different boundaries and rules about what they would discuss and what they wouldn't. Some, for example, would never talk about home life, others avoided politics, some avoided religion and so on. However what was very rarely publicly discussed by any seafarers was their personal life or more accurately their personal problems (bereavement, divorce, arguments with wives/girlfriends) and when such discussion was public, it was apparent that some seafarers were not at all comfortable and visibly demonstrated this by either leaving the setting or asking the seafarer, who was relating his worries, to desist. In this context it seemed that a worry shared was a worry that multiplied. While some shared concerns were discussed, such as fears about events back home during periods of civil unrest, detailed personal problems often remained unshared with any seafarers aboard. I was made painfully aware of this on a number of occasions when seafarers confided in me in relation to situations causing them serious anguish. In two notable cases, these included bereavements that nobody else was aware of, with associated fears of further child deaths (in one case) and guilt at not attending a funeral (in another).

In contrast, humour and joking were hugely important features of all interaction amongst seafarers. Jokes and joking acted as the oil lubricating the wheels of social relationships on board. Seafarers were conscious of the joking strategies they employed and conscious of the importance of humour and a focus on particular 'safe' topic areas in conversation. Amongst these sex and 'girls' ranked highly but so did an interest in other parts of the world, other countries visited, or yet to be visited, and information about the next port, particularly aboard 'tramp' vessels (i.e. those not operating to regular fixed courses/port schedules) where intelligence about the next port was always high on the conversation agenda. Vijay, an officer aboard a bulk carrier put it this way when asked about topics of conversation on board:

> Some jokes, always jokes. [We talk] About girls, maybe. And about different countries, like that. Nothing about home, or anything like that. We don't talk about our home. Not much. Jokes, and about girls. (Vijay – Indian officer, *Santos Sunset*)

Another officer suggested that his recipe for social harmony on board was to:

> Talk properly. Meet each other. Joke around. Don't talk religiously. Don't talk personally. Don't tease anybody. We don't do these things. (Spendit – Indian officer, *Santos Sunset*)

Time and again seafarers of various nationalities and various ranks and aboard different ships drew attention to joking as the social glue bonding seafarers together regardless of nationality and regardless of age, religion, politics, rank.

> This ship is very nice. Everybody is good. Everybody fair to me. Chief engineer very nice. Up till now, no problem. I've enjoyed my life. I have jokes with everybody, play cards. (Ranjit – Indian officer, *Santos Sunset*)

> We talk about our homes, we miss home, and the family. Anything. Depends. Sometimes about girls. And the family. And jokes. (Deppo – Filipino rating, *Santos Sunset*)

> [we talk about] Girls. Sometimes about business. We talk about what we will do when we go home to the Philippines if we have the money, what kind of business you want to establish, that kind of thing. Mostly that. And girls … Well, when we are working we joke also. Always laughing. Filipinos are happy-go-lucky. (Toto – Filipino officer, *Eclipse*)

These rules for the boundaries within which interaction could, or should, occur on board were often referred to by seafarers and bore strong similarities across ships, across nationalities, and across ranks, although they were inevitably variably interpreted and expressed. For example a senior officer of a different nationality aboard a different vessel expressed a similar awareness of what in his terms could, and could not, be discussed or said on board. His reflections also illustrated how these were not hard and fast rules but were contingent on circumstances and upon individual relationships. He explained:

> The general rule is, of course, you don't talk about religion and politics. Sometimes we do, but you don't talk so much about families, you don't ask people about families at home, because it can be a sensitive area. When they start

> talking, maybe you listen, but maybe one day you go away. You talk about
> drinks, your work, and you never criticise persons, you only criticise the work.
> If someone has created something and it's not good enough – 'Look at this wall,
> it can be better, can we do something?' But not, 'Hey you, look at that paint.' But
> it's the same, but you don't get at the person. (Halon – German senior officer,
> *Norwegian Imp*)

Such 'rules' of social interaction were sometimes consciously 'taught' by senior
officers who might take the trouble to explain to young cadets what they should
expect and what to steer clear of. Thus a degree of occupational socialisation relating to learning how to become successfully integrated into the ship's complement
took place (Gould 2010). In this process the issue of 'over disclosure' was an important element as it carried with it consequences for the social stability of the vessel and of seafarers who often described how they survived separation from their
homes and families by mentally switching off from them. They described this to
me on several occasions, as metaphorically flicking a switch in their heads to block
out all thoughts of missing children and partners, worrying about family sickness,
or the frailty of family members. On board many of them chose to focus on work
matters, as far as possible limiting interaction to the superficial (joking, discussing
women, other people or vessels in the company, etc.) and over disclosure by others
was therefore seen as potentially dangerous by many seafarers who felt that personal problems should be kept, well, 'personal'. There was, furthermore, a view in
some cases, that the ship could, and should, provide welcome respite from problems; both talk of them, and consideration of them. As one seafarer explained:

> With your problems, somebody cannot solve, or help you. I don't know. In the
> end everybody has his share of problems, but it might be completely different
> problems. If somebody has a problem at home, maybe the bank is transferring
> the money too late, and there is a problem – I don't know. Or a child needs
> special attention … We are safe on the ship, we hide on the ship. People have
> to solve their problems themselves, we are not counsellors, you know. Maybe
> we would tell them the wrong thing. The chief engineer, the chief mate, we talk
> about work. It's enough. And then a little bit, something not work, but not so
> deep. We talk about what happens in the company, and the retirement fund,
> and the shares, is it a good thing. And what happened on other ships. There is
> enough material to talk about. (German senior officer, *Norwegian Imp*)

Sex was described as an overwhelming preoccupation in terms of conversation. Generally, it took the form of 'tale' telling rather than anything of a significant or personal nature. Seafarers would describe sexual antics in such and such
a place or port and would find their tales believed, or not, to different degrees but
this didn't seem to matter too much. The point was not necessarily to give a true
account but an entertaining one. Sex, that is to say heterosexual sex, was in general
terms widely regarded as a safe topic for conversation amongst all nationalities
and all cultures. Pornographic films were generally found on board and these,
plus the occasional forays by seafarers ashore, fuelled the talk and the tales. Other
topics were not so safe however and seafarers arrived at different decisions as to

which could be discussed and which couldn't. Some, for example, felt that politics and religion should be avoided as topics for conversation, some thought religion safe but politics not, and vice versa:

> *Imran:* Religion, there is no question on board ship about religion. You meet Christians, Hindus, Muslims – we live together. It is a family life here, everybody is the same. They pray in their cabins, and after shower I pray in my cabin. When we come together, we are all the same. We don't talk about religion on board ship.
> *Helen:* Are there other things you deliberately don't talk about?
> *Imran:* We don't talk about religion. I think that's the best way. Mostly our topics are not with religion, on board ship. We talk about funny things, things we do, sometimes Indian politics, who is a good prime minister, and what place is very good in India, which party is coming up and which party is going down. All these topics are there.
> *Helen:* So you feel safe to talk about politics?
> *Imran:* Yes. [But] Not religion.
>
> (Imran – Indian officer, *Santos Sunset*)

As a result talk in the public domain was recognised as rather superficial and shallow by some, particularly those who had been at sea for some time and had become weary of tall tales and oft-repeated gossip. While they recognised its form as safe they nevertheless became frustrated by it and it was not unusual for seafarers to dismiss public conversation as the 'same old rubbish'. However where seafarers established more close personal relationships they were able to move beyond such superficiality and enjoy a deeper level of communication and more stimulating exchanges of views and information and of personal biography:

> When we work, sometimes we discuss regarding the things, professional things, we exchange our views, what it should be and should not be. Those things we exchange. Specially with the second officer. In leisure time, we don't discuss professional matters. We discuss instead about current matters, world news. What happened to such and such. People captured by terrorist groups. International news. We gossip about schooling also, our school days. We are from different countries. But I know more about his childhood, he told me all these things. He did his schooling in … and he stayed with these people. Students. Boarding. So they can't go home, they have to stay there. Girls and boys. He tells me the stories of this. (Sanji – Bangladeshi officer, *Santos Sunset*)

Social embeddedness aboard was therefore highly variable but generally could be characterised as constrained and highly formulated. Seafarers could experience social isolation as a consequence of their rank and nationality. The example of the small number of officers aboard the *Eclipse* who could not integrate with other officers because they were of a different nationality is an important one. These men were also excluded from the ratings of shared nationality because of their rank. Mixed nationality ships were seemingly characterised by a particular social distance amongst seafarers, a polite avoidance of a range of topics that might be contentious and a formality and politeness in interacting with members of other nationalities that was not always witnessed amongst 'countrymen'. Seafarers noted, however, that this had considerable benefits in terms of avoiding the development of tensions, which in the confined and tedious environment of the ship could easily escalate into violence where unchecked. Over time people came to understand that mixed-nationality crews were often characterised by fewer tensions, less factionalism, and fewer rows and violence. A chief cook put it this way:

> It would be more dangerous to work with the one nationality. There would be groups, a few groups here and there. But here, with multi-national, there is nothing like that. No violence. Single nationalities, they are throwing knives and things, and I have never seen that with *Xenon* [name of company employing mixed nationality crews] (Nani – chief cook, *Santos Sunset*)

This frequently expressed view may be regarded as surprising as it can be seen to come at a cost in terms of social embeddedness. However it is easier to understand when consideration is given to the fact that for many seafarers the ship is not regarded as a home or a community but is merely an institutional work space where they have to survive until the end of each contract. Superficial contact with others and emotional isolation on board are, in this context, the price they pay for survival in a very challenging, confined, and tedious, environment.

In terms of the idea of transnationalism and its reliance on notions of embeddedness in two social communities at once the degree of embeddedness aboard may be seen to be insufficient to characterise the experience of being a seafarer as a transnational one. Here rank, nationality, language barriers and occupational culture all serve to limit and constrain integration amongst what are relatively small populations of workers. Seafarers may have relatively few chances of interaction in the first place – interaction being inherently limited by the demands of work, by watchkeeping systems (which mean that some individuals work and eat and sleep according to a different cycle to the rest of the crew) and by the challenges of the environment (noise, motion, etc.). True transnationality might be said to occur where individuals feel they have two homes of similar significance to them. In many cases seafarers do not experience the ship as a home and do not feel integrated into the 'community' of seafarers aboard to a significant extent.

Nevertheless for some seafarers a ship despite being an institutionalised workplace is, of necessity, 'home'. Many reside in such vessels for longer periods than they reside at home in the term of their working lives and some described 'home' as being at sea and on board ship. After a long period of time it is the ship that they become acculturated to and their links ashore gradually become weakened. Transnationalism describes a dual psychological, emotional, and to some extent physical, co-location. Therefore, seafarers who feel disconnected from life ashore back in their home towns and communities may not fit into the category of transnationals either. Aboard all deep-sea vessels the possibilities for connections to be maintained with homes and families while at sea were constrained and limited by company policies and practices, by rank, and by nationality.

Staying in touch with 'home'

Once a vessel leaves a port there are few affordable ways in which seafarers are able to maintain contact with family and friends ashore. In the early years of shipping, communication between seafarers and shore-side communities was severely limited and generally took the form of letters. Today a wider variety of forms of communication are available. Some ships have email facilities available and almost all seafarers rely to a greater, or lesser, extent on mobile telephones in order to communicate with SMS (text) messages and by voice.

Having been largely cut off from the wider world while their vessels are 'deep-sea', one of the major preoccupations for seafarers coming into port is communication with family members and friends. Mobile phones appear in the hands of seafarers all over the vessel and they eagerly await the emergence of the symbols telling them that their phones have picked up a signal. In the early part of the twenty-first century (pre-9/11), once alongside many ships were 'serviced' by salespeople boarding with mobile phones and selling call time to seafarers who were unable to get ashore. Today this is seen less often as most ports have introduced strict security in compliance with the International Ship and Port Facility Security Code (ISPS code) introduced following concerns about terrorism. Thus international politics and regulation have further limited the possibilities for seafarers to communicate with families and have further structured seafarers' social space.

Notwithstanding this change, telephones remain a common vehicle for communication between seafarers and their families and they help them to maintain relationships with children as well as partners. However such telephone communication is generally intermittent and of short duration once initiated. The costs of telephoning from deep-sea (via satellite phone) are prohibitive. Seafarers tend to reserve use of the satellite phone (where they are allowed private access to it) for special occasions (such as birthdays) and emergencies.

Despite the heralding of time-space compression as a result of mass telecommunications and technological advancement, seafarers often do not have access to the quality or quantity of communication that might be anticipated by those of us living ashore. Mail services are slow, telephones expensive, email infrequently available (and often only to particular ranks or nationalities aboard) and satellite communication (often the only option when deep-sea) prohibitively expensive and not always accessible. Private correspondence from vessels is not generally regarded as being available with captains and companies reserving the right to screen and vet mail. Where it is available, email may be even less private, as it is often sent via the captain in daily or twice daily uploads via satellite link. The purchase of a satellite mobile telephone is simply not an option for most individual seafarers – the cost of the handset as well as the calls being prohibitive.

Letters have become something of a rarity as the postal service made available to seafarers (and dependent on the office ashore forwarding mail to agents in the vessel's next port) is very slow and some seafarers complain that the office simply do not bother to regularly forward mail. By the time letters arrive seafarers have normally already had several opportunities to talk with family members and their letters simply repeat what is already known as a result. As Jonathan, the bosun on a bulk carrier explained:

> Right now, since this time, most people telephone call. It's much better. So not writing, but mostly telephone calls. That's why it's a little bit expensive. Letters take 45 days, so the news is already old. (Jonathan – bosun, *Santos Sunset*)

However some seafarers still combine the use of telephone and letters, using letters to fill in the details that there is no time for over the telephone. The advent of cheap telephone communication, including texting services, is widely recognised to have altered practices with regard to communication. Nevertheless the excitement of seafarers on receiving something in the post brought aboard by the ship's agent is palpable. Given the absence of shore-leave this has become the main source of excitement for many seafarers when approaching a port. Roman expressed this feeling thus:

> [approaching a port] I always think about back home. How is your family. You are always thinking back home. Because you feel homesick. What is happening now. We are happy when we receive some letters. Or we talk on the telephone. I think they are the happiest things. (Roman – petty officer, *Eclipse*)

Lenny described how he felt on receiving letters and regretted that they were not always forwarded by companies to seafarers. He told me that:

> A letter is the best medicine to cure your boredom ... I think some of the company – I cannot say all, but some – some companies at every port, they send forward the letters. But I think this company are sometimes not available, and they only forward the letters at a convenient port, like Rotterdam. (Lenny – rating, *Eclipse*)

Furthermore seafarers generally don't use the telephone to communicate with friends with whom long distance calls would seem inappropriate. One explained how this, combined with his very short leave periods, meant that he had lost contact with many friends. It is only those with access to free email on board who really manage to maintain very close links with family members and friends. One seafarer who mostly made use of internet cafés or seafarers' 'houses' ashore to send email described how:

> E-mails go to a lot of people ... Mostly friends and to my home as well, my brother and sisters, whoever logs on. (Sutir, *Calmex*)

Another suggested that while he had access to email, a telephone, and a postal service he communicated infrequently with friends and family at home and was rather at a loss as to what to communicate about. He explained:

> I send a letter once in a while. Actually I don't say so much in it. Not so much happens out here. (Vagn, *Eclipse*)

This feeling that there was nothing to say was echoed by others. One for example described how:

> I only phone my parents, every time we are in San Francisco I call for half an hour, which is every 15–20 days, and I think that is long enough because I don't really have that much to say, I just listen to them really. (Sunit, *Calmex*)

While another drew attention to a practice which is not uncommon amongst seafarers and their partners, which is the limiting of communication to aspects of life which are unlikely to cause seafarers worry or anxiety. In this respect the content of the communication was voluntarily censored rather than restricted in quantity:

> My wife, she is a typical seaman's wife, she knows exactly what to tell me and how to keep me normal without upsetting me. That is very very important. She would never ever ask some stupid questions because I am away. I am not at home. So she is able to manage, that is very very important. (Zigi – officer: *Norwegian Imp*)

A different seafarer expressed the same sorts of feelings as follows:

> Actually, my wife knows about Merchant Navy life, so unless it's something serious, she never inform me. Suppose … my father was die at home, she not inform me. When my contract finish and I go home, then I come to know. Same like my mother die and I was at sea, she not inform me. (Conin – Officer, *Calmex*)

In writing about life at sea in 1973, Mariam Sherar a Professor of Sociology in New York, listed a series of advertisements she had found in publications circulated to seafarers. These contained the following entries:

> Your mother passed away in November. Contact your family or phone …

> Your wife passed away in October. Very important you contact …

> Please call home immediately concerning baby's eye operation.

> Your son Frank, jr. Is getting married on (date) to … He is hopeful that you will be able to attend the wedding. (Sherar 1973: 24)

Clearly the revolution that has subsequently taken place in telecommunications and information technology has dramatically impacted on seafarers' contact with their families and generally speaking, such messages are no longer required or found. Nevertheless the separation that seafarers experienced from loved ones while at sea is significant, and seafarers who are regularly away for long periods of time often feel that their shore-based relationships become increasingly eroded. Telephoning partners from the ship in order to share long conversations is not tenable as a result of access and cost. However, these are not the only constraints. Time differences and claims upon time also come into play. Seafarers cannot rely on being able to talk with their loved ones when off duty and partners cannot necessarily be available at the times when seafarers are able to call. The following field note is illustrative:

> He described how he had phoned home the previous day and his wife was at work. They talked for some time but the hospital where she works was very busy and she had to go before he really wanted her to. He called her back again and once again she had to go to attend to a patient's relatives. He said later in his cabin he kept thinking about wanting to finish the conversation and so he called her again at 03.00 Philippines time. He said she didn't mind but he felt a bit bad because she hadn't got to bed until 01.00. (Sampson field note, *Norwegian Imp*)

Given the scenario described it is easy to see how social relationships may deteriorate over time as isolated partners learn to cope alone and may increasingly resent the intrusion and inconvenience which may be associated with the maintenance of regular contact with their seafarer spouses or boyfriends. One captain explained that he felt that over time seafarers merely became regarded as 'the bank' by their families as they were unable to retain relationships of any quality with partners or children and merely served in the role as breadwinner. This gradually emerged as a rather common experience though not always expressed with such stark cynicism.

Transnationalism and embeddedness

The tests of transnationalism may be multiple but rely on a fundamental premise of social embeddedness across national boundaries. This implies embeddedness in two places at one time. In the case of seafarers, foreign-flagged ships can be construed as extensions of the 'foreign' lands whose flags they fly although they are not much affected by the 'colour' of the flag flown. They are spaces which are occupied nevertheless by a mixture of nationalities and have been previously characterised (Sampson 2003) as the archetypal 'hyperspaces' existing beyond borders in the same way as airports (Kearney 1999b). Foreign-flagged ships can thus be understood to be transborder spaces. However while seafarers occupy these spaces, the superficiality of their social relations on board and their limited connections to others on the vessel suggests that they cannot be considered to be socially embedded in the 'shipboard society'. Few seafarers maintain links with people they have met aboard a vessel once they return home (although I have found evidence of one or two longer-term friendships forged on board) and there are few instances of former shipmates contacting those remaining aboard once they have gone home. Just as rank limits the possibilities for integration aboard, so too does nationality. Rank appears to be the stronger constraint, for example, captains and chief engineers rarely seemed to enjoy easy social relationships with anyone other than each other, whereas cross-nationality friendships and associations are slightly more common. However, nationality can combine with rank in powerful ways to exacerbate social divisions and it can also serve to mediate divisions of rank causing them to be reinterpreted according to divisions in nationality. As a result, the combination of rank and nationality can serve to considerably isolate individuals aboard and act as a force for segregation.

Other factors also serve as barriers to social integration. Foremost amongst these is the occupational culture of seafaring which causes those well-socialised into it to desist from discussing personal issues with others, and also causes them to generally discourage the practice on board. Thus beyond discussions of work and work-related tasks, social conversation is often limited to a range of superficial topics such as sex, company matters and tale telling. Unsurprisingly there are examples where individuals forge deeper friendships aboard and undoubtedly share details of personal lives and worries as well as discussing the range of subjects generally regarded as 'off-limits' such as religion. These are the exception however and as such they represent examples of individuals transcending the limitations of the structured space aboard. This highlights the extent to which the structured nature of space does not prohibit the development of social relations it merely serves to militate against the proliferation of such relationships on board.

In addition to rank, nationality and occupational culture there is evidence that language barriers can arise as a result of a lack on fluency in a shared language on board. The evidence seems to suggest, however, that this particular issue does not serve to divide seafarers strongly and can be overcome. Thus it is primarily rank and nationality that tend to influence the experience of seafarers aboard and to delimit their social interaction and participation. Occupational culture and communication problems are also significant but to a lesser degree. However, it is also apparent that in a few cases seafarers can seemingly transcend all of these factors and forge friendships across nationality and rank of a deeper and more binding nature.

In relation to the other element of transnational lives – the extent to which multi-stranded relationships are maintained ashore – these too are disrupted by factors other than those relating to individual characteristics. Companies control access to mail and letters cannot be relied upon to be entirely private and can be opened by company personnel and in theory (though never witnessed) there was an understanding that captains too could open letters aboard. Email access is determined in many cases by rank aboard (though there are examples of universal access) and sometimes by nationality (Swedish officers aboard the *Eclipse* had access to email while Filipino officers did not) and access to satellite telephones is by permission from the captain. Furthermore in recent times communication with those ashore has been further limited by international regulations as a result of the ISPS code and is also limited in the context of fast vessel turnaround by the provision (or lack of provision) of telephone services in ports.

Thus the possibilities for the emergence of transnationality are limited by structural constraints on physical, social and communicative space both on board and ashore in ports. These are of greater relevance to the emergence of transnationalism than the individual characteristics or orientations of seafarers who were generally speaking (though not universally) quite open to developing socially embedded relationships across borders and with others of different cultures and nationalities. That they were often unable to do so and were also challenged in the maintenance of relationships ashore, seemed to relate more to broader factors beyond their control, which were mediated by rank and nationality and their consequent status in the social hierarchy, than to individual attributes or access to resources – what we might usefully term 'social capital'.

Figure 12 (above): A rating on deck
Figure 13 (below): Deck maintenance

Figure 14 (above): Rigging the gangway
Figure 15 (below): My first ship (left) tied up in Patagonia

Figure 16 (above): Awaiting departure in hot Mexico sun
Figure 17 (below): The North Atlantic on a tanker

8

The transnational household?

The focus of work on migration is often upon the lives of migrants themselves and it is easy to overlook the impact of migration upon the communities, friends and families left behind when workers depart in search of new job opportunities. Yet the impact of migration is considerable on both 'sending' and 'receiving' communities. Communities where large numbers of workers leave for job opportunities elsewhere are required to adapt in order to effectively function. New ways may have to be found for family life to continue undisrupted. When women migrate for jobs as nurses, entertainers, and nannies, men may find themselves undertaking roles which are not traditionally allocated to them (taking the lead in child-rearing, cleaning, cooking, for example). Similarly, women may adopt new family roles with the departure of men. Grandparents too may play a part when their children call upon them for help, and greater reliance may be generally placed upon the extended family in supporting families where one or both parents have left to benefit from employment opportunities elsewhere.

As communities adjust to the long absences of adults of working age so too may they become increasingly reliant on the remittances sent home by migrant workers. In many communities in India where migrant work is commonplace it is relatively easy to spot the large houses of affluent 'contract' workers who often make the purchase or development of a new home their first spending priority. However, the financial dimension of migration has yet greater significance with remittances providing capital for new business ventures and money to support education, healthcare and more general community events and concerns, such as religious activities and festivals.

Having considered the possibilities for transnationalism amongst transmigrant seafarers passing through, and temporarily residing in, North Germany (Chapter 4), and those residing and working aboard ships (Chapters 5, 6 and 7) it is therefore worth turning attention to seafarer families in order to reflect upon the possibilities for people indirectly associated with migrants to become transnational to some extent themselves. Here the idea of a transnational social field (Crang, Dwyer and Jackson 2003) is relevant and the potential for such fields is explored in conjunction with the testimony offered by seafarer wives (and occasionally children). This testimony also facilitates further consideration of the extent to which seafarers themselves genuinely reside in two co-locations, living lives which are embedded in two places in a meaningful sense while they actively engage in seafaring.

In India, the predominant cultures strongly delineate gender roles and family responsibilities and thus the prolonged absence of male members of the household may have particular significance. Furthermore, the occupation brings seafarers, working aboard foreign-flagged ships, into contact with a range of other cultures giving rise to the possibility that such exposure may impact upon their own values and norms and thus on their expectations of their families and domestic roles and responsibilities. Seafarers' partners in India are particularly interesting when considering the idea of the transnational social field as they frequently have the opportunity to join ships with their spouses and sail themselves (unusually regardless of rank in some companies) bringing them into direct contact with the multinational 'community' found aboard many foreign-flagged vessels and making transborder space more directly accessible to them than to other, less mobile, seafarers' partners. These facets of the lives of seafarers and their partners give rise to interesting questions about the impact of workers' involvement in global labour markets on local relations, domestic settings and specific communities. In the context of shipping, and seafaring, the question can be couched in terms of the impact of economic globalisation on local cultures and transnationality.

There are many negative aspects to both economic globalisation and engagement in a labour market that necessitates prolonged absences from home. These have been discussed here (see earlier chapters) and elsewhere (Banuri and Schor 1992, Thomas, Sampson, Zhao 2003, Thomas 2003, Neyzi 2004). Surprisingly, however, the experiences of Indian seafarers' partners suggest that there may also be positive consequences resulting from these circumstances and from involvement in international labour markets and multinational work settings. The positive effects of globalisation have sometimes been touched upon by researchers focusing on elite groups of workers employed in globalised sectors such as banking and finance, and building design (Beaverstock and Smith 1996, Kennedy 2004) but they have rarely been considered in relation to the less glamorous end of the employment spectrum, and more particularly in relation to *families or partners*. Where indirect links between family life and economic globalisation have been of interest to sociologists, research has tended to focus on transnational rituals and ceremonies, such as those attending marriage, deaths and religious rites of passage, for example circumcision, (Fog-Olwig 2002, Mand 2002, Salih 2002, Sutton 2004, Voigt-Graf 2004) and in general the impact of economic globalisation and of transnationalism on the detail of family life remains under-explored (Gardner and Grillo 2002).

The social and economic contexts of Mumbai and Goa

The contexts in which women lived in Goa and Mumbai differed enormously. Mumbai is a modern city 'hosting' a number of 'resident' multinational companies.

It acts as a magnet to a diverse range of artists and within this relatively liberal cultural, and economically prosperous, context it can offer residents a freedom from informal social control that is not widespread across India. However many people are far removed from the cosmopolitan lifestyle of some of the city's modern urbanites and live in severe poverty. The population of Mumbai is significantly skewed having the highest number of slum dwellers of any city in India. In 2001 there were 5,823,510 slum dwellers reportedly resident in Greater Mumbai.[1]

A number of shipping companies locate their main offices in Mumbai or run crewing operations there. It is therefore a convenient base for seafarers and many officers[2] can be found scattered across the city. They tend to live in relatively expensive apartment blocks protected by security guards. Nevertheless these apartments tend to be small and sparsely furnished. One family lived in two non-air conditioned rooms in a security protected block. A field note records that:

> [The family] lives in a two room apartment (non-air conditioned) in a building which is one of several forming an 'enclave' with security at the gate. Kids play in communal playgrounds attached to each building … Furniture etc. was very sparse but they had a new looking TV etc. Not really very luxurious … (Sampson field notes, 2000)

This apartment was very similar to others in Mumbai where the quality of life seemed less good in general than for those seafarers (of equivalent rank) and their partners living in Goa.

Goa is a very small State which feels very rural in comparison to the bustle of the city of Mumbai. It too has attracted a number of multinational companies and specifically to a location known locally as 'silicon valley' predictably specialising in computer-related products. It seems that many Goans see themselves as different to other Indians and this seems to partly result from the local history, and Portuguese influence, and partly from higher levels of affluence and better infrastructure in Goa than found elsewhere. The toughest jobs in Goa (road building, rice planting and brick-making out in the hot sun, for example) are generally done by regional migrants from states such as Kerala. Despite its green and rural feel the population is divided almost equally between those resident in rural areas (50.2%) and those resident in urban areas (49.7 per cent).[3] Many people speak Portuguese and excellent English. This is a result of the region's Catholic influence and the number of convent schools that use English as the medium of instruction.

The relative affluence of Goa has been established as a result of the relatively high proportions of men who have earned dollars working for foreign shipping companies or alternatively for companies based in the Gulf States and this kind of 'migrant contract' work is held to be commonplace. In Goa seafarer families live in different contexts according to their rank. The families of ratings and petty officers tend to live in villages in the southern parts of the state and are the most likely, of all the participants, to live in so-called 'joint households'. Their circumstances range from the relatively affluent, where seafarers have enjoyed considerable continuity of employment, to relative impoverishment where seafarers are constantly faced with long periods of unemployment. In the home of a regularly employed steward[4] and his family one might be impressed by the splendour of the light airy house and the large rooms furnished with locally produced carved wooden furniture lending a grand air to the place. A field note records details of such a home and the pride in it felt by the residents:

> They live in a very nice house – nice furniture, big rooms, solid wood double beds, carved doors and carved banisters. The family name was Smith[5] and they had named their house 'Smith's Castle'. (Sampson field note, 2000)

Not all lower-ranking seafarers (ratings) could afford such investments however and the house of a family in different circumstances was probably more typical of the living arrangements for ratings. The house was smaller and meagrely furnished with plastic chairs and tables replacing the carved wood of the Smiths. The walls had not been painted for some time and the children had scribbled over them in crayon. The house was situated amongst others in a small village settlement and was surrounded by little land. Nevertheless this house compared very favourably to others owned by non-seafarers.

Officers and their families tend to live in large houses in the northern part of Goa and sometimes in airy apartments or in housing developments referred to as 'colonies'. These 'colonies' share some of the features of the housing developments in Mumbai but with less emphasis on security, and with more spacious design. Officers in Goa enjoy a somewhat lavish lifestyle and frequently have the assistance of a variety of employees in the maintenance of their homes and gardens. Their houses are generally characterised by marble-clad bathrooms, manicured gardens and an array of staff. This contrasts starkly with the situation of most officers resident in Mumbai.

A strong similarity in the lifestyles of Goans and residents of Mumbai was apparent, however, when considering the importance of the family and family bonds and obligations. Across India a pattern of 'joint family' households is traditional and reportedly remains relatively commonplace. When women marry they generally reside with the family of their husbands and play a lesser role in the lives of their own parents and siblings. This model can work very advantageously as women cooperate in undertaking demanding, and labour-intensive, domestic chores and child care. Joint families can also provide newly married women with important sources of support and succour particularly if their husbands are absent. However, such arrangements can bring with them complications, stresses and sometimes unhappiness and abuse (Bumiller 1991, Kapadia 1995, Lahiri-Dutt and Samanta 2002, Voigt-Graf 2004). In unforeseen ways, the issue of family living arrangements was one that emerged as central to the concerns and experiences of many of the women I talked with in India.

Adapting to life as a seafarer's partner

Gender roles are relatively strongly demarcated in India as compared with Europe or the Philippines which is where many of the seafarers working alongside

Indian seafarers come from. As such the interpretation and/or reinterpretation of gender norms, expectations and attitudes is likely to shed some light on the extent to which seafarers and seafarers' partners respond to exposure to other 'foreign' cultural attitudes, values and beliefs. Such analysis is complicated, however, by the fact that the very absence of a male partner gives rise to changes in behaviour amongst women ashore who often have no choice but to learn to manage for themselves.

As with seafarers' families in the UK (Thomas 2003) most seafarers' wives in India have learned to become more independent as a result of their husbands' absences and are used to shouldering the burden of responsibilities while their husbands are at sea. They have learned to manage finances, deal with mechanics, electricians and plumbers, change light bulbs, pay bills, negotiate with bank managers, and generally undertake a whole range of what are traditionally masculine roles. However what is of particular interest in this context is how they adjust in relation to their husbands' returns and how they present themselves in relation to their public personas both in the absence, and the presence, of their husbands (all partners were married and co-habitation was not prevalent as a pattern).

The experiences and behaviours of women inevitably varied considerably. While some reverted to their 'feminine' role once their husbands returned home on leave, many others explained that they were unable to do so, or chose not to do so. Regardless of their response to their husbands' return, all women living independently from their in-laws described lives in which their social networks and contact with the outside world had expanded as a result of establishing single-family households. Nevertheless many said that they remained conscious of the continued pressure from their communities to conform to traditional gender roles. Many women who remained under the close surveillance of their partners' families maintained public images which conformed to strict notions of appropriate behaviour for married women in the absence of a partner.

In contrast to this public front however, which emphasised the apparent helplessness or insignificance of women, restricting them to the domestic domain of the housewife, many women felt that they were capable of doing 'anything' now that they had learned to manage independently in their husband's absence. Suki, for example, described how:

> I compare myself to my family, my sisters, that they still depend on their husband. Which I don't, I can just get out, do anything on my own, so it makes a real difference (Suki – Indian seafarer's partner)

Christine also saw big differences in herself and these were evidently plain to her relatives who, in her case, approved and had apparently taken to citing her as a role model. She recounted how:

> Yes they approve. Nothing wrong in it. In fact they encourage more of their people to be like us. My sister they say to her 'she can stay alone with two children, why can't you stay? Why do you need all the family support? She has also gone to a new place with small children, with a husband sailing, not knowing

anybody around. She has managed, why can't you?!' (Christine, Indian seafarer's partner)

Although women often described feeling capable of anything it transpired that many chose to deliberately present a different image to their husbands and/or the outside world. Some women felt that their independence posed a threat to the identity of men as 'heads of households' and even as useful members of the family. This is not a syndrome that is peculiar to India and it has also been identified as a feature of seafarer family life in the UK (Thomas, Sampson and Zhao 2003, Thomas 2003). In India, however, it seemed that the challenge to gender roles was experienced more strongly as there was a much more clearly segregated understanding of gender roles and their meanings. Women suggested that in modern India they are (still) encouraged to submit to their husbands' authority and often to 'adjust' to living with their husbands' families whatever the circumstances. It was clear that for most women their understandings of what it was to be a 'man' led them to generally support such notions even when their own self-development (in terms of expertise, confidence, competence etc.) made such submission personally problematic. One very organised and independent woman who described taking on a whole variety of household tasks in her partner's absence described how she felt this had compromised her partner's role in the household. She explained:

> Certain things which I would not have looked into otherwise, I have learned to look into also. In fact I will tune up the car before his arrival, so that he doesn't have to bother with it. By now I have got so used to doing things on my own that sometimes I must forget he is around and that he can do it. I know if I can open it, I go ahead and get it done. Don't wait for him. He tells me 'you don't need me at home at all!' When we are at the bank, because I am used to doing everything, I just go ahead to the counter, do whatever has to be done. He is with me but he is just standing. And sometimes if he is angry, or in a good mood but just teasing me, or speaking to my mum, he says 'your daughter doesn't need me actually. I am just here, she doesn't need me for anything, she can handle all things on her own'. (Olivia, Indian seafarer's partner)

Her partner's reported response to her independence suggests that there is a feeling amongst some seafarers that they are less embedded in not just their communities but also their families as a consequence of their regular absences. In this instance Olivia's husband appeared to feel marginalised and there were other reports of husbands feeling somewhat disengaged from their spouses. Another very competent woman, Suki, joked that:

> Now he says that I am so independent, at times he gets afraid about it. He calls me a 'monster' like I changed ... (Suki, Indian seafarer's partner)

The accounts of several women suggested that not only could they manage perfectly adequately while their husbands were away but that they found the return of their partners difficult to adjust to. Some seafarers who had returned home 'on leave' were seen by their partners to be in the way, and a nuisance, on their return from sea. For families which had adjusted to new rhythms of daily life the sudden return of a husband could feel like 'interference', as this extended quote from Gina demonstrates:

> I am more distant in a way … Maybe if he was around, you'd be leaning on his shoulder more often. I am very independent. Many times he tries to do things, I tell him, 'Keep out of my kitchen, you just keep an eye on the kids or something.' You don't want him there. He says, 'I am here to help you out.' But independence is there. So you tell them, 'Hang on, I'll manage.' And that gets to them too. These guys have come down, and we tell them we can manage, so it's 'So you don't need us around.' I think it's part and parcel. Automatically after a month you kind of settle down, and you accept them poking their nose in here, and touching this and interfering there. Then they go, and you feel like the ground under your feet has slipped off. You get back to normal … It's nice, when he's around, and you can depend on him. But I find the seafarers get more irritable as the months go by, they tend to – well, the wife doesn't always have time for them, the kids get in their hair. I think it gets to them, they want to go back within three months, that's what I normally feel. And they get in your hair sometimes … Sometimes I say, 'I think three months leave is enough for you guys, after that you start eating our heads, please go back!' They say, 'Look at you wives. We're away for eight months, and then after three months you want to chase us back.' I say, 'I think we need a break, and so do you guys.' … Because you are so independent, and you're doing it for eight months, especially regarding things in the house. And the kids. We get set in our ways. So it gets to you, you get a little angry at times. 'I've done it and it's been peaceful all this time, and now you come and change it.' And he says, 'I'm just telling you, you don't have to change it.' But just the thought of him telling me, I think he feels it's wrong, that's how he's seeing it. Misunderstandings do take place. But it's all part and parcel …
> (Gina, Indian seafarer's partner)

As a result of their sensitivity to this sense of 'disengagement' and loss of role some women described how they took steps to try to ensure that their partners felt valued in the household. They talked about 'pampering' them and making them feel 'special'. Christine, for example, described how on a seafarer's return:

> You have to readjust your routine when they come back. You have to give them a little more time, a little pampering, make them feel wanted. They all want that. Over the years you realise that. So you have to cut all your social outings which have been going on over those months. The time has been your own, and when they come little adjustments have to be made … sometimes you have to pretend, sometimes it is genuine. But then to keep the peace in the house, over the years, you learn to do these things. That's what I feel, they want to feel wanted, they want to feel important when they come back from the ship to the family … They have been away for long stretches, when they come back they want that attention. So it's better to give it to them [laughs] … I do feel that when they come back, a little juggling has to be done, for the time being. To do the food that they like, give them the attention. (Christine, Indian seafarer's partner)

These kinds of accounts were repeated in different ways by several women in Goa and Mumbai. They highlight the problems encountered by seafarers in reintegrating into family life and the community after long periods at sea. Such was their feeling of marginalisation that seafarers themselves made direct reference to a phenomenon whereby they saw themselves and their colleagues as merely becoming the family 'bank': the 'cash cow' to be milked by many relatives in extended families (see Chapter 7).

Seafarers' partners did, at times, discuss and highlight an independence which was described as unavailable to women married to shore-based workers in India. However, in many cases, this independence was restricted to the periods of time when their partners were absent, and a number of women actually faced severe restriction when their partners returned. Not only were partners not working and therefore present in households for much of the time that they were on leave, some also seemed to react to their temporarily absent status by being particularly restrictive and jealous of their wives once they came home. This created a paradoxical situation in some cases where women married to seafarers were both freer and yet more constrained than other women in the community; freer to do as they chose while partners were absent but under their constant surveillance and restriction upon their return. While nobody acknowledged it in so many words several women seemed relieved when their husbands' periods of leave came to an end. This implies that it was the absence of partners which significantly impacted upon the wives of seafarers in India rather than a change in partners' values or attitudes. Indeed some seafarers' partners seemed to experience stronger restraint exercised by their partners rather than 'liberation' as a consequence of their partners' engagement in seafaring. Thus some accounts of life with their husbands resonated with domination and were sometimes even suggestive of hidden violence. One young woman (Esther) talked about the way she had tried to change after her marriage to conform with her husband's expectations. While she talked sadly of her circumstances she also wanted to convey that she felt that she had previously been wayward in her behaviour and that her decision to police herself and constrain her activities was quite 'proper', and to be silently applauded, even while it seemed to make her extremely unhappy. This account, and several like it, seem to indicate that the different gender roles observed by seafarers while working abroad and aboard (some will have even sailed with women seafarers) leave some of them quite untouched or may even encourage them to seek stronger observance of traditional Indian gender roles and norms when back at home with their own families. It is possible that exposure to alternative views of the 'place' of women may be experienced as threatening by some men who work all the harder to retain traditional conservative values in their own households. Describing the periods of time when her husband was at home Esther said:

> Mostly we are alone in the house, and without me he never goes out also. He is always with me, market, buying anything or to anybody's house he is with me ... [He gets angry about] misbehaviour. He doesn't want me to go out. When he is in the house he wants me in the house. Or if I go somewhere else, it makes him

angry. Other things like, if he doesn't get them in order then he shouts ... I don't like it to happen but sometimes it happens. Most of the time I avoid arguments. Arguments make life very difficult. Especially my husband he gets angry very soon. I know him very well! From the beginning. So I am very careful. I get very scared of him. (Esther, Indian seafarer's partner)

While other women did not talk so openly of being afraid of angering their partners they nevertheless described how they 'managed' their activities when their partners were around curtailing regular activities with friends and even risking friendships in the process. One explained that:

I have to re-schedule all my routine because when I know he is not here I am a little bit free. I don't have to be home when he comes back from the office ... and when he is back [from sea], I find friends getting very upset. 'Your husband is here now we can't do this we can't do that!' (Olivia, Indian seafarer's partner)

Many women seemed to struggle with frankly discussing their domestic situations in relation to their own household roles, and that of their partners. In particular they seemed reluctant to voice discontent even where they hinted strongly at its presence. This contrasted both with the frankness with which they were willing to discuss other aspects of their lives as seafarers' partners (for example fidelity) and with the success of others in interviewing wives about personal, and relatively intimate, issues in European societies (Finch 1993, Dunscombe and Marsden 1996, Thomas 2003). It seemed to be particularly important to many seafarers' partners to maintain a public front of domestic harmony and this may well have reflected a notion that family strife or discord is something for which they, as women, would be to blame. Children also seemed complicit in promoting an image of 'happy families' free from any strife. In the course of one interview a very gentle woman's daughter (Mona) repeatedly spoke in her mother's place constantly attempting to project an image of her mother and father as a devoted couple, something which did not come across very strongly from her mother's account. At one point in the interview when I asked her mother (Monica) whether she and her husband tended to have conflicts and if so what about she intervened in the following way:

Monica: Sometimes he tells me he is going for the weddings or dancings ... he tells me ... [interrupted by daughter]
Mona: What she means is my Daddy says sometimes on the ship when they have a chance to go to parties. She knows her husband is not doing anything bad. If he was doing anything bad he would not have told her. But she says 'why do you have to go there? Why do you do this?'
Monica: Otherwise [if he was doing something 'bad'] he would not tell me. He is good [laughs hollowly].
(Monica and Mona, Indian seafarer's partner and daughter)

These efforts to project a positive image of matrimonial and familial relations may account for the fact that in describing their domestic roles women often said their husbands were helpful in the house and shared household tasks while the evidence of their detailed descriptions seemed to suggest otherwise. On some occasions accounts were supported with examples of practical aid, but there were many times when the impression that was given was that men would, at best, keep their partners company while they cooked or cleaned, perhaps lending the occasional hand by fetching and carrying or even helping with food preparation. However, they rarely seemed to take primary responsibility for household tasks although occasionally some men undertook the 'marketing' (grocery shopping) and some women told me that their partners regularly took the children to school. There were also a number of women, without any domestic help, whose husbands did not help with household chores at all during their vacations. In many houses it was the women who prepared food (except where they had paid help) and often they would not sit down to eat with their husbands, children, and guests. Exceptions to this were found and they seemed to sometimes (but not exclusively) relate to experiences of partners sailing together.

While there was quite a range of domestic arrangements, and despite the fact that the involvement of men in the household was very limited, on balance it did seem that seafarers generally shouldered more of the responsibility for household work, when they were home, than most local men. An example was provided by Susanna, a fitter's[6] wife living in a 'joint household' with her mother-in-law. She described her marriage as a 'love match' and she had a good government job as a bookkeeper. While in many respects she seemed to live quite a traditional lifestyle, going to work but never socialising while her husband was away, she also described him as a tremendous support and help while he was home on vacation and she was going out to work. She explained:

> He [her own husband] is very helpful when he is at home …Even at home he helps me, cooking also and taking the children's lessons also. Everything, he does everything…He gets up at 5.30. My children … at 7 o'clock … Sometimes he makes chapattis also. He helps a lot … [when he is away] I also get up at 5.30. Then I make everything ready for them [the children]. Then I wake them up and take them to the bathroom. When he is not here I have to do it … To make chapattis it takes a lot of time! (Susanna, Indian seafarer's partner)

Despite such exceptional accounts of direct involvement in cooking and 'everything' it seemed that where men did help in the house they were more usually involved in tasks directly relating to the care and discipline of children, financial matters, grocery shopping, and practical maintenance. Disputes between husbands and wives were rarely said to be anything other than trivial and were most likely to relate to the discipline of children. There was no obvious difference between the reported helpfulness of ratings and petty officers and the reported helpfulness of officers, on the domestic front, despite the fact that ratings and their families were much more likely to be living with 'joint family' arrangements than officers and that many officers' families paid for domestic assistance.

Across the range of domestic circumstances represented, some families still lived in a style which they recognised as traditional and which resonates with the accounts of women's lives presented by authors such as Bumiller (1991) and Lahiri-Dutt and Samanta (2002). However, others had negotiated different house-hold divisions of labour which incorporated more significant contributions from male partners during their time at home. The independence they had acquired as-sisted some women in being assertive in their households and insisting that their partners made a contribution. One woman, Claire, was married to a chief cook.[7] She described how in the early days of their marriage her husband had been most unwilling to lend a hand during his vacations. Despite the fact that it was difficult for her to argue with him in the joint household in which they lived with his parents she insisted that he do more to help and in the end her will prevailed. She told me:

> When he comes home he likes to rest. I tell him I also want rest. Sometimes he does the cooking, when he's in the mood, and the children love it. He's a good cook ... [In the beginning when the kids were young] I had to feed the children, and do the cooking, and then he's also at home ... we used to argue. I said 'Why should I do all the cooking, and look after them, you do a little bit of my work'. At first he wouldn't ... then I used to find it very difficult. Then after a time he did. (Claire, Indian seafarer's partner)

As well as identifying some differences in their private behaviour (which could be attributed to their connection with seafaring) some couples also identified dif-ferences in their attitudes to behaviour in public settings. An interesting example of this related to alcohol consumption.

Attitudes to alcohol consumption varied in Goa and Mumbai. Many people in India do not approve of alcohol consumption at all and are tee total while others think that it is unseemly for women to consume alcohol, particularly in public. Such is the strength of this view that it can feel uncomfortable for a female 'out-sider' to drink alcohol at some social gatherings.

Thus in some settings (often where husbands were present) the pressure for women not to drink alcohol was immense while in others, groups of women (of-ten without their husbands) felt able to surreptitiously drink beer. However some seafarers described a relaxed attitude to alcohol and often in these cases so, too, did their partners. This was especially true of officers' wives who had often sailed with their partners aboard ships with multinational crews in the company of men and women who openly consumed alcohol. Vera laughed as she described how her husband's attitude to alcohol initially worried her but only until she took to drinking with him:

> It used to worry me when he used to drink, but then I felt if you can't beat them, then join them. So I also have a drink with him. I drink rum, gin, vodka, and he drinks only beer. I used to drink beer before, but I found it very fattening, so stopped ... we go out and have a drink and smoke ... When he comes home he brings me a carton every time ... At one time he had a pancreas problem so he had to stop drinking. He stopped for about ten years but he never stopped smoking. (Vera, Indian seafarer's partner)

While some seafarers' partners seemed to feel free to engage in marginally deviant social behaviours (such as drinking alcohol) with their husbands and sometimes in public, with and without husbands, others by contrast seemed particularly concerned to behave in socially exemplary ways when their husbands were away. It seemed as if the awareness amongst them that they may be viewed with suspicion by the local community (they were conscious both of the reputation of seafarers and threats to their own reputation given the prevalence of gossip), countered any influence that might otherwise have arisen from being in direct or indirect contact with alternative views about gender roles and norms. In discussion of the image of seafarers, women were particularly conscious of issues of promiscuity and this seemed to rub off on them and promote a desire to develop a particularly squeaky clean image. Serena, for example, explained that:

> Some people here in Goa, you know they have this low mentality because you are a sailor's wife 'they must be having wives in every port' you know, that kind of attitude. (Serena, Indian seafarer's partner)

While another suggested:

> Some [people] had misconceptions, like a seafarer had a girl in every port and they are not good character and so on…This happens with other professions also. Only the seafarer's profession is much talked about. I think in other professions too there are people who get away with all these things – bad character and womanising and everything – but nobody talks about it. But for seafarers they all talk about it openly…Of course when you are just married and not known your husband for long, so it does worry you – that they may have relation with somebody. Of course!…I used to talk with him but he had trust with me, and I had trust in him, and we belonged to good families, so it was never thought that they would indulge in such a thing. (Christine, Indian seafarer's partner)

Changes in outlook: the indirect impact of economic globalisation

There is little doubt that seafaring often had both a positive and a negative impact on the lives of many seafarers' partners. In terms of their direct living arrangements this duality was clearly revealed, for example in relation to social freedoms and restrictions as already discussed. It was also revealed in other ways. For example, where they lived in joint families, the jobs of their husbands often meant that early in their married lives women were left 'alone' (without their husband) in a family of people who were strangers to them. As a result, those in unhappy joint families felt particularly lonely and isolated while their husbands were at sea. On the other hand seafaring had a positive effect on the lives of many women in freeing them (often later in the course of their married lives) from these same traditional living arrangements in joint households, and possibly making seafarers more open to the idea of single-family households having been exposed to the idea of them at sea when discussing family life with friends and colleagues. It was only the relatively high earnings of officers, petty officers and ratings in stable employment, that enabled them to set up new and separate households with their spouses and children without abandoning the care and support of their parents and siblings. The issue of joint, or single, family life was one that emerged as central to the experiences of the women I met with. While many women were understandably, but visibly, reticent in their public criticisms of members of their wider kinship networks, those living in single-family units invariably expressed pleasure and relief at having a 'place' of their own. It remained unclear whether this was a result of any external cultural influence or a reaction to the issues arising from partner absences. The following comment from Susheela, who was married to a chief cook, is illustrative of the particular issues faced by seafarers' partners marrying into joint households and the relief many felt on being able to leave them. In describing the early years of her arranged marriage while her husband spent many months at sea Susheela said:

> I was with another family, alone. I didn't know them properly. I felt quite off-weather [off colour/under the weather] having no one to talk to, to talk confidentially with. At least when he was there at home I could adjust myself in the house. It was a new house altogether. It was really tough ... we were all together, joint family, all of them...I was pleased to get my place. There were too many. My children and their children were growing up, they fight, and then something happens and the parents argue. It is really tough. (Susheela, Indian seafarer's partner)

Once she had moved into her own home she, and others, described a strong sense of self-reliance and independence. They felt liberated as a result of managing independently in their husbands' absences.

Most foreign companies operating in the Indian labour market allowed officers' wives to sail with them. As such, it was common for officers' wives and even for some wives of ratings to have experienced life on board ship. For most, this was an extremely pleasurable experience which served to broaden their outlook and to give them a better understanding of the work of their partners. On board they were overwhelmingly welcomed by seafarers who generally escorted them ashore if their husbands were busy, and might dance with them, tease them, and generally treat them as part of the 'family'. One woman had some very funny accounts of her first experience on board a vessel as a newly married woman. She had no idea of what to expect on a ship and she was a gullible target for the seafarers' humour. She described a variety of incidents but the one which made me laugh the most related to having her leg pulled about the electricity bill on board (ships generate their own electricity and are clearly not connected to a grid). She explained how:

> I remember once – I used to get scared in the night, initially when I first joined the ship ... and I got scared. So I would sleep with all the lights on. My husband said, 'Why did you keep all the lights on?' ... After some days, we were just sitting in the smoke room, all the officers, and they were talking about the very big

electric bill, so many dollars, they printed it out, and they gave it to me! I was newly married. I was so scared! So then I closed down all the lights, except the toilet light, I kept it on … 'Why did you put off all the lights?' I said, 'They gave me the electricity bill.' He said, 'It doesn't matter.' … I was so happy he spoke like that. After that, the radio officer came and said they were just fooling. I never knew that. I didn't know anything about the shipping line. It was new to me.

There was a lifebuoy, and I asked one, 'What is that?' It was the third officer, working there. And all of them were standing there. Even the captain. It was the first time I joined, everything was new to me. And they knew that. So I asked him, and they said, 'It is a lifebuoy.' So I said, 'What does that mean?' They said, 'It's a big soap for washing the ship with.' And I said, 'It's hard, how can you wash it with that?' They all laughed. Sometimes they used to make a fool of me like that, I didn't know anything. I was new! (Angela, Indian seafarer's partner)

Women who had sailed described visiting different ports in different parts of the world, meeting people from different regions and sampling different foods, local customs, and cultures. For Suki the idea of travel was a major attraction of marrying a seafarer and she clearly enjoyed her sea-time, she explained:

My vision was always to go abroad. I wanted to join the airlines, that also my father didn't let me. So then I got this [proposal of marriage] … we got married in September, December he joined, about ten days after that I joined him … first trip was enjoyable, because it was our honeymoon but he was so busy because he just got his masters [captain's position], and the trip was just around India, from Calcutta … then we changed the ship then went up to Italy, and Singapore and it was good. And then one lady joined us and it was a smaller ship, better ship, so it was nice … we have parties so that's the time when so many people, all of us, especially [at] big parties, barbecues … all of us like dance around together or whatever … it is no problem thought … it sort of becomes like a family because you are all the time together … (Suki, Indian seafarer's partner)

These experiences often impacted greatly on the women who had sailed with their husbands and especially in mixed-nationality crews and on internationally trading vessels. They described becoming more open-minded and developing a broader outlook on life, in short becoming more cosmopolitan (Hannerz 1990, Holton 2002) as a result of their experiences. Suki, for example, noted that:

I saw the world differently. Like in India it is totally different. Then you meet different kind of people, their cultural difference from us, so it was really good. You know what India is, so when you see places you feel totally different. It widened my horizons. So it made me think differently. (Suki, Indian seafarer's partner)

Christine described how one of the compensations of being married to a seafarer related to travel opportunities for both her and her children which she regarded as highly educational:

You get to travel around a lot which I feel in other jobs you may not be able to do. The children also get to travel, to learn many things, which in other jobs the families are not so lucky … It has broadened my outlook. We belong to families that were not exposed to much, just the house, the family, the town we lived in. We had not travelled around much. So travelling of course broadens your outlook, you learn many things … Until the time we had got married, we had not travelled out from the city, so we did not know how to go about it. Though we were educated, we didn't have much confidence. But now I feel I could go anywhere. I don't need anybody. I can find my way around, I can take things on myself, I can manage things. Which we could not do before with the upbringing we had. (Christine, Indian seafarer's partner)

It was curious that while women readily acknowledged that *they* had changed and become more 'broadminded' as a result of the chosen career of their partners they were sometimes less quick to suggest that seafaring had changed their partners or made them different to their shore-based peers. This reluctance was not universal however and some suggested their husbands' perspective on life was different as a result of their careers. Suki, for example, exclaimed that:

It's [the seafarers' perspective] totally different … Because they see the world differently compared with shore-based. People who are ashore they hardly, they are always are in here [India]. Their life is totally different compared to them. (Suki, Indian seafarer's partner)

Where they were initially reluctant to recognise difference, on better acquaintance and reflection, it was quite common for some women to suggest that their husbands were relatively broad minded in comparison with other men in the community. The following comments are illustrative:

He [my husband] is more broad-minded. Because I have seen many…they won't allow their wives to talk to others or to go alone to functions and all, I have seen many. Many of my friends also, their husbands are also like that. (Caroline, Indian seafarer's partner)

He is very open towards things and more broad minded and of course you can talk about anything. Some women are scared to tell their husbands because maybe they may get angry, but it is different with me. (Serena, Indian seafarer's partner)

He was quite broad-minded, you know, in the beginning. But I think travelling of course broadens your outlook. Women also, he thought they should be given all liberties and privileges in life that men are getting. It broadens the outlook. (Christine, Indian seafarer's partner)

There were also some specific examples of learned ideas, habits, or behaviours that seafarers' partners attributed to their mixing with other nationalities and these were usually regarded in a positive light. Monica, a steward's wife, and Mona, her daughter, talked about some of the things Michael (husband/father) had said about working with other nationalities and in other countries and what he had seen and done. They became quite animated as they described how:

[Mona] He always says that when you move around you come across many different people, and you get some ideas. It's very good to mix with people. You can adjust to the situation. He always feels that. He says it is good to meet with people [Monica] He learns Portuguese songs ... [Mona] He tells us about foreign decorations [the conversation took place just before Christmas]. In Goa we do the decorations only during Christmas but he says in foreign countries one month before they do the decorations. He tells us that. In Goa we do it only two days beforehand. In foreign countries it is one month before ... he tells us about that, the decorations, and when they have parties on the boat he says the decorations are there. He shows us. It's something we don't know about, ideas, foreign countries. He tells us what it is. He says Singapore is a very nice place. He would like to take us to Singapore and good shopping there. (Mona and Monica, Indian seafarer's daughter and wife)

Others described their partners' different tastes in food. Susanna, for example, described how her husband, who was a fitter and nothing to do with catering on board ship, had learned to cook 'foreign' dishes and how at home he would make:

Mushroom soup! I like that. He used to make it on the ship. The cook showed him how to do things, and asparagus, and chicken soup also. I like the mushroom soup. I don't like the chicken or asparagus! (Susanna, Indian seafarer's partner)

It was ultimately apparent that seafarers *were* regarded as more open to difference, more open to strangers, and more 'broad-minded', than non-seafarers and non-seafarer households. Christine, who was born in the same town as her husband in Kashmir described the contrast she had identified on returning back to her original community between her immediate and her extended family. A difference that she felt was apparent to all. She explained:

In certain respects I feel I have moved on. But then when you are with them [in Kashmir] you behave as one of them. But then you feel you have moved ahead of them because they are still a closed community, the thinking is the same. Whereas we have moved out and travelled, and our outlook has changed. We feel different ... They notice we have become more independent, more confident ... all those things they do notice. (Christine, Indian seafarer's partner)

This sense of independence and confidence has been reported elsewhere in connection with migration and people's experiences of surviving in challenging social environments away from all of their traditional networks of support, away from family and from friends. Morawska reports, for example, that women migrants from Poland to the USA reported more 'autonomy and self assurance' (Morawska 2004: 1381). One of her interviewees echoing very closely the sentiments of several of the women interviewed in India explained that she:

... became here more ... daring ... I am not afraid of new situations as before; I believe I could now cope in any country. (Morawska 2004: 1381)

Transnational lives by association?

In a very fundamental way the lives of seafarers' wives differed markedly from those of many other women married to shore-based (non-migrant) workers in India. Like their UK counterparts (Thomas et al 2003) the absence of their partners for long periods of time ensured that they learnt to cope with the demands of daily family life alone and to shoulder the burden of responsibility for the care and welfare of their children. This in itself caused shifts in domestic relationships and altered the pattern of the domestic division of labour upon a seafarer's return. Where seafarers' wives had set up single-family households and had moved away from a life shared with their husbands' relatives there appeared to have been much scope for them to become highly independent and to live fairly non-traditionally as women within the community. However, the response of some seafarers to their own frequent absences and perhaps to their exposure to alternative gender norms in other cultures seemed to be highly defensive and very constraining in relation to the social space they allowed to their partners. Some seafarers' partners were highly restricted in their daily lives and activities and some seafarers expected very traditional arrangements to be in place in relation to the domestic division of labour when they returned home.

There were some examples of women who identified change in their lives as directly associated with the transnational connections of their husbands and indeed the connections that they themselves may have been exposed to, as a result of having sailed with their husbands. However these women were in a minority and it is very difficult to infer from the data that association with transborder seafarers had impacted significantly on the majority of women. Changes where they were identified were relatively small – changes in food tastes, in habits (such as drinking/smoking), in attitudes to domestic labour. What seemed of much greater overall significance in relation to the social space available to seafarer partners was the absence of husbands as a consequence of their employment at sea, and the type of household they resided in (i.e. joint or single-family households). In some cases, where women were not strongly policed by partners or partners' relatives, space expanded and women were able to lead active and interesting social lives. In others, however, space contracted as without their husbands as chaperones women did not venture out into the community more than was absolutely essential in relation to employment or the servicing of the household.

The findings did more to confirm the extent to which seafarers were no longer embedded in social and domestic arrangements at home than it did to suggest that the wives and partners of seafarers were somehow engaged in activities which might be seen to relate to the creation of transnational social spaces. Just as men had talked about becoming nothing more than the family 'bank', women too hinted at the distance which could come to characterise their relationships with husbands who were tolerated while at home, and sometimes even 'pampered' and made to feel 'special', but who in reality disrupted the daily rhythm of life and the social activities of partners and of children. In short there did seem to be some evidence that travel and exposure to other cultures impacted directly and indirectly on seafarers' partners but this seemed to be highly variable in character and the potential for private spaces to be flexibly interpreted and determined was apparent, leading to a myriad of social arrangements and patterns of behaviour and making it difficult to disentangle the influence of transnationality from other influences such as the mere absence of partners for long periods of time. In contrast, evidence of the distance that developed between seafarers and their families over longer careers at sea was less ambiguous and more apparent.

Notes

1 This constitutes 35 per cent of the total slum population of India and 49 per cent of the total population of Greater Mumbai (calculated from India census data 2001).
2 I was unable to make contact with any ratings living in Mumbai. Traditionally ratings have not been drawn from the city and the high cost of real estate is likely to militate against families moving into the city to take up residence.
3 Calculated from India census data 2001.
4 A steward works in the galley and is classified as a rating. May also be termed 'messman'.
5 Pseudonym.
6 This rank falls between rating and officer.
7 A chief cook would normally be regarded as a petty officer.

9

On transnationalism, people and space

When I stood at the quayside surveying the rusty little reefer that I was about to board, back in 1999, I had no idea what to expect having negotiated my way onto the decks towering above me. I had never been on a cargo ship. I thought I might be afraid once out at sea in heavy swell or severe storms; I thought I might be sea sick; I thought I might be bored. I was none of these things. I was won over by the sea and by the seafarers. John Masefield's words resonated with me back on land, as I looked out at the ships, rising and falling with the swell, at anchor off the coast of Falmouth, the shoreline of Singapore, the Bay in San Francisco.

I hadn't known what to expect at sea but I had known what I was looking for. I wanted to understand how these workers lived: how they survived at sea and how they coped with the long absences from home, friends, and family, which were associated with their work. As I came to understand the industry better, I wanted to understand not just the lives of transborder seafarers on ships but also of transmigrants seeking work at sea and largely residing in Germany. Beyond this, the lives of seafarers' families became important to me in relation to questions of transnational social fields and the extent to which transnationalism may become unbounded. As I worked at understanding the data I was collecting, I began to realise that transnationality as a concept needed to be pared down to the bare essentials in meaning in order to be usefully applied in the data analysis. Concurrently, questions of space emerged as central to the consideration of the qualitative nature of the lives and experiences of both seafarers and their families.

Throughout this book I have made a sustained effort to delimit and clearly define the concept of transnationalism, pinning down precisely what is meant by the term and how it should be employed. Certainly it relates to migrants and is a state which may conceivably be attained by them as they become simultaneously embedded into two different countries. Pries has outlined various ideal types relating to migration ranging from emigrants/immigrants through return migrants/sojourners, recurrent migrants, diaspora migrants, all the way to transmigrants. Transmigrants, according to Pries, display an ambiguous stance in relation to both regions of departure and regions of arrival; move for economic reasons; and may not be certain of the planned duration of migration which may be sequential as well as indeterminate (Pries 2004: 10). Within his categorisation it is clear that

most of the seafarers (but not those Cape Verdeans in Germany who held European passports) considered in this text are not transmigrants at all but are 'recurrent
migrants'. Pries describes the characteristics of recurrent migrants as follows:

> [the recurrent migrant] departs the region of origin only for seasonal or oc-
> casional stays, remaining abroad for less than one year and maintaining strong
> household ties in the region of origin. He/she lives provisionally outside a typi-
> cal household structure and accepts exceptional working and living conditions,
> maintaining social, political, and cultural differences to the region of arrival.
> (Pries 2004: 11)

Such a definition clearly fits the status of the seafarer working at sea and most
of those who are searching for work in European hub ports. These workers also
demonstrate some of the characteristics described by Pries as associated with
transnational transmigrants, however, and the definitions he supplies in separat-
ing out transmigrants and recurrent migrants are somewhat narrow and in some
senses overly limiting. At the other end of the spectrum Crang, Dwyer and Jackson (2003) seek to broaden the approach to who, or what, might be defined as
transnational and develop the notion of the transnational social space. Engagement in such spaces might, they suggest, render individuals transnational regardless
of the residential/migration statuses so carefully outlined by Pries (see Chapter 2).

In undertaking empirical work reference to the precise definitions of key terms
may be important and in this case the concept of the 'transnational' needed to be
taken into consideration and arguably specified. However it is equally, or perhaps
more, important to recognise that the usefulness of ideal types does not merely relate to the categorisation of individuals, but to the clarification of concepts
and conceptual boundaries. Work which attends carefully to strict definitions of
transnationality quite often reveals the difficulty in finding *any* individuals who sit
comfortably within the boundaries of an ideal type labelled as 'transnational' or
'transmigrant'. Pries himself acknowledges that in his study of Mexican migration
to the USA 'quantitative evidence [of transmigration] remains scarce' (Pries 2004:
30). Similarly rigorous work by Morawska carefully considering the assimilation
of migrants in the USA as a receiving society and what she terms their transnationalism (i.e. in her conceptualisation their connection to home or sending societies) reveals that of seven different groups of migrants to the USA (Indians,
Jamaicans, Poles, Russian Jews, Dominicans, Undocumented Chinese, Cubans)
only Cubans can be considered to be both home and host focused. This may be
ascribed to their very particular context in relation to the politics of their homeland. As she puts it:

> The simultaneous home-and-host country orientation of ethnic path adaptation
> of first-wave Cuban émigrés in Miami has been an outcome of their enforced,
> involuntary departure from Cuba and the dependence of their enduring, pas-
> sionate involvement in anti-communist politics aimed at undermining the de-
> spised Castro regime on sustained collaboration with U.S. government agencies,
> combined with significant investment in the ethnic enclave economy and local
> politics in Miami. (Morawska 2004: 1399–1401)

In contrast to the orientation of Cuban migrants, Morawska identifies that it is more common to identify migrants as 'home focused' or 'host focused' rather than 'doubly focused' even where they hold dual nationality and in this sense her research reflects the essence of much empirical work on transnationality which frequently fails to confirm the idea that transnationals are focused significantly upon life in both home and host societies. The lack of empirical evidence relating to the presence of 'true' transnationals dispersed around the world in significant numbers is both at once important and insignificant. The importance is self-evident perhaps as it brings into stark relief the shortcomings of the idea and an obvious critique of the concept. However the reasons why the failure to find significant numbers of transnationals is not of any great consequence are less self-evident and require some explanation.

The difficulties associated with categorising people whose status and identities are dynamic and characterised by overlap as much as by fracture are to be expected. It is unsurprising therefore that carefully configured definitions of transnationalism nevertheless fail to 'capture' significant numbers of people once operationalised in the field. This failure does not, however, render the concept of the transnational migrant redundant. There is little doubt that changes in labour markets and the concurrent revolution in telecommunications and information technology have significantly transformed the experiences of migration. The possibility that migrants might be in a position to settle in, or work in, new places without severing links to their homes, and countries of origin, opens up the potential for the emergence of new kinds of identities, politics, networks and communities. These may offer huge possibilities for the enhancement of social life and improvements in the circumstances and lives of individual migrants and their extended families. Exploring these possibilities in connection with the concept of transnationality allows for the consideration at a deeper level of the complexity of the impact of migration upon groups of workers and their families. It offers us a lens through which to consider in some detail the impact of the globalisation of labour markets upon workers themselves. In this research, it has only been through such a consideration, that the dangers of marginalisation associated with the new context of migration have emerged. It is via the consideration of transnational connections and their detailed meaning, and significance, that the mechanisms for a 'double' kind of social exclusion that may be associated with transmigration, in a variety of forms, have become apparent. Thus the concept of transnationalism is arguably of considerable significance within social science and need not be abandoned nor completely reconfigured simply because few migrants (including those considered in this research) appear to fall into the ideal type category that may be associated with it.

Across the shipping industry globalisation has transformed the labour market for seafarers. While seafarers working aboard ships and searching for work in hub ports such as Hamburg may not be archetypal transnationals or transmigrants they do constitute groups of recurrent migrants with dual affiliations: to North Germany and Cape Verde, for example, but also to the multicultural hierarchically ordered ship and the comfort of shore-based 'sending' communities.

On the whole, exposure to the globalised labour market for seafarers can be seen, perhaps paradoxically, to have confined and restricted the social spaces that seafarers can access. Such spaces are heavily structured by immigration laws, by occupational hierarchy, by cultural intolerance and by discrimination. Furthermore, the failure to represent migrants (such as the seafarers residing in Northern Germany) at a cultural and political level serves to be exclusionary, causing them to look towards their original homelands for affirmation rather than integrating more fully into new host societies (Morawska 2004). This 'structuring of space' is an aspect of the lives of transnationals, transmigrants and recurrent migrants that is under-explored in much research which has tended to emphasise agency on the part of migrants and the role of various forms of capital in influencing migrant success in accessing social space. Important exceptions to this come in the detailed work of social scientists considering either the sending or the receiving societies' characteristics (or both) in more detail. Morawska (2004) identifies a range of factors influencing integration including both the 'structural' characteristics of sending and receiving societies and the individual characteristics of migrants. While presentationally very different to the data discussed here, these factors echo many of the conditions identified as key to the 'porosity' and 'stickiness' of the societies which the seafarers included in the research entered and left (respectively). They include for example: 'structural and dynamics of the economy; civic-political culture and practice regarding immigrants particularly of different race; openness/closure of local political systems; (in)visibility of immigrant groups in host perceptions' as well as more individual characteristics such as 'cultural capital; social capital' and so forth (Morawska 2004: 1399). Li in contrast focuses our attention clearly on the politics and discourse of receiving societies with his concentration upon Canada and reminds us that the outcome of immigration while in part reflective of the actions of individual migrants 'also depends on how much the resident population is prepared to open the door to welcome outsiders at the gate' (Li 2003: 2). He goes on to state that:

> The 'warmth of the welcome' as Reitz (1998) calls it, depends upon the institutional features of the receiving society, including educational opportunities, welfare accessibility and labour market arrangements. (Li 2003: 3)

Similarly while other work does not necessarily focus on the structuring of space (including the 'institutional features of society'), there are, nevertheless, examples where the importance of factors such as immigration status and associated limitations on employment emerge in accounts of migration and transnationalism. Tajima, for example, discusses migrant Chinese 'newcomers' to Japan in relation to employment status and visa restrictions (Tajima 2003) while the relevance of the legal framework characterising the European Union is explicitly referenced by Gustafson in his discussion of 'retirement migration' (Gustafson 2008: 456). Notwithstanding these examples it is surprising perhaps how much work does not sufficiently attend to such issues and there is a particularly strong argument for their greater consideration in work focused upon transnationalism.

Space as a term has self-evidently been most used in relation to the disciplines associated with physics and geography. There is also, however, a long-standing interest in space within the social sciences. In this sense space is generally differentiated from other forms of space by terming it 'social space'. A cursory exploration of 'social space' quickly reveals that even within the social sciences the term has been used in a multitude of ways with different points of interest and focus. Writers in the Bourdieu camp (see Veenstra 2007), for example, consider social space as a stratified medium and concentrate on the various ways by which it is accessed and delineated, i.e. through the possession and expression of various forms of capital. In stark contrast, Lefebvre and others have had an explicit interest in the relationship between states, modes of production and space, and have called for the development of a theory of the production of space (Lefebvre 2009). Lefebvre's influence can be seen in recent papers considering the production of residential or urban space and the role of the state within this process. Sin, for example, considers the role of the extremely powerful Singapore state apparatus in setting the agenda for the construction of ethnically mixed residential spaces via the use of a powerful discourse. Amongst other things, he concludes that:

> The Singapore government attempts to create, legitimize, appropriate and reproduce a hegemonic form of discourse. In a very real sense, the government's portrayal of ethnic regrouping is an attempt at disciplining the social landscape using spatial, social and ideological strategies. (Sin 2003: 540)

In this work on seafarers, the importance of states in the production of space has emerged from a concern which has arisen, from the data itself, with access to social space. Principal findings emerging from the data have related to the extent to which groups are excluded or included in social interaction as it plays out at every level of society, i.e. from the level of the private (friendships and family life) to the variegated forms of the public, for example, from the level of the local street corner, to that of national and international politics. The notion that space is subject to powerful influences in relation to its 'shape' (which is a consequence of its production) and in relation to which groups gain access to it, is one that is supported in the adoption of the term 'structured' space. This term is utilised to emphasise that space is influenced by *more* than just states, although they are a very dominant influence, and that we need to combine an interest in how space is produced with how it is accessed in order to better understand how the fabric of social space is woven in society.

While within physics it is well understood that space is infinite, social space may be understood here to be bounded and linked with the notion of places be they rural or urban, or something more confined and specific such as a ship. Social spaces vary in size and type and to borrow momentarily from Lefebvre might be bounded by rooms, buildings, neighbourhoods, cities, districts, nations, continents, representing for him a 'hierarchized morphology' (Lefebvre 2009: 236). While this study of seafarers shares some of the characteristics of Lefebvre's notion of social space it perhaps resonates more strongly with Flores' adaptation of Gottdiener's conceptualisation, where space is argued to be:

[…] a physical location, a piece of real estate, and simultaneously an existential freedom and a mental expression. Space is both the geographic site of action and the social possibility of engaging in action. (Gottdiener 1985: 123, quoted in Flores 2003: 89)

Interaction in society and congruent access to participative space is a key element of concern in an era of globalisation as mass movement can be seen as liberating in opening up new social spaces, or constraining in relation to their closure. In many discussions of transnationality and in common with studies of immigration and the successful integration of migrants into host societies, there has often been a focus in the literature on the characteristics of migrants themselves (for example the 'possession' of social capital) and the extent to which these impact upon migration outcomes. In many respects an understanding has built up amongst academics, and policy makers, that social capital and access to social networks amongst migrants of similar backgrounds in host societies, provides a 'soft entry' into new communities. This cosy and rather prevalent view has been convincingly questioned in recent times as researchers demonstrate how immigrant communities may themselves be fractured and infused with tensions and conflicts (e.g. Christiansen 2008), and how the host society may impact in negative ways on the kinds of networks which formerly characterised the social fabric of migrant communities 'back home'. McMichael and Manderson offer an account, for example, of Somali refugees settling in Australia and deliver a series of quotes illustrating the extreme isolation and loneliness experienced by the Somali women they talked with. In doing so they uncover the extent to which the habits of refugees may change with a move to a new society and that even where kin are present migrants cannot necessarily rely on isolated individuals to support them. For example, one of their interviewees poignantly commented that:

The people in Somalia love each other. Here you are not supported because the person you are asking for support needs support themselves … I can't avoid being depressed by the separation from people, from my family and from my husband. (McMichael and Manderson 2004: 93–4)

Notwithstanding the growing evidence that social capital is not as freely accessible to migrants as once may have been imagined, it nevertheless remains a factor which has the potential to impact considerably on their lives. This research, too, bears testimony to the relevance of such characteristics. The example of transmigrants in Germany illustrates, for example, the ways in which the social outcomes of transmigrants may vary according to capital (for example differential access to social networks according to nationality) and individual characteristics such as age. What emerges even more strongly, however, is the impact of the 'structures' of societies themselves upon transmigrants. Such 'structures' may be political and legal (for example immigration and work permit restrictions) or cultural relating to the social porosity of society and the extent, for example, to which it is rendered impermeable by the prevailing cultural attitudes, norms and values. Loic Wacquant indirectly reminds us of the prevalence of both kinds of 'structures' in his reflections upon the experiences of Black Americans migrating from the oppressive regimes of the South (where they were banned from many places and thus most effectively excluded from specific participative spaces) to northern states of the USA. Here they may have expected to find equality and the possibility of participating fully in society but on the contrary what they found instead was that they were excluded from much social space by virtue of discriminatory attitudes and practices. He observes that:

> ... as migrants from Mississippi to the Carolinas flocked to the Northern metropolis what they discovered there was not the 'promised land' of equality and full citizenship as they had fervently hoped, but another system of ethnoracial enclosure, the ghetto, which, though it was less rigid and less fearsome than the one they had escaped, was no less encompassing and restricting. (Wacquant 2009: 201)

Thus while the most effective ways of reducing access to space may on the surface appear to be to formally bar access to places (through laws of segregation but equally through rules of group membership etc.) other powerful mechanisms of social exclusion also operate. Most pervasively, exclusion of the poor characterises capitalist societies. Struggles over land rights poignantly illustrate the relationship between struggles over space/place and impoverishment. In Guatemala returning refugees struggle with a variety of interest groups to occupy space and colonise 'place' and Stepputat notes that 'Governments too have ideas about how returnees should fit into national space' (Stepputat 1994: 177). In Brazil the landless mobilise to colonise areas where they might scratch a living while the affluent increasingly occupy apartment blocks behind high walls and security gates. Additionally however, other forms of vulnerability beyond poverty serve as exclusionary forces. Women and people with disabilities may, for example, exclude themselves from particular places for fear of attack or harassment and thus from the possibilities of particular forms of social participation. As Koskela argues, fear leads women to restrict their own 'access to and activity within public space' (Koskela 1999: 111). Furthermore she suggests that:

> ... public space can be considered as one territory to which men hold greater rights than women: a territory from which women are often excluded by harassment and fear of male violence (Koskela 1999: 111–12)

The rise of gated communities has similarly been understood to derive from the power of discourses of violence producing fear amongst the white middle class in US cities (Sin 2003). More obviously, perhaps, undocumented migrants while being present in places may actively absent themselves from social space as a consequence of fear as Coutin's work suggests. Such undocumented migrants may be described as not fully arriving 'even when they reach their destinations' (Coutin 2005: 195). Thus while deportation might most effectively remove them as a presence from unwilling 'host' societies, even where they remain undetected, and therefore physically present, their lack of social rights and the denial to them of social services renders them largely socially absent:

Unauthorized migrants are absented physically by being detained or deported and socially by being denied particular rights and services. The prohibition on arriving at their destination shapes unauthorized migrants' journeys, causing these migrants to hide even before they appear. (Coutin 2005: 196)

In this research, transmigrant seafarers in Northern Germany were subject to both kinds of exclusion (i.e. exclusion from places and exclusion from spaces) as they were excluded by dint of immigration law from particular places – places of work – and they were also marginalised as a consequence of poverty and of fear of harassment, and a sense that German society was hostile to them and to their self-expression and self-realisation. Access to space was structured by the state but also by the 'society'.

Aboard ships custom and practice in relation to occupational hierarchy and the 'rules' laid down locally by captains similarly had the effect of excluding particular seafarers (those of lower rank) from particular places and therefore social spaces on board. Ratings could not enter the messrooms designated for officers unless called upon to serve food there or to clean. Similarly lower ranks did not have access to officer lounges although some officers frequented the social spaces 'allocated' to ratings. The occupational culture of seafaring, and the emphasis on unspoken 'rules' of social interaction on board also served to restrict space, and thereby social space. Seafarers notionally had equal access to shared facilities such as gyms. However, the unspoken rules of interaction and their relationship with hierarchies produced an uneven access with ratings absenting themselves, should officers wish to use equipment, or seeking to avoid using facilities at times when officers were known to be present. Similarly at social events ratings tended to suppress their own self-expression and restrict the extent to which they occupied social space as long as officers were present. Once alone such self-censorship was lifted and they emerged from the sidelines and the shadows of social space to take a more central part in interaction. Unlike the experiences of transmigrants ashore, the state, as such, played little role in the shaping of social space for seafarers on board ship. Ships, particularly those flying flags of convenience, largely exist beyond state influence at the level of 'the social', and complex issues of jurisdiction may even disrupt, and/or prevent, intervention where serious social misdemeanours (such as homicide) occur.

In each case, however, both aboard and in Northern Germany, seafarers' own resources (their 'capital') impacted upon their capacity to occupy and to negotiate social space. It *impacted* on their capacity to occupy and negotiate space but it did not *determine* it. In some respects some of the structural features of the space available to those ashore, and on board, were determined by forces that were too strong for individuals to influence. Thus access to social space was a result of both the production and form of such spaces and the ability of individuals to 'colonise' them.

While the experiences of seafarers in Germany and those sailing with multinational crews emphasise the ways in which social space becomes restricted in particular circumstances, the data collected on seafarers' families in India emphasises the opposite effect. In doing so it focuses attention upon the ways in which social space may be opened up for the partners of seafarers as a consequence of their spouses' exposure to transborder employment and work within multicultural contexts. It also highlights the differences between public and private social space with private social space being demonstrably more flexible and more negotiable than public social space. Thus for seafarers' partners, husbands' departures from the family home could allow them to move into a new family role associated not just with greater responsibility but with increased social freedoms and access to wider social networks. This was not inevitably the case, however, and in some circumstances family members actively intervened to try to ensure that even in the absence of a seafarer his wife would live a socially restricted and constrained life centred almost exclusively on 'the home'. In India seafarers' wives' access to social space was shaped not only by local customs, norms and values, but also by individual family members who retained a huge amount of influence within domestic settings. Like the ship, therefore, access to social space was determined less by the state and more by prevailing norms and the impact of influential and powerful individuals within largely private and isolated spaces.

The consideration of social space emerged here as a concern because of an interest in the applicability of the concept of transnationality. In thinking about whether seafarers and their partners ashore in Germany, on board transborder workplaces (ships), or at home, could be considered to be transnationals, not only did the meaning of transnationalism come to be given careful consideration but the quality of the connections and interactions between groups and individuals had to be closely examined.

Transnationalism is often characterised in the literature as 'liberational', at least by implication. There is no doubt that the notion of the potential expansion of social space and the creation of social fields is a seductive one. However, the present limitations placed on the potential for migrants to co-exist across borders are significant. Waldinger and Fitzgerald remind us that the practical realities of current international politics mean that, what we might think of as, containerised states remain in the ascendant:

> Migrants do not make their communities alone. Intellectual fashions notwithstanding, states and politics conducted within their borders fundamentally shape the options for migrants and ethnic trans-state social action. (Waldinger and Fitzgerald 2004: 1178)

While constraints imposed by nation states, by cultural practices, norms and values, and so forth, may be overcome by particular individuals, blessed with particular resources, at particular times, their influence is nevertheless compelling. Faist argues that the exclusion of migrants from host societies via discriminatory practices within a context of a multicultural rhetoric or nation-state politics (Faist 2000: 218), is in some sense a precondition for the development of transnational spaces in as much as it predisposes migrants to retain links with their original 'homelands' as a consequence of their lack of integration into new 'host' societies. This suggests however that transnational communities occupying such spaces may be little more than communities excluded from both host and homelands as there is a wealth of evidence to suggest that having left homelands migrants frequently find themselves unable to reintegrate properly with their remaining friends, family and community members. Seafarers for example may feel they become no more than the 'family bank'. Seafarers' wives may secretly crave their husbands' departure in order to allow them to return to richer, more stimulating social lives. In short migrants can easily become 'strangers' in their 'own lands'. In such circumstances it is apparent that transnational arrangements cannot be conceived of as positive new forms of embeddedness, fostering enriched social relations.

Understanding that transnational spaces are in fact spaces characterised by severe restriction and limitation is important in considering suggestions that transnationalism 'from below' may require new governance structures relating to citizenship and judicial processes. Pries suggests that:

> Transmigration makes us aware of a new 'transnationalism from below' that is being constructed by decentralised and barely visible social practices, symbolic systems, and artefacts belonging to millions of private social actors. Can and should new governance structures be developed for transmigrants, like global or pluri-national citizenship or global or pluri-national courts of justice. (Pries 2004: 32)

The potential for the marginalisation of transmigrants needs to be given closer attention in relation to such suggestions to ensure that any steps taken along such lines lead to the expansion and not the further contraction of the social space accessible to transmigrants, recurrent migrants, transnationals and their like. At present it seems that globalisation, while bringing with it the possibility of an increase in the mobility of labour with the development of globalised and internationalised labour markets, also carries a potential for the degradation of life for many migrant workers who may find that after a period of recurrent migration they no longer feel at home in the land of their forebears while being marginalised within the countries where they work. At sea it is possible to find seafarers who feel they no longer belong 'ashore' with their families. Here and across a range of studies one can find examples of migrants who feel different to, and separate from, the communities they have left as well as the communities they have sought to join. So it seems that there is growing evidence that just as urbanisation and the national mobility of labour disrupts communities and extended families, and carries with it the potential for alienation, so too does globalisation further this process, bringing with it the possibility of the creation of a generation of 'the dispossessed'. Seafaring, it seems, may be good for many groups of people, including seafarers' families and their shore-based communities. In the final analysis, however, the advantages of a life at sea for seafarers themselves are less readily apparent and many may be justified as regarding their pursuit of a seafaring career as an act of great personal sacrifice.

Bibliography

Alba, R. (2005) 'Bright vs. blurred boundaries: Second-generation assimilation and exclusion in France, Germany, and the United States', *Ethnic and Racial Studies* 28 (1): 20–49.

Albrow, M. (1996) *The Global Age: State and Society beyond Modernity*, Cambridge: Polity Press.

Alderton, T., Bloor, M., Kahveci, E., Lane, T., Sampson, H., Thomas, M., Winchester, N., Wu, B. and Zhao, M. (2004) *The Global Seafarer: Living and Working Conditions in a Globalized Industry*, Geneva: ILO.

Almazan, A. (2000) 'Training IMO warns Philippines', *Lloyds List*, 30 March.

Appadurai, A. (1990) 'Disjuncture and difference in the global cultural economy', pp. 295–310 in Mike Featherstone (ed.), *Global Culture: Nationalism, Globalisation and Modernity*, London: Sage Publications.

Arnold, G. (2012) *Migration: Changing the World*, London: Pluto Press.

Ballard, R. (1987) 'The political economy of migration: Pakistan, Britain, and the Middle East', pp. 17–41 in J. Eades (ed.), *Migrants, Workers, and the Social Order*, London: Tavistock Publications.

Banuri, T. and Schor, J. (eds) (1992) *Financial Openness and National Autonomy* Oxford: Oxford University Press.

Basch, L., Glick Schiller, N. and Szanton Blanc, C. (1995) *Nations Unbound: Transnational Projects, Postcolonial Predicaments, and Deterritorialized Nation States*, Basle: Gordon and Breach.

Beaverstock, J.V. and Smith, J. (1996) 'Lending jobs to global cities: Skilled international labour migration, investment banking and the City of London', *Urban Studies* 33(8): 1377–94.

Becker, H., Geer, B., Hughes, E. and Strauss, A. (1961) *Boys in White: Student Culture in Medical School*, Chicago: University of Chicago Press.

Belcher, P., Lane, A.D., Sampson, H., Thomas, M., Veiga, J. and Zhao, M. (2003) *Women Seafarers: Global Employment Policies and Practices*, Geneva: ILO.

Benton, G. and Gomez, E.T. (2000) 'Chinatown and transnationalism', unpublished paper.

Bergantino, A.S. and Marlow, P.B. (1997) *An Econometric Analysis of the Decision to Flag Out*, Cardiff: SIRC.

Beynon, H. (1973) *Working for Ford*, Harmondsworth: Penguin.

BIMCO/ISF (2005) *Manpower Update – The Worldwide Demand for and Supply of Seafarers*, Coventry: Warwick Institute for Employment Research.

Bloor, M. and Sampson, H. (2009) 'Regulatory enforcement of labour standards in an out-sourcing globalised industry: The case of the shipping industry', *Work Employment and Society* 23(4): 711–26.

Bumiller, E. (1991) *May You Be the Mother of a Hundred Sons: A Journey Among the Women of India*, New Delhi: Penguin.

Bunnell, T. (2007) 'Post-maritime transnationalization: Malay seafarers in Liverpool', *Global Networks* 7(4): 412–29.

Burawoy, M., Blum, J., George, S., Gille, Z. and Thayer, M. (eds) (2000) *Global Ethnography: Forces Connections, and Imaginations in a Postmodern World*, Berkeley and Los Angeles, CA: University of California Press.

Child, I. (1943) *Italian or American? The Second Generation in Conflict*, New Haven, CT: Yale University Press.

Christiansen, C. (2008) 'Hometown associations and solidarities in Kurdish transnational villages: The migration-development nexus in a European context', *The European Journal of Development Research* 20(10): 88–103.

Chung, Y.K. (1988) 'An ethnographic exploration of women and work in a high technology factory in Singapore', *Studies in Sexual Politics* 23: 1–89.

Clifford, J. (1992) 'Travelling cultures', pp. 96–112 in L. Grossberg, C. Nelson and P. Treicher (eds) *Cultural Studies*, New York and London: Routledge.

Clifford, J. (1997) *Routes, Travel and Translation in the Late Twentieth Century*, Cambridge, MA and London: Harvard University Press.

Coutin, S. (2005) 'Being en route', *American Anthropologist* 107(2): 195–206.

Crang, P., Dwyer, C. and Jackson, P. (2003) 'Transnationalism and the spaces of commodity culture', *Progress in Human Geography* 27(4): 438–56.

Dunscombe, J., Marsden, D. (1996) 'Can we research the private sphere? Methodological and ethical problems in the study of the role of intimate emotion in personal relationships', pp. 141–55 in L. Morris and E. Stina Lyon (eds), *Gender Relations in Public and Private: New Research Perspectives*, London: Macmillan.

Eades, J. (1987) 'Anthropologists and migrants: Changing models and realities', pp. 1–16 in J. Eades (ed.), *Migrants, Workers, and the Social Order*, London: Tavistock Publications.

Ellis, N. and Sampson, H. (2008) *The Global Labour Market for Seafarers Working Aboard Merchant Cargo Ships 2003*, Cardiff: SIRC, www.sirc.cf.ac.uk, accessed 11 November 2011.

Fabricant, C. (1998) 'Riding the waves of (post) colonial migrancy: Are we all really in the same boat?', *Diaspora* 7: 25–51.

Faist, T. (2000) 'Transnationalization in international migration: implications for the study of citizenship and culture', *Ethnic and Racial Studies* 23(2): 189–222.

Favell, A. (2003) 'Games without frontiers? Questioning the transnational social power of migrants in Europe', *European Journal of Sociology/Archives Européennes de Sociologie* XLIV(3): 397–427.

Finch, J. (1993) '"It's great to have someone to talk to": Ethics and politics of interviewing women', pp. 166–80 in M. Hammersley (ed.), *Social Research: Philosophy, Politics, and Practice*, London: Sage.

Fix, M., Papademetriou, D., Batalova, J., Terrazas, A., Lin, S. and Mittelstadt, M. (2009) *Migration and the Global Recession*, Washington DC: Migration Policy Institute.

Flores, W. (2003) 'New citizens, new rights: undocumented immigrants and Latino cultural citizenship', *Latin American Perspectives* 129, 30(2): 87–100.

Fog-Olwig, K. (2002) 'A wedding in the family: Home making in a global kin network', *Global Networks* 2(3): 205–18.

Gardner, K. and Grillo, R. (2002) 'Transnational households and ritual: An overview', *Global Networks* 2(3): 179–90.

Gekara, V. (2007) 'Increasing shipping skills in the UK: "Bursting" the industry myth of diminishing interest', SIRC Symposium Proceedings, 4–5 July, pp. 29–44, Cardiff: SIRC, www.sirc.cf.ac.uk, accessed 17 July 2011.

Gekara, V. (2010) *Globalisation, State Strategies And Labour in the Shipping Industry: The UK Response to Declining Shipping Skills*, Cardiff: Cardiff University.

Giddens, A. (1990) *The Consequences of Modernity* Cambridge: Polity Press.

Goodman, J. (1997) 'National multiculturalism and transnational migrant politics: Australian and East Timorese', *Asian and Pacific Migration Journal* 6(3–4): 457–80.

Gottdiener, M. (1985) *The Social Production of Urban Space* Austin, TX: University of Texas Press.

Gould, E. (2010) *Towards a Total Occupation: A Study of Merchant Navy Officer Cadetship*, Cardiff: Cardiff University.

Gustafson, P. (2008) 'Transnationalism in retirement migration: the case of North European retirees in Spain', *Ethnic and Racial Studies* 31(3): 451–75.

Hannerz, U. (1990) 'Cosmopolitans and locals in world culture', pp. 237–51 in Mike Featherstone (ed.), *Global Culture: Nationalism, Globalisation and Modernity*, London: Sage Publications.

Hannerz, U. (2003) 'Being there … and there … and there! Reflections on multi-site ethnography, *Ethnography* 4(2): 201–16.

Hannerz, U. (2004) *Foreign News: Exploring the World of Foreign Correspondents* Chicago: University of Chicago Press.

Hansen, H.L. (1996) 'Surveillance of Deaths On-board Danish Merchant Ships 1986–93: Implications for Prevention' *Occupational and Environmental Medicine* 53(4): 296–75.

Heaton, P. (1981) *The Redbrook: A Deep-Sea Tramp*, Abergavenny: P.M. Heaton Publishing.

Held, D. and McGrew, A. (2001) Entry, pp. 324–370 in J. Krieger (ed.), *Oxford Companion to Politics of the World*, second edition, Oxford: Oxford University Press.

Held, D., McGrew, A., Goldblatt, D. and Perraton, J. (1999) *Global Transformations: Politics, Economics and Culture*, Cambridge: Polity Press.

Hirst, P. and Thompson, G. (1999) *Globalisation in Question*, second edition, Cambridge: Polity Press.

Hollinger, D. (1995) *Postethnic America: Beyond Multiculturalism*, New York: Basic Books.

hooks, b. 1990 *Yearning – Race, Gender, and Cultural Politics*, Boston, MA: South End Press.

ICONS (2000) *International Commission on Shipping, Inquiry into Ship Safety: Ships, Slaves and Competition*, Charleston, Australia: ICONS.

India Census data (2003), http://censusindia.gov.in/2011-common/censusdataonline.html, accessed 13 June 2012.

Kahveci, E. (2005) 'Abandoned seafarers: The case of the Obo Basak', *Proceedings of the Seafarers International Research Centre's Fourth International Symposium*, pp. 28–51, Cardiff: SIRC, www.sirc.cf.ac.uk, accessed 1 July 2011.

Kahveci, E. (2007) 'Welfare services for seafarers', *Proceedings of the Seafarers International Research Centre's Fifth International Symposium*, pp. 10–28, Cardiff: SIRC, www.sirc.cf.ac.uk, accessed 17 July 2011.

Kahveci, E. and Nichols, T. (2006) *The Other Car Workers: Work Organisation and Technology in the Maritime Car Carrier Industry*, Basingstoke: Palgrave Macmillan.

Kapadia, K. (1995) *Siva and her Sisters: Gender, Caste, and Class in Rural South India*, Oxford: Westview Press.

Kearney, M. (1995) 'The local and the global: The anthropology of globalization and transnationalism', *Annual Review of Anthropology* (24): 547–65.

Kearney, M. (1999a) 'Borders and boundaries of state and self at the end of empire', pp. 520–38 in Vertovec and Robin Cohen (eds), *Migration, Diasporas, and Transnationalism*, Cheltenham: Edward Elgar Publishing.

Kearney, M. (1999b) 'The local and the global: The anthropology of globalization and transnationalism', pp. 503–19 in Steven Vertovec and Robin Cohen (eds), *Migration, Diasporas, and Transnationalism*, Cheltenham: Edward Elgar Publishing.

Kellner, D. (2005) 'Globalisation and the postmodern turn', www.gseis.ucla.edu/courses/ed253a/dk/GLOBPM.htm, accessed 24 July 2005.

Kennedy, P. (2004) 'Making global society: Friendship networks among transnational professionals in the building design industry', *Global Networks* 4(2): 157–79.

Khor, M. (1996) 'Globalisation: Implications for development policy', *Third World Resurgence* 74 (October): 15–21.

Kim, J.H. (2004) '"They are more like us": The salience of ethnicity in the global workplace of Korean transnational corporations', *Ethnic and Racial Studies* 27(1): 69–94.

Knudsen, F. (2004) *If you are a good leader I am a good follower: Working and Leisure Relations between Danes and Filipinos on board Danish Vessels*, http://static.sdu.dk/mediafiles/Files/Om_SDU/Institutter/Ist/MaritimSundhed/Rapporter/report92004.pdf, accessed 31 December 2011.

Koskela, H. (1999) '"Gendered Exclusions": Women's fear of violence and changing relations to space', *Geografiska Annaler* 81 B(2): 111–24.

Lahiri-Dutt, K. and Samanta, G. (2002) 'State initiatives for the empowerment of women of rural communities: Experiences from eastern India', *Community Development Journal*, 37(2): 137–56.

Landolt, P. and Da, W.W. (2005) 'The spatially ruptured practices of migrant families: A comparison of immigrants from El Salvador and the People's Republic of China', *Current Sociology* 53(4): 625–53.

Lane, T. (1986) *Grey Dawn Breaking: British Merchant Seafarers in the Late Twentieth Century*, Manchester: Manchester University Press.

Lefebvre, H. (2009) 'Space and the State', pp. 223–53 in N. Brenner and S. Elden (eds), *State Space World: Selected Essays/Henri Lefebvre*, trans. Gerald Moore, Neil Brenner and Stuart Elden, Minneapolis: University of Minnesota Press.

Leichtman, M.A. (2005) 'The legacy of transnational lives: Beyond the first generation of Lebanese in Senegal', *Ethnic and Racial Studies* 28(4): 663–86.

Levitt, P. (2001) 'Transnational migration: Taking stock and future directions', *Global Networks* 1(3): 195–216.

Levitt, P. and de la Dehesa, R. (2003) 'Transnational migration and the redefinition of the state: variations and explanations', *Ethnic and Racial Studies* 26(4): 587–611.

Levitt, P. and Glick Schiller, N. (2003) *Transnational Perspectives on International Migration: Conceptualizing Simultaneity*, Centre for Migration and Development Working Paper, 03–09, http://cmd.princeton.edu/papers/wp0309j.pdf, accessed 11 November 2011.

Li, P. (2003) 'The Place of Immigrants: The Politics of Difference in Territorial and Social Space' *Canadian Ethnic Studies* XXXV(2): 1–14.

Luibheid, E. (2004) 'Childbearing against the state? Asylum seeker women in the Irish republic', *Women's Studies International Forum* 27: 335–49.

Mand, K. (2002) 'Place, gender and power in transnational Sikh marriages', *Global Networks* 2(3): 233–48.

Marcus, G. (1995) 'Ethnography in/of the world system: the emergence of multi-sited ethnography', *Annual Review of Anthropology* 24: 95–117.

Masefield, J. (1902) *Salt-Water Ballads*, London: Grant Richards.

Massey, D. (1994) *Space, Place, and Gender*, Cambridge: Polity Press.

Mclaughlin, J. (1999) 'Refugees clash with Dover locals', *The Independent*, 15 August, www.independent.co.uk/news/refugees-clash-with-dover-locals–1112868.html, accessed 3 February 2012.

McMichael, C. and Manderson, L. (2004) 'Somali women and well-being: Social networks and social capital among immigrant women in Australia', *Human Organization* 63(1): 88–99.

Mitchell, K. (2000) 'Transnationalism', pp. 853–55 in R.J. Johnston, D. Gregory, G. Pratt and M. J. Watts (eds), *The Dictionary of Human Geography*, fourth edition, Oxford: Blackwell.

Moeran, B. (2006) *Ethnography at Work*, Oxford: Berg.

Morawska, E. (2004) 'Exploring diversity in immigrant assimilation and transnationalism: Poles and Russian Jews in Philadelphia', *International Migration Review* 38(4): 1372–1412.

Newton, S. (2004) *The Global Economy, 1944–2000: The Limits of Ideology*, London: Arnold.

Neyzi, L. (2004) 'Fragmented in space: The oral history narrative of an Arab Christian from Antioch, Turkey', *Global Networks* 4(3): 258–97.

O'Donnell, M.A. (2001) 'Becoming Hong Kong, razing Baoan, preserving Xin'an: An ethnographic account of urbanization in the Shenzhen Special Economic Zone', *Cultural Studies* 15(3–4): 419–43.

Okamura, J.Y. (1998) *Imagining the Filipino American Diaspora: Transnational Relations, Identities, and Communities*, London: Taylor & Francis.

Ong, A. and Nonini, D.M. (eds) (1997) *Ungrounded Empires: The Cultural Politics Of Modern Chinese Transnationalism*, London: Routledge.

Panayides, P. (2001) *Professional Ship Management: Marketing and Strategy*, Aldershot: Ashgate.

Pollert, A. (1981) *Girls, Wives, Factory Lives* London: Macmillan

Portes, A. (1995) 'Transnational communities: Their emergence and significance in the contemporary world system', *John Hopkins University Working Paper Series 16.*

Portes, A. (1996) 'Global villagers: The rise of transnational communities', *The American Prospect* 25 (March–April): 74–7.

Portes, A. (1997) *Globalization from Below: The Rise of Transnational Communities*, ESRC WPTC–98–01 working papers,www.transcomm.ox.ac.uk, accessed 6 July 2006.

Portes, A., Fernandez-Kelly, P. and Haller, W. (2005) 'Segmented assimilation on the ground: The new second generation in early adulthood', *Ethnic and Racial Studies* 28(6): 1000–40.

Portes, A. and Zhou, M. (1993) 'The new second generation : Segmented assimilation and its variants among post-1965 immigrant youth', *The Annals of the American Academy of Political and Social Sciences* 530: 74–96.

Pries, L. (2004) 'Determining the causes and durability of transnational labour migration between Mexico and the United States: Some empirical findings', *International Migration* 42(2): 3–39.

Radice, H. (1999) 'Taking globalisation seriously', *Socialist Register*.

Rafael, V.L. (2000) *White Love and Other Events in Filipino History*, London: Duke University Press.

Reiser, O.L. and Davies, B. (1944) *Planetary Democracy: An Introduction to Scientific Humanism and Applied Semantics*, New York: Creative Age Press.

Roth, W. (2009) '"Latino before the world": The transnational extension of panethnicity', *Ethnic and Racial Studies* 32(6): 927–47.

Salih, R. (2002) 'Reformulating tradition and modernity: Moroccan migrant women and the transnational division of ritual space', *Global Networks* 2(3): 219–31.

Sampson, H. (2003) 'Transnational drifters or hyperspace dwellers: An exploration of the lives of Filipino seafarers aboard and ashore', *Ethnic and Racial Studies* 26(2): 253–77.

Sampson, H. (2005) 'Left high and dry? The lives of women married to seafarers in Goa and Mumbai', *Ethnography* 6(1): 66–85.

Sampson, H. and Bloor, M. (2007) 'When Jack gets out of the box: The problems of regulating a global industry', *Sociology* 41(3): 551–69.

Sampson, H. and Schroeder, T. (2006) 'In the wake of the wave: Globalisation, networks, and the experiences of transmigrant seafarers in Northern Germany', *Global Networks* 6(1): 61–80.

Sampson, H. and Tang, L. (2011) *New Shipboard Technology and Training Provision for Seafarers*, Cardiff: SIRC, www.sirc.cf.ac.uk, accessed 1 December 2011.

Sampson, H. and Thomas, M. (2003) 'Lone researchers at Sea: Gender, risk, and responsibility', *Qualitative Research* 3(20): 165–89.

Sampson, H. and Wu, B. (2003) 'Compressing time and constraining space: The contradictory effects of ICT and containerization on international shipping labour', *International Review of Social History* 48 (supplement): 123–52.

Sampson, H. and Zhao, M. (2003) 'Multilingual crews: Communication and the operation of ships', *World Englishes* 22(1): 31–45.

Sander, H. (1996) 'Multilateralism, regionalism, and globalisation: The challenges to the world trading system', pp. 17–36 in H. Sander and A. Inotai (eds), *World Trade after the Uruguay Round: Prospects and Policy Options for the Twenty-First Century*, London: Routledge.

Schirato, T. and Webb, J. (2003) *Understanding Globalization*, London: Sage.

Scholte, J.A. (2000) *Globalisation: A Critical Introduction*, London: Palgrave Macmillan.

Schrank, R. (1983) *Industrial Democracy at Sea*, Cambridge, MA: MIT Press.

Schmidt, R. and Voss, B. (2000) *Archaeologies of Sexuality*, London: Routledge.

Sedgwick, M. (2007) *Globalisation and Japanese Organisational Culture: An Ethnography of a Japanese Corporation in France*, Abingdon: Routledge.

Selkou, E. and Roe, M. (2004) *Globalisation, Policy and Shipping: Fordism, Post-Fordism and the European Maritime Sector*, Cheltenham: Edward Elgar.

Sherar, M.G. (1973) *Shipping Out: A sociological Study of American Seamen*, Cambridge, MD: Cornell Maritime Press.

Sin, C.H. (2003) 'The politics of ethnic integration in Singapore: Malay "regrouping" as an ideological construct', *International Journal of Urban and Regional Research* 27(3): 527–44.

Spruyt, J. (1994) *Ship Management*, London: Lloyds of London Press.

Spybey, T. (1996) *Globalisation and World Society*, Cambridge: Polity Press.

Stepputat, F. (1994) 'Repatriation and the politics of space: The case of the Mayan diaspora and return movement', *Journal of Refugee Studies* 7(2–3): 175–85.

Strangleman, T. and Warren, T. (2008) *Work and Society: Sociological Approaches, Themes, and Methods*, Abingdon: Routledge.

Sutton, C.R. (2004) 'Celebrating ourselves: The family reunion rituals of African-Caribbean transnational families', *Global Networks* 4(3): 243–57.

Tajima, J. (2003) 'Chinese newcomers in the global city Tokyo: Social networks and settlement tendencies', *International Journal of Japanese Sociology* 12: 68–78.

Tanker Operator (2009), www.tankeroperator.com/news/todisplaynews.asp?NewsID=1450, accessed 2 September 2009.

Tapias, M. and Escandell, X. (2011) 'Not in the eyes of the beholder: Envy among Bolivian migrants in Spain', *International Migration* 49(6): 74–94.

Taylor, P.J. (2000) 'Izations of the world, americanization, modernization, and globalization', pp. 49–70 in C. Hay and D. Marsh (eds), *Demystifying Globalization*, Basingstoke: Macmillan.

Thomas, M. (2003) *Lost at Home and Lost at Sea: The Predicament of Seafaring Families*, Cardiff: SIRC.

Thomas, M., Sampson, H. and Zhao, M. (2003) 'Finding a balance: Companies, seafarers, and family life', *Maritime Policy and Management* 30(1): 59–76.

Thomas, W.I and Znaniecki. F. (1958) *The Polish Peasant in Europe and America*, New York: Dover Publications.

Ulseth, O. (2002) 'The International Ship Register – a force for quality', *MARE Forum 2002* Athens, http://odin.dep.no/nhd/english/news/speeches/024081-090018/dok-bu.html, accessed 5 November 2005.

UNCLOS (1982) *United Nations Convention on the Law of the Sea of 10 December 1982*, Part VII, Section 1, Article 91, www.un.org/depts/los/convention_agreements/texts/unclos/UNCLOS-TOC.htm, accessed 3 February 2012.

United Nations Conference on Trade and Development Review of Maritime Transport (UNCTAD) (2006) Geneva: United Nations, http://unctad.org/en/docs/rmt2006_en.pdf, accessed 3 December 2010.

United Nations Conference on Trade and Development Review of Maritime Transport (UNCTAD) (2008), http://unctad.org/en/docs/rmt2008_en.pdf, accessed 3 December 2010.

Veenstra, G. (2007) 'Social space, social class and bourdieu: Health inequalities in British Colombia, Canada', *Health and Place* 13: 14–31.

Vertovec, S. (1999) 'Conceiving and researching transnationalism', *Ethnic and Racial Studies* 22(2): 447–63.

Voigt-Graf, C. (2004) 'Towards a geography of transnational spaces: Indian transnational communities in Australia', *Global Networks* 4(1): 25–49.

Wacquant, L. (2009) *Punishing the Poor: The Neoliberal Government of Social Insecurity*, London: Duke University Press.

Waldinger, R. and Fitzgerald, D. (2004) 'Transnationalism in question', *American Journal of Sociology* 109(5): 1177–95.

Werbner, P. (1999) 'Global pathways: Working class cosmopolitans and the creation of transnational ethnic worlds', *Social Anthropology* 7(1): 17–35.

Westwood, S. (1984) *All Day Every Day: Factory and Family in the Making of Women's Lives*, London: Pluto Press.

Winchester, N. and Alderton, T. (2003) *Flag State Audit 2003*, Cardiff: SIRC.

Winchester, N., Sampson, H. and Shelly, T. (2006) *An Analysis of Crewing Levels: Findings from the SIRC Global Labour Market Study*, Cardiff: SIRC, www.sirc.cf.ac.uk, accessed 1 December 2010.

Yegenoglu, Meyda (2005) 'Cosmopolitanism and nationalism in a globalized world', *Ethnic and Racial Studies* 28(1): 103–31.

Index